Improving Software Organizations

The Agile Software Development Series

Alistair Cockburn and Jim Highsmith, Series Editors
For more information check out http://www.aw.com/cseng/

Agile software development centers on four values identified in the
Agile Alliance's Manifesto:

- Individuals and interactions over processes and tools
- Working software over comprehensive documentation
- Customer collaboration over contract negotiation
- Responding to change over following a plan

The development of Agile software requires innovation and responsiveness, based on generating
and sharing knowledge within a development team and with the customer. Agile software
developers draw on the strengths of customers, users, and developers, finding just enough
process to balance quality and agility.

The books in **The Agile Software Development Series** focus on sharing the experiences of
such Agile developers. Individual books address individual techniques (such as Use Cases),
group techniques (such as collaborative decision making), and proven solutions to different
problems from a variety of organizational cultures. The result is a core of Agile best practices
that will enrich your experience and improve your work.

Titles in the Series:

Alistair Cockburn, *Surviving Object-Oriented Projects*, ISBN 0-201-49834-0

Alistair Cockburn, *Writing Effective Use Cases*, ISBN 0-201-70225-8

Lars Mathiassen, Jan Pries-Heje, and Ojelanki Ngwenyama, *Improving Software
Organizations: From Principles to Practice*, ISBN 0-201-75820-2

Alistair Cockburn, *Agile Software Development*, ISBN 0-201-69969-9

Improving Software Organizations

From Principles to Practice

Lars Mathiassen
Jan Pries-Heje
Ojelanki Ngwenyama

✦✦Addison-Wesley

Boston • San Francisco • New York • Toronto • Montreal
London • Munich • Paris • Madrid
Capetown • Sydney • Tokyo • Singapore • Mexico City

The publisher offers discounts on this book when ordered in quantity for special sales. For more information, please contact:

Pearson Education Corporate Sales Division
One Lake Street
Upper Saddle River, NJ 07458
(800) 382-3419
corpsales@pearsontechgroup.com

Visit AW on the Web: www.awl.com/cseng/

Library of Congress Cataloging-in-Publication Data

Mathiassen, Lars et. al.
   Improving software organizations : from principles to practice / Lars Mathiassen.
      p.   cm. — (The Agile software development series)
   Includes bibliographical references and index.
   ISBN 0-201-75820-2
   1. Computer software—Development.   I. Title.   II. Series.

QA76.76.D47 M372 2002
005.1—dc21   20011040189

ISBN 0-201-75820-2
Text printed on recycled paper
1 2 3 4 5 6 7 8 9 10—MA—0504030201
First printing, September 2001

Contents at a Glance

Contents

Foreword

When Watts Humphrey enticed me to replace him as the director of the Software Process Program at the Software Engineering Institute in 1991, I began receiving weekly calls from organizations asking, "Now what?" I would invite them to explain what they were asking about and they would reply, "We have just completed a software process assessment—you know, the SEI thing—now what?" After I encouraged them to make improvements to some of their most pressing findings, they would invariably ask, "How do we do that?" I would ask if they had a process group in place, and they would reply "No, should we?" I would press the point with, "Wasn't someone assigned responsibility before the assessment to do something about the findings?" Not surprisingly the usual reply refrained their original query, "No! Now what?" By the end of the call I knew they were frustrated that I had not offered explicit guidance, and I was frustrated that there was little reported experience to support any guidance I might offer.

In those early days most of the advice we offered was based on the technology transfer literature. However, there were two problems with this advice. First, improving an organization's processes was not always like deploying a new technology. In fact, the technology transfer literature was rife with examples of transfer failures caused when technologies required major changes to an organization's processes. Second, as we produced the CMM, we realized that introducing new technologies was a risky undertaking until an organization had reached at least level 3. In essence, the models that worked for technology transfer were primarily designed for organizations with defined processes. These were not the organizations calling us. What advice should we offer to organizations in the throes of level 1 adhocracy?

Fortunately, companies began reporting their software process improvement experiences over the next several years in journals and at conferences. Some people who had been in improvement groups began publishing books on their experiences and lessons learned. However, there was no source that integrated and compared software process improvement experiences from multiple companies. This book fills that void.

Improving Software Organizations: From Principles to Practice is one of the best books ever written on software process improvement. It describes real industrial experiences and admits to the problems that were experienced in implementing software process improvement and how they were addressed. Perhaps the greatest lesson in this book is that none of the reigning models of how to conduct improvement programs is sufficient to guarantee success. While most of the models seem academically proper, the action research reported here uncovers the very real limitations in their effectiveness. True to the tenets of good action research, the final chapters induce the lessons learned across this broad research program. Confidence in the generalizability of these lessons across companies is difficult to establish without the broad cooperation and support that was achieved in Denmark during the late 1990s.

With so many companies in so many nations spending so much money on software process improvement, why did an industry-leading book emerge from a country with a comparatively small population? First, because the country cared. The Danish government invested in learning how to increase the capability of its companies to compete in software development. It recognized that organized research and learning would serve the country's industry better than isolated reports delivered at foreign conferences.

Second, because management cared. The four companies that participated in producing the lessons presented in this book realized the critical role that software played in their businesses and that software process improvement was critical to their competitiveness. They believed that the rate of learning from comparing mutual experience exceeded the learning to be gleaned from their individual experiences. Management believed that the benefits gained from participating in precompetitive research far exceeded the risks of sharing internal experiences, not all of which were positive.

Third, because academia cared. The action research tradition pioneered in Scandinavia is displayed at its most beneficial in this book. Danish researchers ventured beyond their laboratories and campuses to take the risk of applying their ideas in actual practice. This book stands as a testament to the national benefits that can accrue from energetic collaborations between government, industry, and academia. Does publishing these lessons reveal national secrets to countries that didn't pay for the research? Of course it does. But little competitive advantage will be lost, since these companies will be implementing a whole new round of improvements by the time you read this book.

This book is a critical resource for software organizations across the globe. It is important not only because of its valuable lessons, but also because it demonstrates the power of pre-competitive collaborative research. Research I wish I had had access to when I was responding to those phone calls in 1991.

Dr. Bill Curtis
Ft. Worth, Texas

Preface

Global competition and customer demands for better software quality are pushing companies to undertake software process improvement (SPI) initiatives. However, the scale and complexity of SPI organizational change can be daunting, and when it is not managed with great skill, the effort is likely to fail. Software development managers and engineers know too well the feelings of frustration associated with investing valuable resources and not achieving the desired SPI outcomes.

In this book, *Improving Software Organizations*, we discuss ways to understand and develop the core competencies required to succeed with SPI. Our approach is pragmatic and action-oriented. We examine SPI experiences from real-world situations and distill from them essential lessons for planning, implementing, and managing SPI initiatives to successful completion.

Our book is a result of a collaboration between four Danish companies—Danske Data, Brüel & Kjær, Ericsson Denmark, and Systematic Software Engineering—three universities—Aalborg University, Copenhagen Business School, and Technical University, Denmark—and an R&D organization, Delta. The project was part of the Danish National SPI Initiative and lasted from January 1997 to December 1999. It was funded in part by the government of Denmark through the Danish National Center for IT Research. During the three-year project, scientists and engineers from the companies and universities worked together on SPI projects within the companies.

A primary objective of our collaboration was not only to successfully implement SPI in the companies but also to develop principles and strategies for effectively executing SPI initiatives. From the beginning, we set out to examine and develop solutions for difficult practical problems reported by other SPI experts. In these pages, we present our findings and reflections based on our experiences practicing SPI. We hope that you find our book informative and that the information in it supports your own efforts to solve the practical problems involved with planning and implementing your own SPI programs.

THE FOUR COMPANIES

Following is general information about each company. As you'll see, the companies vary in size and in the products they make. They also have various objectives and approaches to SPI. Such variety offers us a unique opportunity to examine a broad range of SPI issues of interest to both software managers and engineers. You are thus likely to find many issues and problems presented in this book that are similar to those facing your own organization, as well as solutions that you can adapt and implement.

Brüel & Kjær A/S

Brüel & Kjær is a leading manufacturer of high-precision measuring instruments. These technically advanced instruments are used in many industries—including automotive, telecommunications, electricity, and aerospace—as well as in environmental measuring and university and industrial research. Brüel & Kjær's measuring instruments are based on both embedded real-time software and Windows NT applications. The Brüel & Kjær product line covers the entire range of measurement equipment, from simple transducers to highly advanced software for calculating and presenting measurement results.

Brüel & Kjær's main office is in Nærum (just north of Copenhagen), and the company operates more than 50 sales offices and agencies worldwide. In 1998, Brüel & Kjær was divided into two separate companies:

- Brüel & Kjær Sound and Vibration Measurement
- Brüel & Kjær Condition Monitoring Systems

Sound and Vibration is the larger of the two companies, with 550 employees. Approximately 80 of these employees are development engineers, of whom 40 are software developers. Annually, 10 to 15 development projects are carried out, with 4 to 8 people in each project group. Condition Monitoring Systems has some 50 employees, of whom 10 are software developers. Over the past 10 to 15 years, Brüel & Kjær has been transformed from a company focused on hardware, mechanics, and electronics to a company focused on software. Today, two out of three engineers at Brüel & Kjær are software engineers. Most Brüel & Kjær employees have an engineering education; a few have backgrounds in business or computer science.

In the mid-1990s, Brüel & Kjær transformed itself from a departmental organization to a project-oriented organization. As part of this process, the entire middle management layer was replaced. Several other employees were trained in project management and given responsibility for managing development projects in the new organization. During the 1990s, Brüel & Kjær carried out several other organizational change initiatives. In 1994, the company successfully completed ISO 9000 certification.

When assessed in October 1996, Brüel & Kjær was measured at level 2.25 on the Bootstrap scale. It was the only one of the four collaborating companies that started the SPI project at maturity level 2. In the fall of 1999, Brüel & Kjær was again assessed using the Bootstrap model, and the result showed an increase of maturity to 2.5.

Danske Data A/S

Danske Data is a subsidiary of Danske Bank Group, a financial institution that provides all types of financial services (banking, mortgaging, insurance, and so on). The primary business function of Danske Data is the development of information technology (IT) systems for Danske Bank Group, including Danske Bank, the largest bank in Denmark. Danske Data was originally the IT department within the bank, but on July 1, 1996, it was spun off as an independent company.[1] The company has approximately 900 employees located at four development centers and is one of Scandinavia's largest IT companies.

Software development projects at Danske Data vary widely in size; most are small and short-term, but there are also some major projects that have strategic implications for the entire corporation. Project teams of 3 to 5 people typically handle the smaller projects, which usually take 6 to 12 months. Large projects, such as the Year 2000 compliance project, typically involve as many as 150 people and last 6 months to 3 years. Danske Data has four development divisions, each headed by a senior vice president. Each individual division is led by a vice president and organized into departments, typically with 20 to 50 people divided among five or so projects. Project managers oversee regular projects, and the vice president manages high-profile projects. Software developers at Danske Data typically have a bachelor's degree in either an IT-related field or banking.

---

1. In Summer 2000—after the SPI project ended—Danske Data was again brought in as part of Danske Bank.

Danske Data develops software mainly for mainframe computers but also develops some applications for client/server environments, such as Internet banking. Danske Data mainframe applications run 24 hours a day and process a daily average of nine million transactions from about 11,000 workstations. The company's mainframe installation is the largest in Northern Europe and is divided between two operation centers. Systems developed for this platform are based on an advanced event-oriented database principle, something that increases data processing flexibility. Security and reliability are the two main system requirements because data are mirrored in real time between the two operation centers in Århus and Copenhagen. Modern methods for modeling data, functions, and workflow are used along with the all-important business model—information framework—which is crucial to getting stakeholders from the user organization involved in the development process.

In May 1997, Danske Data conducted its first assessment of software process maturity. It used both the Capability Maturity Model (CMM) and Bootstrap assessment approaches, which showed the company to be right between level 1 and 2 (1.5 using the Bootstrap scale). Danske Data was again assessed in October 1999 and was at that point at level 2.0.

Ericsson Denmark

The Ericsson Corporation is one of the world's largest suppliers of telecom equipment. During the past 20 years, the company has gradually transitioned from hardware-only products to embedded software products and pure software products. Ericsson's major product areas are fixed and wireless switching equipment, mobile phones, telecommunication management systems, PBX systems, transmission equipment, defense systems, and Internet solutions—all of which rely heavily on software. Ericsson Denmark has a mid-sized systems development division within the Ericsson Corporation and employs approximately 500 people working in five product groups.

In early 1996, Ericsson Corporation changed its organizational structure from a line to a matrix organization. In the period following—from 1996 to 1998—Ericsson Denmark's staff increased from 250 to 400, and each of its product groups reported to corresponding business units located in other countries. Both the Ericsson Corporation and Ericsson Denmark have a long history of improving software development. In 1992, the company took the first steps to set up a corporatewide SPI program, the Ericsson System Software Initiative (ESSI). From the beginning, ESSI was a strategic effort that ensured alignment, deployment, and follow-up on corporate SPI goals. ESSI's first intervention was in Ericsson's largest and most complex software development area, the telephone exchange software group. An aggressive goal was defined to reduce fault density in telephone exchange software products by 50% annually.

Another important ESSI initiative focused on CMM as a long-term strategy for improving software development performance. The initiative was supported by the creation of an international corps of trained CMM assessors tasked with determining the level of software process maturity throughout the company. At the end of 1996, the ESSI program had been operational worldwide for a couple of years, and most of the company's international software development sites had shown good progress toward reaching the corporate fault density goals.

Ericsson Denmark was assessed at level 1 in 1995 and at level 2 in June 1998. In between the two assessments, the division underwent both Light Assessments and UltraLight Assessments.

Systematic Software Engineering

Systematic, founded in 1985, produces and integrates software for complex information and communications systems. Systematic's international customers include military institutions and suppliers as well as data communication, transportation, and manufacturing companies and organizations in the finance and health care sectors. As a systems integrator, Systematic has established a core competency in the management and implementation of complex software projects that require high reliability and secure communications 24 hours a day. Systematic is recognized by its customers for the timely delivery of quality, cost-effective products.

In 1996, Systematic employed 137 people. Of these employees, 105 were software engineers and 32 worked in finance, administration, internal IT, quality assurance, canteen, and cleaning. By 1999, the number of employees had grown to 155. At Systematic, all software development takes place in project teams, led by a project manager. Most managers started with the company as software engineers and were later trained internally for management responsibilities. In 1998–99, project teams ranged in size from 2 to 18 members and projects lasted from two months to three years. Typically, project members were not rotated out; they stayed with the project from the analysis phase through requirements specification, design, programming, test, documentation, installation, and user training. This practice reflects the company's belief that such consistency ensures maximum commitment and development of staff competence.

Despite the small number of graduates in computer science and systems engineering in Denmark, two-thirds of Systematic's employees hold master's or doctoral degrees. To facilitate high flexibility and preparedness for change, the company recruits highly educated people with knowledge of state-of-the-art technologies. One of the main reasons Systematic undertook SPI was to help meet its goal of becoming an internationally recognized software supplier and systems integrator in communications and interoperability between defense units, and in electronic commerce and data interchange between enterprises. In 1992, Systematic's quality assurance system was certified in accordance with ISO 9001 and the military standards AQAP 110 and 150. The ISO 9001 certified quality management system is the basis of numerous elements in Systematic's quality assurance procedures.

In 1997, Systematic conducted its first software process maturity assessment using both the CMM and Bootstrap approaches and was rated to be just under Bootstrap 2. In 1998 and 1999, the company conducted additional Bootstrap assessments, and in 1999 the company was assessed to be at level 2.5 (using the Bootstrap maturity scale).

THE STRUCTURE OF THE BOOK

The book is divided into five parts. Part I consists of Chapters 1 and 2 and introduces the major learning points of our three-year collaborative project. In this first part, we present an overview—a map—of the theories and models that inspired us and formed the basis of our practice in the projects. Part II, Learning from Experience, is divided into four chapters. Each of these chapters characterizes the SPI experience of one of the four collaborating companies and is named accordingly. For example, Chapter 3, The Correct Effort, describes how Ericsson Denmark attempted first to follow standard advice, only to discover that adherence to general prescriptions did not bring the desired results. Thus, it had to deviate, ultimately producing a truly "correct" effort through innovation and adaptation to its particular circumstances.

Part III, Initiating Learning, focuses on how to structure learning conditions and initiate learning in SPI initiatives. We discuss maturity level assessments as an important mechanism for learning. We have used a broad range of assessment methods. Some were inspired by formalized approaches, such as CMM or Bootstrap (discussed in Chapters 7 and 10), whereas others were invented in project groups (Chapters 8 and 9). Finally, Chapter 11 discusses how to select an appropriate assessment strategy. Part IV, Organizing for Learning, goes beyond assessments and takes a more reflective look at SPI: In Chapter 12, we reflect on knowledge transfer; in Chapter 13, we discuss customer maturity; and in Chapter 14 we focus on organizational learning in the SPI context.

Part V examines interesting details in different techniques for SPI. Chapter 15 presents a framework for implementing SPI programs, and the remaining chapters offer detailed discussions of how to carry out risk assessments (Chapter 16), how to implement a metrics program (Chapter 17), and how to improve requirements specification (Chapter 18).

This book is based on a truly collaborative effort. The team of engineers and scientists that have authored the chapters is listed at the very end of this book. Three of the authors—Lars Mathiassen, Jan Pries-Heje, and Ojelanki Ngwenyama—have edited this book assisted by Keri Schreiner who has interacted closely with the authors to help them write for practitioners. Finally, the staff at Addison-Wesley has provided valuable support in designing and producing the book.

PART I

Learning to Improve

Chapter 1

Learning SPI in Practice

Lars Mathiassen, Peter Axel Nielsen,
and Jan Pries-Heje

According to the common rhetoric of software process improvement (SPI), there are a few basic steps to improving your software development process. First, you assess your organization's current capability to develop quality software. Based on this, you derive a stepwise, focused strategy for improving this capability. You then make improvement efforts an integral part of your organization's long-term goals. The result? Both the quality of your services and the productivity of your processes increase.

SPI rhetoric is certainly powerful and appealing, and it inspires many software organizations to engage in improvement initiatives. However, even though most organizations struggle to meet expectations, many of them eventually fail.

Starting SPI is not difficult. You begin by assessing your current processes. Typically, enthusiasm at this point is high. Most of your colleagues will be eager to learn about the strengths and weaknesses in the way projects are organized and carried out. However, turning assessment insights into action is the point at which many organizations fail. Others manage to initiate focused improvement projects, only to find that implementing new ideas is very difficult (see Chapter 15). Even when you succeed in implementing an idea in an individual project, you are still a long way from institutionalizing improvements. In addition to the predictable challenges at each stage, you're likely to encounter other challenges. These include conflicts between SPI efforts and other traditional improvement initiatives, and the tendency for resources to grow scarce as the first wave of energy for SPI dies out. Clearly, SPI success involves more than simply choosing the right methods and collaborating with the best experts (see Chapter 16).

The authors of this book have all been actively engaged in SPI research and practice for several years. Our experiences have taught us what it takes to go from SPI rhetoric to success with actual initiatives. In some ways, SPI's main goal works against success: SPI seeks to change existing practices. In this change process, deeply rooted values and traditions—including traditional improvement efforts—are necessarily critiqued and challenged. For most organizations, SPI is a radically different improvement philosophy, and as such it must be learned. Learning SPI can help you prepare for the changes and challenges ahead.

How does SPI differ from traditional approaches to improvement? Based on our experiences, we have identified five core SPI principles. These principles express SPI's underlying values—values that organizations must adopt to succeed with SPI. The five principles are

- Focus on problems.
- Emphasize knowledge creation.
- Encourage participation.
- Integrate leadership.
- Plan for continuous improvement.

Practicing these principles is an acquired skill. We examine each principle in more detail and discuss the factors that support and undermine them. We also provide insights drawn from the broader field of organizational learning that help explicate each principle's underlying rationale.

1.1 FOCUS ON PROBLEMS

Problem solving is the essence of improvement. SPI starts with an organization's existing practices. SPI practitioners diagnose these practices to evaluate their strengths and weaknesses; then they identify and prioritize possible improvements and establish teams to design and implement new or better processes. Practice is the SPI group's starting point as well as their goal, and their customers are practitioners, be they software engineers or software managers. Figure 1.1 illustrates the problem orientation of SPI efforts.

This SPI principle has several immediate implications:

- There are no generally-applicable solutions. The SPI group must take into account the organization's specific traditions, values, and capabilities.
- Many different and competing viewpoints are involved. Different actors and groups within the organization have different perceptions of the problems and of the usefulness of possible solutions.
- The ultimate measure of success is practice. Is the SPI initiative actually improving the organization's capabilities? The SPI group must constantly ask this question to keep an improvement initiative on track.

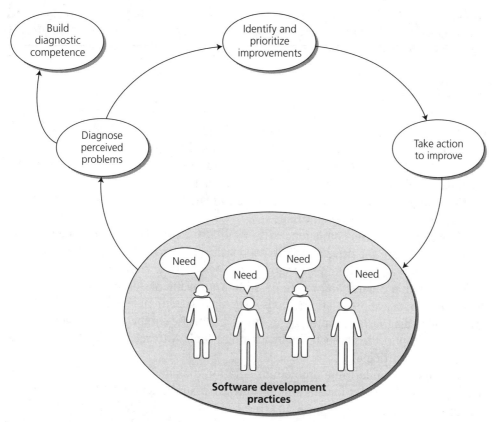

Figure 1.1 *SPI should focus on problems*

Examples from Practice

For years, Danske Data's methodology department had developed methods and tools to support software practices. Its first SPI assessment showed that these methods and tools were state-of-the-art. However, as Chapter 5 explains, few projects used the tools and methods. Furthermore, the methodology department did not feel obligated to en-sure that its inventions were used. The SPI initiative questioned the department's tra-dition of solution orientation. How well did the department members understand current practices? What did they conceive as the result of their efforts? What were their underlying success criteria? Such questioning led to many discussions and ulti-mately to changes in both the improvement efforts and the methodology department.

Brüel & Kjær's project managers were skeptical about using methods and were in no way motivated to engage in improvement programs (see Chapter 6). Because project managers were key players in the organization, their attitude toward SPI was crucial to the effort's success. The SPI group had no choice but to build a constructive alliance with the project managers. They therefore decided to engage project managers in a dialog to identify their most immediate problems and needs.

Key Factors

Organizations that are learning to be problem-oriented should start with perceived problems and build diagnostic competence. To identify problems, SPI group members must understand and address the software practitioners' perception of which practices need improvement. Two obvious strategies help here. You can analyze and formulate problems and develop improvements in direct response to practitioner perceptions, and you can engage practitioners in dialog about other, less obvious, but equally important improvement issues.

Building diagnostic competence also facilitates a problem orientation. Your SPI group should have the drive and skills to identify problems in current practices. You should develop and maintain strong relations to practice, know how to relate problems to possible causes, and relate possible improvement actions to specific problems. You can use appropriate methods—such as assessment techniques (Chapter 7) and problem diagnosis (Chapter 9)—to build diagnostic competence into your group, or you can import the competency by inviting people with relevant backgrounds and experience to participate.

Factors that undermine problem orientation include the silver bullet syndrome and a general disrespect for SPI among software practitioners. Traditional methodology departments typically believe that they can resolve problems by applying technology. Their primary strategy is thus technology push. This silver bullet approach is rarely compatible with problem orientation.

The problem-oriented approach is also undermined when SPI or the SPI practitioners lack credibility among software practitioners. A negative image of SPI among practitioners can result when the SPI group offers too little or inappropriate information, does not demonstrate useful results, or fails to interact with software practitioners.

Broader Insights

The underlying rationale for a problem-oriented approach to SPI conforms with general lessons from organizational learning. Argyris and Schön (1996) suggest that the real challenge in any form of organizational learning is to effectively address the gap between espoused theories and theories-in-use. Espoused theories express what people believe and think they do; theories-in-use is what they actually do. Hard as it is to admit, most of us realize on some level that self-deception, lack of discipline, and environmental factors often make it difficult to follow best practices. We keep doing what we are used to doing even though we know that other approaches are more effective.

As individuals and as organizations, we are constantly facing the challenge of understanding and bridging the gap between espoused theories and theories-in-use. State-of-the-art software engineering knowledge is not the only nor the most important source of learning. The key to effective organizational learning is to understand the difference between what we already know we should do and what we actually do. With problem orientation, we confront that gap. If we don't, we risk getting stuck with general solutions and personal beliefs.

Many methods can help you practice a problem-oriented approach. Widely known in the SPI community, the IDEAL model—Initiate, Diagnose, Establish, Act, and Learn—describes in detail a problem-oriented model of how to organize SPI (McFeeley 1996).

You can also use other, more general approaches to inspire your SPI initiative. One approach is Soft Systems Methodology (Checkland and Scholes 1990), which applies rich pictures, multiple perspectives, system modeling, and debates to drive complex problem-solving processes. This method takes as a starting point an unstructured situation in which problems have yet to be identified. Thus, problem owners and their different perceptions of problems play a key role in the process.

1.2   EMPHASIZE KNOWLEDGE CREATION

In essence, improvement is knowledge creation. SPI is driven by knowledge about practices and perceived needs, insights gained during the improvement process, software industry standards, and state-of-the-art methodologies and tools. SPI efforts also depend on the implicit, individual knowledge of participants. However, the general idea is to make knowledge explicit and to share knowledge.

To create useful knowledge, you must be observant and systematic. Some knowledge will, of course, remain tacit in individual skills and organizational capabilities. You should, however, make an effort to learn from practice, to make the implicit explicit, and to build widely shared knowledge about software development and SPI. Also, your SPI group should understand knowledge itself in a broad sense, ranging from experience to general, established theory. Finally, your SPI effort's knowledge creation process should be cyclical in nature, as Figure 1.2 shows.

Your SPI group's knowledge creation process must be deliberately designed and nurtured. We recommend that you pay particular attention to the following questions:

- How do you capture and evaluate your experiences?
- How do you combine them with other experiences and with your underlying theories?
- How is your thinking influenced by knowledge from outside the organization?

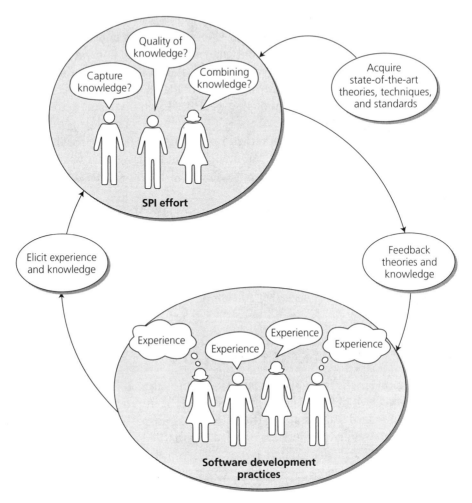

Figure 1.2 *SPI should emphasize knowledge creation*

- What is the quality of your knowledge?
- How does your knowledge feed back into the SPI efforts?

Examples from Practice

As part of its SPI initiative, Danske Data established the Project Management Competence Center (see Chapter 5). The PMC Center's purpose was to be a meeting point
where project managers could exchange ideas and solutions and discuss problems, is-

sues, and challenges. Thus, through the PMC Center, Danske Data could better organize and use its project-management knowledge and bring in outside information to inspire project activities. However, the main motivation for establishing the PMC Center was to harness competence already present in the organization, much of which resided with a few knowledgeable and powerful project managers. PMC Center activities would help explicate this knowledge and make it available to all project managers. Danske Data also developed a project-manager training program in which experienced project managers led many of the key sessions.

Systematic was slower to realize the importance of the knowledge creation principle in its SPI effort (see Chapter 4). Several years ago, Systematic established a quality management system and was quickly certified as compliant with the ISO 9000 standards. When Systematic started its SPI effort, Systematic managers believed that the organization could reach CMM level 2 and even level 3 just as easily. It took a while for the SPI group to realize that this was not the case. Gradually, they concluded that the new change process was quite different. To succeed, common software processes had to be found, described, and institutionalized, and that would require a tremendous amount of work. This understanding emerged slowly as old knowledge was forced to give way to new experience. The company's experience in launching the ISO certification effort required a lot of process description and some management pressure. However, the knowledge explicated in the descriptions was at that time largely shared. With the SPI effort, processes were not in place in advance and the knowledge did not even exist. Thus, new knowledge had to be introduced and shared across the organization.

Key Factors

Two factors are key to facilitating a knowledge creation approach to SPI: systematic evaluation and state-of-the-art knowledge. When you systematically evaluate software practices ("diagnose" in the IDEAL model) and specific SPI initiatives ("learn" in the IDEAL model), you create a foundation for learning from experience. This learning in turn can lead to increased understanding of what it will take to improve your organization's software practices.

You can also import state-of-the-art theories and techniques from outside the organization. Such external knowledge can provoke your organization to change and can introduce what industry leaders consider common knowledge. The purpose is to transcend your organization's existing software practice when internal knowledge building is insufficient (for more on this, see Chapter 12).

Knowledge creation is undermined by myths and the "not-invented-here" syndrome. Building local knowledge is important, particularly when it is done publicly. Half-baked stories of the successes and failures of various past efforts can, however, reinforce myths and ruin good initiatives. It is therefore important that you create knowledge openly and that conclusions are tested in public. Otherwise, all knowledge will be equally important, there will be no sense of knowledge quality, and, ultimately, all knowledge will be equally meaningless and bound to remain private or localized in subcultures.

Most software practitioners are proud of their practices and results, and they often invent new approaches to deal with challenges they face. All this is positive, but if they value only in-house solutions—and thus the not-invented-here syndrome dominates—practitioners considerably reduce their ability to learn from state-of-the-art theories and techniques and thus limit improvement possibilities.

Broader Insights

The value of knowledge creation is clearly expressed in the SPI literature. Humphrey (1989) argues that SPI initiatives must be guided by two types of knowledge: normative models (understanding the map) and systematic assessments (understanding the landscape). Assessments are particularly important here because they provide insight into current software practices; for examples see McFeeley (1996) and Chapters 7, 8, 9, and 11.

Checkland distinguishes between the perceived world and the ideas and concepts relevant to appreciating it (Checkland and Scholes 1990). People create the perceived world through interpretations based on ideas and concepts, and their experiences of the perceived world in turn yield new ideas and concepts. According to Checkland, intellectual work is not simply a matter of making sense of the perceived world; sensemaking is a purposeful activity that brings experience and theory together in a framework. Individuals conceptualize frameworks and use them to support reflection and thinking, something that leads to action.

Nonaka and Takeuchi (1995) focus on the nature of human and organizational knowledge and explain how knowledge is created in daily organizational life. Their primary distinction is between tacit knowledge and explicit knowledge. Based on this distinction, they discuss four fundamental knowledge creation processes:

- *Socialization* occurs when one person's tacit knowledge is directly adopted by others as tacit knowledge.
- *Externalization* occurs when an organization explicates tacit knowledge as concepts and models.
- *Combination* occurs when an organization brings together different sources of explicit knowledge to create new forms of explicit knowledge.
- *Internalization* occurs when individuals adopt explicit knowledge in practice, thereby making it part of their tacit knowledge.

To create and manage knowledge successfully in your SPI efforts, you must ensure that all these processes are working at the individual and organizational level (see Chapter 14).

1.3 ENCOURAGE PARTICIPATION

Participation makes improvement happen. The point of SPI is to change the way practitioners develop software. However, changing human behavior is not an easy task. SPI initiatives provoke the same types of resistance to change as traditional IT implementations (Levine 1997). The factors that make IT projects successful are similar to those that help SPI succeed. The main difference between the efforts is the target customer: IT projects address the way the users work; SPI initiatives address the way software practitioners work.

One way IT projects cope with resistance to change is to encourage user participation. Early in the process, they involve the people whose behavior needs to change (see Figure 1.3). As obvious as this sounds, it is difficult to practice for many reasons. For example, if your SPI customer group is very large—thus making it impossible to involve everyone—who should participate? If you involve only representative practitioners, will they maintain the practitioner perspective over the long run, or will they themselves become change agents? Allocating time is also a problem. Software practitioners have their own work to do, and SPI work is typically logged as overhead. Given this, do you have a plan for keeping them motivated?

Examples from Practice

At Brüel & Kjær, participation became the cornerstone for most improvement activities (see Chapter 6). An improvement group analyzed problem reports and identified the most promising requirement specification techniques. But instead of forcing the best techniques on the projects, the support team asked project members which techniques they preferred. Table 1.1 shows the questionnaire the team used to discuss the techniques with project members. Each project then selected five or six techniques. The support team held a workshop and used some of the techniques to elicit and check a requirements specification. Not only did the result lead to better requirement specifications and better products, but also the improvement effort was so successful that many other projects asked to learn the same techniques (see Chapter 18). Letting project members pick which techniques they wanted to learn created the commitment needed for this improvement initiative to succeed.

Another example of participatory improvement comes from Ericsson Denmark (Chapter 3). Ericsson Denmark had long tried to move from one maturity level to the next but had made little progress. This changed when project managers became

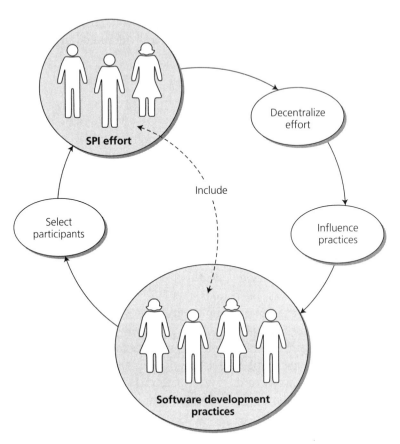

Figure 1.3 SPI requires participation

Table 1.1 Brüel & Kjær's Requirement Techniques Questionnaire

To what extent will this be a change in the way *you* usually work?
To what extent do you think this will be a change in the way *other people at B&K* usually work?
Please evaluate this statement: The technique described here is effective and usable.
How certain is it that the use of this technique will lead to the expected prevention of errors?
Do you have the necessary time in the project to adapt and use this technique?

involved in doing UltraLight Assessments on their own projects (see Chapter 10). Each month, every project manager assessed his or her own project and presented the results to management. Because of project managers' commitment and involvement, Ericsson Denmark successfully advanced to the next maturity level a few months later.

Key Factors

As these examples show, the involvement of professional practitioners and a decentralized improvement effort are key factors in the participatory approach. The intent is not merely to persuade practitioners to practice new processes; you must involve practitioners in actually designing and developing new processes based on their own experiences and professional judgment. When the people who will use the new processes help create them, the processes are much more likely to be integrated into future practice. To succeed, you need more than just good practitioners—you need professional practitioners who are engaged both in getting the job done and advancing the profession.

Decentralizing the improvement effort facilitates participation throughout your organization and helps you to capture and account for local variations in current practices. However, inviting participation can lead efforts in unexpected directions. To see such developments as opportunities rather than threats, your organization must be decentralized because opportunities are much easier to appreciate locally. This, in turn, requires that you be able to coordinate your effort and dynamically adjust your tactics.

A participatory approach is primarily undermined by bureaucracy and firefighting. Strongly formalized assessments and centralized, management-driven SPI programs tend to make things too rigid and distant from practitioners' daily practice on software projects. To support participation, you should limit bureaucratic arrangements and approaches. Bureaucracies are excellent ways of implementing rules and routine, but SPI follows few rules, and it focuses on problem definition and problem solving rather than on routine.

Even when resources are directed toward SPI participation, practitioners are often submerged in day-to-day work, and finding time to participate in SPI activities is difficult. Also, a culture that acclaims firefighters as heroes offers individuals little incentive for investing their time in long-term improvement activities. At the start of Danske Data's 1997 improvement effort, management directed several people to devote 30% of their time to the SPI initiative. At a first glance, this sounds satisfactory. But—not surprisingly—we quickly found that "part time is no time" (Johansen and Mathiassen 1998).

Broader Insights

The idea of participation is well established in the software profession. Mumford's now classical work on involving users in systems development efforts (1983) has had a major impact on the profession. In Scandinavia, participation is now more or less characteristic of systems development. Bjerknes et al. (1987) and Greenbaum and Kyng (1991) provide many examples and practical approaches in support of active user involvement. Unfortunately, user participation often degrades into platitudes such as"build a prototype," "enlist a sponsor," and "create user-friendly interfaces" (Hirschheim, R., and Newman M., 1988). To succeed, participation must go beyond persuasion or motivation; it is a powerful strategy for building useful knowledge and must be treated as such.

1.4 INTEGRATE LEADERSHIP

Ultimately, improvements must be integrated at all levels. To succeed, your SPI efforts must be consistent with your organization's strategy and vision of the future. Although SPI is focused on software practices, software organizations have other concerns as well. New technologies emerge, new markets develop, and alliances and mergers with other companies occur. Moreover, in many organizations, software development is not the core business but rather is one among many functions aimed at the organization's overall goals. Given this, SPI initiatives risk getting in the way of other organizational initiatives. To prevent this, leadership should be integrated at all levels (see Figure 1.4).

Our primary concern here is management's ability to use leadership to motivate and set direction. When your SPI vision and your organization's overall strategic vision are aligned, management can be integrated at all levels. In our experience, a good vision is closely linked to how leaders perceive the existence of people in the organization. It is not enough to build a vision. As a leader, you must base your vision on the organization's reality and present the vision in a way that motivates others to both understand and believe in it.

Examples from Practice

At Danske Data, top management endorsed and supported the SPI initiative from the start. For example, the CEO spoke at the workshop where Danske Data's standard for project management was created (see Chapter 5). This ensured that the initiatives around project management—such as establishing the PMC Center—were consistent with the overall company strategy. However, it is also fair to say that in this case, middle management did not share the SPI vision and generally ignored the SPI effort's existence.

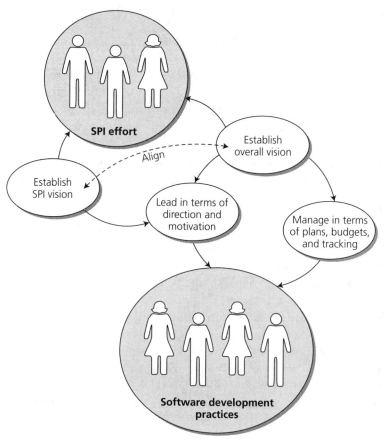

Figure 1.4   *SPI Requires Integrated Leadership*

Another example of leadership comes from Systematic. From the beginning, Systematic's CEO was keen to achieve CMM maturity level 3 (see Chapter 4) and to include customers in the improvement process (see Chapter 13). These aims were woven into all the organization's plans and actions. Because the organizational vision and the SPI vision were aligned, Systematic could set ambitious goals and move forward. Furthermore, Systematic's CEO walked his talk. When an assessment identified project management as a problem, the CEO invited several suppliers to compete to deliver a project-management training program. Within a year, more than half of Systematic's project managers had completed 12 days of intensive training.

Key Factors

The most important leadership quality is the ability to communicate. Managing, controlling, and monitoring do not a leader make. Leaders need vision and the skills to communicate that vision throughout organization. According to Kotter, any type of change requires 75% leadership and only 25% management (Kotter 1996). SPI visions, plans, and achievements should be widely communicated. To maintain attention and commitment, you should produce results regularly and disseminate them widely.

Leadership is undermined by a lack of management commitment and the Balkan syndrome. At Ericsson Denmark, management was committed, but the commitment was wildly unfocused. At one point, there were six key process activities (KPAs) on the SPI agenda, plus several critical success factors and a few "vital few actions" (see Chapter 3). This scattered commitment made the SPI effort confusing at both the project and the organization level. It was not until the responsible manager outlined a simple and clear strategy—achieve maturity level 2 before summer—that change and improvement began. Such a lack of management commitment is not limited to top management; it might also apply to middle management or any type of supporting staff.

The Balkan syndrome is common in software organizations. It occurs when each group or department has its own way of doing things and develops individual professional standards. Without strong leadership, improvement efforts tend to diverge and common commitment disappears. Although you must take variations and differences into account, you should do so only when necessary. When projects learn from each other and processes are reused across the organization, you can better focus energies when difficult challenges arise.

Broader Insights

This principle is grounded in strategic theories that consider not only an organization and its environment (see Ansoff 1988) but also internal factors such as organizational structures, production processes, and technology (c.f. Chandler 1962, Scott 1987). Furthermore, we view the strategic plan not as the most important part of strategy but rather as an outcome of an ongoing process of integration and reorientation. For SPI to succeed, it must be an integral part of the organization's strategic leadership.

Organizational leadership involves the ability to build a shared vision and to identify prevailing mental models that need to be challenged. In a learning organization, leaders "are part of changing the way business operates, not from a vague philanthropic urge, but from a conviction that their efforts will produce more productive organizations, capable of achieving higher levels" (Senge 1990).

1.5 PLAN FOR CONTINUOUS IMPROVEMENT

Improvement should be a continuous effort. It is easy to imagine the end of an SPI project, when you count your successes and failures. It's equally obvious that improvements are in some sense endless: As you alleviate some problems, others become visible. Both views make sense.

Organizing your SPI efforts as projects that have an end point lets you stop, step back, and evaluate your SPI initiative and its progress. When an SPI project ends, you can move responsibility for the new processes into the organization itself. Nonetheless, as Figure 1.5 shows, SPI initiatives are necessarily ongoing because there are always new problems and challenges, and solutions to old problems must be maintained and further developed.

Examples from Practice

Although our experiences span only a few years, it is clear to us that a continuous approach is important. At Danske Data (Chapter 5), recent discussions have focused on

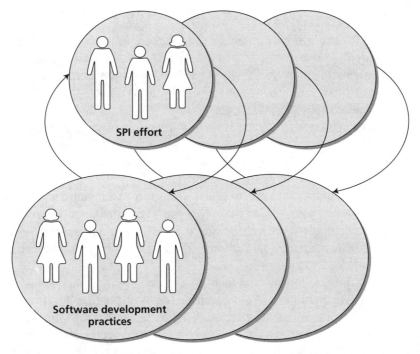

Figure 1.5 *SPI should be continuous*

how to organize the SPI effort in the coming years. Danske Data has long had a large methodology department. Initially, the SPI group attempted to dissociate itself from this department because it was not well regarded by software practitioners. However, the SPI effort has been gradually reorganized to include the methodology department so that it can fill the growing demand for maintaining new software processes. In some ways, the methodology department and the SPI initiative have merged. In other respects they are distinct initiatives. In any case, the SPI effort has now become a stable part of the organizational structure.

Another event at Danske Data supports this view. After two and a half years of SPI effort, a Bootstrap assessment showed that the company had reached its goal of maturity level 2. The CEO then decided to go after level 3. Evidently, the SPI effort will be ongoing for some time. A question remains, however, as to how far Danske Data will or should go on the conventional maturity ladder. Metaphorically speaking, it is not important to reach the summit. What matters is that you stay on an ascending path that is appropriate for your organization. Reaching one goal thus creates another, higher goal that has meaning for your processes and their context.

Key Factors

The key factors in a continuous approach are stepwise improvement, top-management commitment, and a sustainable improvement organization. Maturity models such as CMM, Bootstrap, and SPICE (Software Process Improvement and Capability Determination) embody the essence of stepwise improvement. All experiences suggest that such ladders take years to climb.

A continuous approach thus requires commitment from top management. A local or bottom-up initiative can be effective for a while, but it easily loses momentum. As time goes on, the focus on SPI initiatives will decrease unless they succeed in becoming part of the organization's strategic thrust.

To successfully climb the maturity ladder, you must install and maintain impeccable improvement processes. To do this, you need a sustainable improvement organization that is adaptable to changing circumstances. Management must directly allocate resources to such an organizational unit and must help it create and maintain organizationwide SPI awareness.

Factors that undermine the continuous approach are inadequate results and a marginal SPI effort. If results are not documented or the return on investment is poor, your SPI effort is unlikely to survive past the first project. In most cases, you cannot simply document improved maturity on a normative scale. Practical, convincing results are needed, and it is typically best to establish a simple metrics program that can help you argue for continuing your efforts (see Chapter 17).

Even when an SPI effort is showing results, organizational politics or other organizational issues can still marginalize it. Brüel & Kjær's SPI effort went from marginal to central and widely known and back to marginal (see Chapter 6). At this point, it looks as if Brüel & Kjær will most likely discontinue its six-year SPI effort.

Broader Insights

The IDEAL model clearly expresses SPI's continuous nature (McFeeley 1996). The main theory underlying the continuous approach is Humphrey's CMM (Humphrey 1989). The CMM is specific to software development, but it shares a basic structure with Crosby's five-level model of quality systems (Crosby 1979). The idea of continuous, stepwise improvement is also common to many other quality models.

In his work on Soft Systems Methodology, Checkland has been particularly clear on how alleviating some problems makes way for others (Checkland and Scholes 1990). Effective problem-solving approaches are therefore continuous. Checkland and Scholes also distinguish between two types of problem solving: intervention and interaction. The interventionist mode is external and uses problem solving to structure an internal inquiry. The interaction mode is internal and uses problem solving to make sense of experience. The latter mode is similar to the continuous approach, whereas the interventionist mode corresponds more with a focused collaboration with SPI consultants over a limited time.

Theories of organizational learning view learning as continuously present and as a significant factor in organized work and behavior (see, for example, Argyris and Schön 1996, Senge 1990).

1.6 LEARN TO IMPROVE

Our five principles are strongly interdependent. If your organization fails to practice one of them, you seriously reduce your chances of successfully implementing the others. For example, if you fail to focus on problems, the following occur:

- You cannot create new knowledge based on your organization's software practices.
- A primary motivator for having practitioners participate disappears.
- Management is more likely to reduce improvement initiatives to traditional support functions with little strategic importance.
- You are left with only an overall concern for improving software practices, and that concern cannot drive a continuous, long-term improvement effort.

If you fail to adopt other principles, similar weaknesses will result. The five principles are a coherent philosophy of SPI that we have developed through practice. The underlying values are different from or even contradictory to the values of conventional improvement approaches. It is therefore not simply a question of deciding to practice SPI. Learning SPI is a demanding process; it questions personal and professional beliefs and challenges existing traditions.

If you start your SPI initiative as a series of projects, you can maintain your focus and allow for dynamic changes as your particular process evolves. Above all, SPI requires committed, patient participants. To learn SPI, you must be prepared to improve both software practices and existing improvement traditions. To prepare yourself for such a challenge, in Chapter 2 we offer an overview of the existing SPI literature and recommend that you take advantage of the knowledge it contains. Ultimately, however, each organization must find its own path to SPI success. Your primary and most important role will be that of change agent. The best change agents avoid becoming dogmatic SPI followers. Rather, they learn what they can, listen to the many voices within their own organization, and, based on both, they chart the best path toward change.

1.7 REFERENCES

Ansoff, H.I. 1988. *The New Corporate Strategy.* New York: John Wiley & Sons.

Argyris, C., and D. Schön. 1996. *Organizational Learning II.* Reading, MA: Addison-Wesley.

Bjerknes, G., P. Ehn, and M. Kyng, eds. 1987. *Computers and Democracy.* Aldershot, UK: Avebury.

Chandler, A.D. 1962. *Strategy and Structure: Chapters in the History of American Industrial Enterprise.* Cambridge, MA: MIT Press.

Checkland, P., and J. Scholes. 1990. *Soft Systems Methodology in Action.* New York: John Wiley & Sons.

Crosby, P. B. 1979. *Quality Is Free: The Art of Making Quality Free.* New York: McGraw-Hill.

Greenbaum, J., and M. Kyng, eds. 1991. *Design at Work: Cooperative Design of Computer Systems.* Hillsdale, NJ: Lawrence Erlbaum.

Hirschheim, R., and Newman, M. 1988. "Information Systems and User Resistance: Theory and Practice, *The Computer Journal* (31:5), pp. 398–408.

Humphrey, W. S. 1989. *Managing the Software Process*. Reading, MA: Addison-Wesley.

Johansen, J., and L. Mathiassen. 1998. "Lessons Learned in a National SPI Effort." *Proceedings of EuroSPI '98*, Gothenburg, Sweden.

Kotter, J. 1996. *Leading Change*. Cambridge, MA: Harvard Business School Publishing.

Levine, L. 1997. "An Ecology of Resistance." *Proceedings of the Second IFIP 8.6 Working Conference on the Diffusion and Adoption of Information Technology*, Ambleside, Cumbria, UK.

McFeeley, B. 1996. *IDEAL: A User's Guide for Software Process Improvement*. Handbook, CMU/SEI-96-HB-001. Pittsburgh: SEI.

Mumford, E. 1983. *Designing Human Systems: The ETHICS Method*. Manchester, UK: Manchester Business School.

Nonaka, I., and H. Takeuchi. 1995. *The Knowledge-Creating Company: How Japanese Companies Create the Dynamics of Innovation*. Oxford, UK: Oxford University Press.

Scott, W.R. 1987. *Organizations: Rational, Natural and Open Systems*. Upper Saddle River, NJ: Prentice-Hall.

Senge, P. 1990. "The Leader's New Work: Building Learning Organizations." *Sloan Management Review*. Fall: 7–23.

Chapter 2

Mapping SPI Ideas and Practices

Ivan Aaen, Jesper Arent, Lars Mathiassen,
and Ojelanki Ngwenyama

Our experience using SPI in four organizations has taught us that each organization must find its own approach. An organization must learn to practice SPI in its own particular context and must be open to changes in software practice, culture, and management style. However, an organization need not pursue SPI in a vacuum. Regardless of the particulars of an organization, in implementing SPI it will deal with a standard set of ideas. These ideas have been extensively explored in the literature over the past 15 years as SPI has become a widely used approach to improve software engineering quality and productivity. Many practitioners, consultants, and researchers have engaged in developing relevant frameworks, reporting specific experiences, and reflecting on SPI's strengths and weaknesses in maturing the software engineering discipline. As a result, the literature on SPI is extensive.

Organizations undertaking SPI initiatives can look to this literature for both inspiration and guidance. In doing so, they can avoid the pitfalls that have led other organizations to failure and can learn from successful initiatives that bear on their situation. However, following this advice is difficult because the literature is extensive and rapidly expanding, and the authoritative sources offer considerably different descriptions of SPI's underlying rationale. To remedy this situation, we present here a guide to SPI literature that focuses on management, approach, and perspective (MAP). This MAP is based on Aaen et al. (2001).

We also offer a practical framework for evaluating your ongoing SPI initiatives: Which SPI ideas have you applied appropriately? Which ideas could you more actively adopt? After introducing our MAP of SPI ideas, we use it to discuss four case studies that reflect the need to tailor SPI to your organization's reality. We have given each case study a unique name that captures the most characteristic feature of the organization's SPI experience. The four cases are

- The correct effort (Ericsson Denmark)
- The ambitious effort (Systematic)
- The grassroots effort (Danske Data)
- The adolescent effort (Bruel & Kjaer)

After describing each case, we show how you can apply MAP to assess the strengths and weaknesses of your own SPI initiative. Such a diagnosis will help you find ways to in;crease your initiative's chances of success and minimize its risk of failure.

In mapping the SPI literature, we distinguish between management ideas (M), which help you manage improvement initiatives; approach ideas (A), which help guide your improvement process; and perspective ideas (P), which help you assess or transform the improvement target: the software operation. The MAP is complete in the sense that it covers the literature's key ideas about how to mature software organizations.

We distilled the MAP from our comprehensive study of the SPI literature and from our experiences practicing SPI. To identify SPI literature, we systematically researched the key software engineering journals, the available books on SPI, and papers published in computer and information systems journals and conference proceedings. To select references, we systematically researched the references included in the specialized SPI literature and in the available surveys of SPI literature (Fuggetta and Picco 1994, Paulk 1999).

Table 2.1 offers an overview of the MAP. Each aspect of it is based on three primary ideas. SPI management is based on the ideas that activities are organized in a dynamic fashion, with a focus on projects; that both overall intervention and specific improvement efforts are carefully planned; and that feedback is ensured through systematic evaluation of the effects on software engineering practices. The ideas behind the SPI approach are that it is evolutionary in nature; it is based on idealized, norma-

Table 2.1   *Mapping Key Ideas in SPI*

Concern	SPI ideas
Management of SPI	Organization, plan, feedback
Approaches to SPI	Evolution, norm, commitment
Perspectives of SPI	Process, competence, context

tive models of software engineering; and that the careful building and development of commitments between the involved actors is essential to success. Finally, the SPI perspective on the improvement target is based on the ideas that the main target is the software process; the key resource is software developers' competencies; and the intention is to change the software operation's context to create sustainable support for the involved actors.

In the following, we present the map in detail. We describe the essence of each of the nine key ideas, discuss counter positions that represent alternative approaches, and outline the benefits and risks related to practicing each key idea in SPI. We subsequently show how this set of ideas can be used to map specific SPI initiatives and generate possible avenues for improvement.

2.1 MANAGEMENT OF SPI

SPI is a challenging and complex change process. For it to succeed, effective management is required. Much of what has been learned about managing the successful transformation of organizations can be applied to managing SPI initiatives. However, even though SPI managers can learn common strategies that have been successful for managing initiatives such as Business Process Reengineering (BPR) and Total Quality Management (TQM), SPI managers must address some unique challenges. First, the duration, scale, and complexity of SPI initiatives are far beyond those encountered in other organizational transformation projects. For example, whereas a BPR project typically has a short and intense life cycle, an SPI project is likely to last for several years. On the other hand, whereas the scope of TQM activities can be very narrow, SPI initiatives affect every aspect of software production. The duration, scale, and complexity of SPI projects argue for strong management, effective organization and planning, and good feedback and control mechanisms. Meeting these conditions does not, in itself, guarantee success, but failing to meet them can be a sure prescription for failure.

Organization

The scale, complexity, and duration of SPI initiatives necessitate a dedicated organizational unit with adequate resources and a well-defined reporting structure. The status and resources that your company devote to the SPI initiative will influence its success or failure. As Humphrey sees it, "If software process improvement isn't anybody's job, it is not surprising that it doesn't get done! If it is important enough to do, however, someone must be assigned the responsibility and given the necessary resources" (Humphrey, 1989, p. 287).

Because SPI is a strategic, organizational transformational initiative and because it entails several different projects in different areas of the company, it must have an infrastructure. An SPI group should be established early—preferably before the first project starts—and institutionalized as a permanent organizational unit. This group will be responsible for planning, implementing, and managing all SPI efforts in the organization at large. Having the status of organizational unit with a clear line of reporting can ensure the authority, legitimacy, and survival of the SPI initiative, which are necessary because SPI projects are generally long-term and often quite political.

A second important condition is that the SPI group have access to and control of necessary resources, including people, budget, space, and computers. The SPI group must have a strong and influential manager and must include several people with specialized technical competence in all SPI practices. The SPI manager will have difficulty attracting and keeping people with the relevant qualifications because such people are generally scarce. Furthermore, if the technical specialists are on loan from other areas in the company, there will always be competition for their skills and knowledge, and that can threaten the survival of the SPI initiative. Therefore, the SPI unit manager must take great care to train, develop, and maintain a set of dedicated SPI experts and to allocate them to specific projects for limited periods.

There are several risks to institutionalizing an SPI group. One risk is that the group can become a centralized and bureaucratic methods department. A second risk is that the group might produce solutions that practitioners deem irrelevant. Involving practitioners in the project should reduce this risk. The SPI group also risks becoming alienated and having its results met with indifference in other parts of the organization. Finally, as a direct consequence of being separate, the SPI project risks ending up on a sidetrack, with little importance in the organization. Nonetheless, lessons learned from SPI practice suggest that disintegrated, asynchronous improvement efforts are not only inefficient but also ineffective for solving organizationwide problems.

Thus, the dilemma is this: How can you organize the effort to achieve the strengths of centralization (specialization and resource base) and decentralization (responsiveness and local acceptance)? One effective strategy is to organize improvement initiatives as coordinated localized projects within specific organizational units of the company. Each project should have its own defined objectives, deliverables, and resources. This strategy allows for intense focus on specific areas of the company, separates the effort from ongoing organizational activities, and increases the visibility of SPI projects.

Organizing SPI initiatives as dedicated, localized efforts provides many benefits for effective process management. First, it ensures that the transformation considers the practicalities of each organizational area. It also allows SPI experts to collaborate closely with the area's software developers to define work procedures that fit their concerns. Second, resource adaptation can be taken into account. For example, when the SPI effort is established as a localized project, the allocation of appropriate resources will be an integral part of that unit's work activity. Third, this organizing strategy helps you to manage the scale and complexity of the transformation and increases your ability to control each project and its outcome. Finally, the strategy enhances organizational learning and knowledge diffusion across various localized projects. As each project encounters and solves specific problems in the implementation life cycle, that knowledge is passed on to others.

Plan

Planning is another important management activity (Zahran 1998). Many SPI programs have failed simply because no action was taken after the initial CMM appraisal (Paulk 1996). Success is more readily achieved when you have a strategy, a clear statement of goals and objectives, and a clear implementation plan. The SPI implementation plan should detail the plan of action, and managers should assign individuals and groups responsibility for specific work and oversight activities. Creating a plan for your SPI effort typically

- Supports a common understanding of goals, target dates, and expected outcomes for specific project activities
- Makes it easier to decompose the project into limited tasks with specific operational objectives
- Supports prioritization and coordination of improvement tasks and helps to clarify interrelationships among tasks
- Helps top management, SPI project members, and affected practitioners to build and meet specific commitments
- Serves as a vehicle for communicating progress to ensure proper visibility and understanding of the SPI effort

Although few (if any) SPI experts would argue against having a well-defined plan, many major SPI initiatives have been started without serious planning. In practice, we have seen unplanned and arbitrary improvements in which organizations follow opportunities as they emerge, almost by accident. We have seen isolated improvements in which changes are implemented without attention to synergy and without regard to other changes, if not in contradiction to them. Creating and using plans in SPI initiatives can help you to build a common understanding among relevant parties about what you are doing and why. As a result, people feel that they are part of a common undertaking. You should base your plans on a consideration of strategy and tactics. When people follow and reflect upon plans, they learn how different strategies and tactics work and thereby increase their capacity to select or devise better ones.

Not only do they learn how to improve, but they also learn how to improve their improvement efforts.

However, a plan in itself is no panacea, and several things can go wrong. Plans can be uncoordinated, meaning that they are not adjusted to other ongoing organizational concerns. As a result, key people can be unavailable when they are needed, or other activities can overshadow or even contradict planned improvement activities. Another risk is that the focus on plans can be overblown, with the actual improvement activities relegated to oblivion. Finally, a strong insistence on plans and plan adherence can kill participants' motivation and commitment—along with their creativity if there is no room for improvisation.

Feedback

The universal raison d'être for SPI approaches is to change existing software practices in order to achieve improvements in quality and productivity. But how do managers know whether they have achieved the objectives set out in the improvement plan? How do they know how much the organization has benefited from the changes? As such questions indicate, you must collect data so that you can analyze and evaluate the SPI effort.

An SPI project's success often depends on obtaining early, observable results that are backed up with data if possible. To keep the effort visible and to motivate and sustain interest in the SPI initiative, managers must show positive outcomes. One way to ensure that you can demonstrate positive results is to have a measurement program that focuses on collecting and analyzing relevant data on initiative outcomes. Such a measurement program should make visible both the SPI effort's progress and the extent to which the goals are being met. The measurement program should also support change management by providing feedback on specific aspects of the SPI efforts that managers can use to fine-tune their efforts. Experiences shows, however, that measurement is a difficult endeavor that should be a dedicated effort or project in itself.

There are several alternatives to measuring SPI effectiveness. One alternative is to strive to achieve abstract goals. This is what people do, for example, when they state a goal to go for level 3, 4, or 5 in the CMM model without a clear understanding of the benefits of such a move. In such cases, the improvement goal becomes elusive and managers find it difficult to mobilize participants in the effort. Another alternative is to rely on people's perception of the effects. Without question, it is very difficult to measure SPI effects, and there is often a temptation to declare success without proper measurements. Such an approach may seem politically expedient to maintain commitment, but it provides little or no value in managing the change process. A third alternative is to rely on religious impulse. The CMM is presented with an almost sacred appeal, wherein striving to be a proper software professional is akin to going to church and obeying the Ten Commandments. Relying on this impulse might help to build commitment to the SPI effort, but it will not guide the process, and it renders particular objectives vulnerable to failings of faith.

Collecting appropriate data can offer your SPI effort at least three benefits. First, by pointing out positive outcomes it can legitimize the effort and give you a basis for defending the resources spent. An organization's practitioners and managers will be more appreciative and protective of the effort when you can demonstrate a return on investment. Second, measurements serve as vital instruments for controlling the effort. Measurements detail the efficiency and effectiveness of SPI strategies and tactics and of the changes made to engineering practice. Third, as suggested earlier, measurements—when used prudently—are important for helping maintain motivation and commitments.

There are, however, several risks in measuring SPI effects. Measurements are generally regarded as a problematic area of software engineering. Many software organizations experience difficulties in establishing well-grounded and justifiable measurements that are both relevant and meaningful. In other words, it might be hard to argue for the measurements' validity. Another problem is in ensuring verifiability in order to establish that measurements are trustworthy, accurate, and reliable. Measurements should be repeatable and comparable. Conforming to these requirements can be very difficult for many SPI efforts. Furthermore, measurement can be an activity fraught with political difficulty. Some individuals will be tempted to use measurements as an opportunity for advancing or protecting their particular interests. Opportunism can lead others to submit irrelevant data or even to commit fraud or submit fake measurements. A systematic, well-designed measurement program can help you avoid these risks while improving the likelihood that the data collected will help you manage the SPI initiative.

2.2 APPROACHES TO SPI

This aspect of the MAP addresses how to design the SPI process. There are three key ideas here. First, change should be achieved in an evolutionary, rather than a revolutionary, manner. Second, you should use norms to guide and control the SPI effort's results. Finally, to create an effective SPI initiative, you must inspire a broad commitment to change.

Evolution

Software process improvement is an evolutionary process in which you implement changes incrementally, over time, rather than in a few dramatic transformations. SPI approaches generally emphasize stepwise improvements within a limited set of process areas. These incremental changes are continuous, concerted, and cumulative; they follow Deming-like cycles of assessing, experimenting, and rolling out; and they address the individual, project, and organizational level.

There are other approaches to organizational change—some revolutionary and others technology-driven—but they have not been very effective in improving software processes. Business Process Reengineering is an example of the revolutionary approach. BPR focuses on obliterating major business processes and redesigning them from the top down (Davenport 1993). An example of the technology-driven approach is when management or experts encourage a team to acquire a specific technology—such as Computer-Aided Software Engineering (CASE)—as a way to improve performance. These two approaches take an instrumentalist approach to change, but the complexities of software processes tend to inhibit the rationalization of BPR strategies and overwhelm the narrow gains of technology-driven approaches.

An evolutionary approach to SPI offers several benefits. When practitioners are actively involved in identifying, designing, and implementing changes, SPI is more likely to succeed. People who participate in developing a new or modified process are generally much more willing and motivated to change their existing practice. Experience-based learning is another important aspect of SPI. Carrying out stepwise, incremental improvements increases the opportunity for participants to learn from successes and failures during experiments with new or modified processes. Finally, evolutionary SPI lets you keep and leverage the best elements of the existing process. As Paulk states, "Begin with the 'as is' process, not the 'should be' process, to leverage effective practices and co-opt resisters" (Paulk 1996).

Still, an evolutionary approach involves risks. When you implement incremental changes to a limited set of process areas, immediate and visible improvements are not always forthcoming. You might even find yourself unable to measure any effect because of measurement uncertainties. Another risk is that if you do not anchor and maintain the incremental improvements as part of the daily practices, the performance increase might be even more negligible. The first wave of changes will probably be noticed, but the second wave might either pass by unnoticed or make people forget what the first wave brought about. Nonetheless, incremental change is generally less risky than revolutionary approaches to change.

Norms

Most SPI approaches assess a software organization's capabilities using best-practices models of software processes as norms or benchmarks. Such benchmarks are also used to formulate a strategy for bridging the gap between norm and practice. Many such models are now available, including CMM, Bootstrap, and SPICE. Best-practices models have also been suggested for related areas, including the People Capability

Maturity Model, the Software Acquisition Capability Maturity Model, and the Systems Engineering Capability Maturity Model.

SPI models of best practices have been criticized for focusing too narrowly on software process change objectives and not enough on business goals. However, such norm-based approaches to SPI offer several opportunities for transforming the organization. They can serve as benchmarks for measuring progress and can help managers create a vision and explicate specific SPI goals tailored to the organizational context. Norm-based models can also support organizations in comparing experiences and achievements from process improvement efforts. By applying a professional standard that is widely used throughout the industry, a company can compare itself against other companies and profile itself accordingly. Norms can also provide criteria for prioritizing improvement areas and implementing stepwise improvements focusing on a limited number of areas at a time. Finally, the Goal Question Metric approach (Basili 1992) was developed to correct the SPI models' lack of attention to business goals. It provides a complementary assessment strategy for linking SPI change objectives to the business goals of software companies.

Norm-based approaches do introduce some risks into the organizational change process, but these risks are manageable. For example, a manager might easily develop an overly ambitious strategy based on the norm. This is because the models' scale and complexity implications are not clear until implemented. There is also a risk that some managers and organizations will follow norms for the sake of recognition rather than because they actually need to change their process. Finally, obtaining reliable results from the assessment process can be difficult and thus can make it difficult to compare actual process capability with the norm.

Commitment

Commitment is the explicit or implicit agreement of participants to strive for expected goals and results. As such, commitment can greatly influence the outcome of large-scale SPI organizational changes. Ways to ensure participant commitment include offering incentive schemes, such as bonuses or career opportunities, and involving practitioners in process assessments and process improvement activities. Successful SPI requires not only individual commitments but also the long-term, strategic commitment of organizational resources to continuous improvement. Senior management must actively support the change initiative with leadership, resources, and strategic management. Grady identifies a set of strategic, tactical, and organizational factors that senior managers must address to create commitment for SPI change (Grady 1997). The strategic factors are vision, strategic focus, and core competence; the tactical factors are customer perception, market share, product cycle time, and profitability; and the organizational factors are organizational maturity, process improvement infrastructure, organizational inertia, stability, and cost/time alignment. If not managed effectively, any of these factors can distract managers enough to jeopardize an SPI initiative. Grady recommends that managers be aware of these business and organization factors and consider what can be done to ameliorate their negative influences.

Are there alternatives to commitment-based improvement? One possibility is to base the improvement effort on power. But Paulk points out that a top-down mandate stating that everyone must follow the new processes is a common recipe for failure (Paulk 1996). Another possibility is personal initiatives to improve practices that individuals consider problematic. Although this approach can improve individual capabilities, without sponsorship and coordination such discrete personal initiatives easily create islands of excellence rather than improved organizational capability. If the entire organization shows commitment to SPI, people will be motivated to share new ideas and experiences, try out new practices, and work together to reach challenging goals (Jakobsen 1998).

Although the commitment process is vital for SPI, it can be carried too far. Managers and practitioners can become so dedicated to solving current problems that they lose sight of the original goal. This can further lead to a loss of perspective on the long-term improvement program and to the gold-plating of solutions to current problems.

2.3 PERSPECTIVES OF SPI

The target of SPI is software engineering practice. The literature views this practice from three basic perspectives that help us build practice models and thereby focus on core issues and assess means and ends. SPI is an abbreviation of software process improvement, which points to the first and most basic perspective: the *process*. The process is simply a view that sums up what people do and which methods and tools they apply during software development and maintenance. The second perspective of SPI is *competence*, which is the knowledge that makes individuals the fundamental asset in the software practice and the primary target of improvement efforts. The last perspective is *context,* the notion that neither general processes nor specific competencies exist in isolation. Practices will always be sustained and developed in interplay with their environment. If you fail to understand the environment, prospects for improving the process or enhancing vital competencies are bleak.

Process

Software processes are a set of activities, methods, practices, and transformations that people use to develop and maintain software and its associated products. One prominent feature of the software process is persistence. A software process is an institution in the sense that its practices become firmly established in the company culture. An institutionalized process is resistant to change. This does not imply that it cannot be changed, but rather that change requires systematic and sustained effort. Just as people are unlikely to change behavior overnight, you are unlikely to make quick, dramatic changes to methods, tools, and the like. Success in SPI requires that infrastructure and culture be built to support the institutionalization of new methods, practices, and procedures. Thus, you must implement policies, standards, and organizational structures to facilitate the SPI process. The primary objective is a new, more mature software process in which individual process components are better defined and more consistently implemented and interacting components produce more predictable and desirable results.

SPI's total process perspective is a holistic view of software engineering that is based on the conventional wisdom that improved processes can lead to better products and projects. However, because of the complexity of this perspective, managers might be tempted to adopt a more narrow focus on a specific aspect of the software process, including products of the process or process components such as people, methods, or tools. With a product focus, you would identify opportunities for improvement aimed at increasing product quality. Similarly, a focus on methods and tools would address questions such as, "Are we using the methods and tools appropriate for the project?" and "Are we using our methods and tools effectively and efficiently?" If your focus were on people, you would view behavioral change as the main vehicle for improvement (Bach 1995). With a people focus, you adopt an organic view of the software organization, in which developers and managers are seen as committed and competent professionals who constitute the software organization's main asset.

The weakness of a narrowly focused SPI strategy is in its bounded view of the software process. Focusing on selected parts of the process fails to yield the necessary synergy and often invites an analysis of simple cause–effect relationships that lose interdependencies and can thus invalidate your findings. Furthermore, many elements of the software process simply cannot be meaningfully reduced to cause–effect relationships. With a product focus, for example, it is difficult to establish adequate criteria for software product quality, and that is the main reason quality is generally seen as a result of combining sound software practices with specific product requirements. Similarly, a focus on methods and tools can create grave problems in that it fails to take people into account when analyzing the performance of specific technologies. The same holds true when the focus is on people at the expense of technology. Thus, these alternative perspectives suffer from similar deficiencies: They see software processes as loosely coupled systems in which people, methods, tools, and products can be studied independently or by taking only a few relationships into account.

Despite the inherent complexities of a holistic approach, the main virtue of the process perspective is that technologies and people are understood in their practical organizational context. However, SPI based on a process perspective does involve risk. The approach's inherent complexities necessitate the involvement of the organization's best people in the SPI effort. Consequently, a conflict may arise between their SPI responsibilities and their software development responsibilities to customers. Another risk relates to the fact that the existing software process is deeply embedded and assumed. The old software process can thus defeat the new process if people act as if it is business as usual. A third risk comes in underestimating the people element and adopting an instrumental view of the practitioners. This approach can produce a lack of participation and commitment. Finally, the broad focus on people, products, and technology can lead to a neglect of the change potential of technology push—using the technological infrastructure to provoke changes in the software process.

Competence

To be of any use, even the best methods and tools require gifted people, and they are key ingredients of any well-functioning software process. Successful SPI therefore requires competency development in relation to the new software process. The goal of developing competencies is to empower people to expertly use and adapt the practices of the new software process. Effective use of new and more sophisticated development technologies also requires new competencies if developers are to benefit from them. These competencies must be developed so that both individual and organizational requirements are met. That is, not only should the individual manager or developer feel empowered, but also the organization as a whole should muster a synergy of competencies to sustain the preferred software process.

Bureaucratization is one alternative to competence as a lever for SPI. A bureaucratic approach is one in which rules and hierarchical management structures implement and sustain the software process. This strategy aims to build structural support for the process via manuals, quality systems, and tools (such as CASE tools). This structural support instructs and guides practitioners through their tasks, but at the same time the process must be preprogrammed, leaving little room for discretion and adaptation.

Building competence can create strong commitments to projects and the software process. Because practitioners understand and appreciate the process, they are empowered to use their discretion and adapt the process to meet the needs of both the situation and their customers. In this way, they participate in a learning organization in which all experiences (good and bad) contribute to the continuous development of a software process that can meet present and future needs.

When SPI is based on building competence, responsibilities should be delegated to the organization's operational level, where competent people with the appropriate insights can effectively address problems and opportunities. In organizations where common values are not sufficiently strong, such empowerment can lead to problems. One possible problem is loss of control, which leads to coordination difficulties; another is goal deflection, in which overall goals for the software process are sacrificed to suit particular objectives in a given situation. Another potential problem is turf guarding, wherein the protection of individual or group interests obstructs organizational or project goals.

Context

An existing software process provides a context for software engineering activities. This context provides a basis for process improvements on a general level, as well as for customizations for specific needs. The context also provides an environment for each element of the software process, making it clear why things are done, how they are done, and when they are done. The context represents the stability of the software process, provides a setting for software engineers, supports the introduction of newcomers, defines training requirements, and offers a basis for customer relationships.

The context is where individual and organizational competencies merge. Through training, documented procedures, the repertoire of methods and tools, and other kinds of support, the software process is stabilized and melded into a whole that allows for both the adaptation of existing practices and the adoption of new practices to suit the situation.

One alternative to providing such a context is to let go of stability and address every project as a unique process. However, this alternative demands that participants have superior qualifications. It also increases process overhead and drastically reduces the possibilities for learning from project to project. Other alternatives would be to rely on heroes (Bach 1995) or on the widespread use of technology. But, as we discussed earlier, such strategies have severe limitations when compared with a more holistic process perspective.

A sustainable and supportive context offers opportunities for building and maintaining a sound and strong software process. It helps you identify best practices, eases the introduction of new employees, and supports systematic reuse, training-program design, and the development and reinforcement of a professional software engineering culture.

Creating such a context also involves risks. One is the possibility of process ossification, in which practices remain, unchanged, long after their justification has passed. Similarly, reuse can lead to activities being performed because they are part of a tradition rather than because they are needed. Finally, the software process can become defined so that competencies are externalized in procedures and discretionary behavior is virtually outlawed. This has led to the criticism that SPI causes organizations to become rigid and bureaucratic. However, documented SPI experiences indicate that such concerns are misplaced for all but a few organizations (Herbsleb et al. 1997).

2.4 MAPPING SPI PRACTICE

Table 2.2 summarizes the MAP and offers an overview of key SPI ideas. The MAP framework provides information about alternatives, opportunities, and risks related to SPI initiatives. You can use the MAP in two ways. First, you can use it as a roadmap for searching, reading, and interpreting the SPI literature. Second, you can use the MAP to evaluate ongoing SPI initiatives. By mapping initiatives into this framework, you can uncover their strengths and weaknesses and identify additional SPI ideas that can improve your ongoing SPI efforts. We use the MAP in the following section to

Table 2.2 The SPI MAP with Aspirations and Pitfalls for Each Idea

Concern	Idea	Aspiration	Pitfalls
Management of SPI	Organization	Create a dedicated effort adapted to the conditions of the organization	Inadequate resources, emphasis, and coordination
	Plan	Plan goals, activities, responsibilities, and coordination	Loss of motivation; diversity or deadlock
	Feedback	Measure and assess benefits	Opportunism; loss of relevance
Approach to SPI	Evolution	Learn by experience and employ stepwise improvements	Burnout and inertia
	Norm	Seek guidance in ideal processes	Hastiness and fundamentalism
	Commitment	Ensure dedication and legitimacy	Goal deflection and gold-plating
Perspective in SPI	Process	Integrate people, management, and technology	Customer disinterest
	Competence	Empower people through competence building	Turf guarding
	Context	Establish sustainable effort	Machine-like bureaucracy

characterize each of the four initiatives presented in Part II. Our introduction to these cases explains why we named the efforts "correct," "ambitious," "grassroots," and "adolescent," respectively. We also show how you can use the MAP framework in SPI practice.

The Correct Effort

Ericsson Denmark was already involved in a corporatewide improvement initiative, Ericsson System Software Initiative (ESSI), when it initiated its SPI project in 1997. The goal of the ESSI program was to improve software quality by 50%, lead-time precision by 50%, and lead time by 20% each year. Depending on their product area, all Ericsson design centers, except for the Aalborg branch, were to meet at least two of these goals. The Aalborg branch was established in 1997 in the northern part of Denmark and was not part of the ESSI program.

As part of ESSI, senior management expected all design centers to implement CMM level 2 processes, and they planned a formal CMM assessment. However, as the deadline for the CMM assessment came closer, management realized that the gap between level 2 and current practices was not decreasing and that a different approach was needed. They stated CMM level 2 as the primary goal for Ericsson Denmark and adopted a more incremental and evolutionary approach, in which improvements were more directly tailored to each project. They followed the advice of external consultants, who said that level 2 is not about defining organizationwide processes but rather is about changing management behavior project by project. They used project assessments to improve project-management practices within each project and to ensure a more consistent implementation of level 2's six KPAs.

The use of project assessments was a huge success. In 1998, a formal CMM assessor team rated Ericsson Denmark as a young level 2 organization. However, the company had yet to institutionalize level 2 practices into a supportive organizational context for good project management, and it did not do this right away. Achieving CMM level 2 seemed to be the important thing for top management, and the organization soon faced the risk of falling back to level 1.

From the start, Ericsson Denmark's SPI initiative focused on SPI management. Still, it was quite difficult to create a well-functioning SPI organization that was strong enough to survive the turbulence of both management turnover and vague and shifting improvement goals. Improvement initiatives were rarely coordinated throughout the organization, and there were too few result-oriented SPI plans with clearly defined goals to guide and focus the improvements.

Only the Aalborg branch established a well-functioning SPI organization with result-oriented SPI plans on both a strategic and a tactical level. The Aalborg branch is now on its way toward CMM level 3, having created a successful context for supporting a healthy software engineering culture with SPI as an integral organizational activity.

The other design centers are learning from the success of the Aalborg branch. Ericsson Denmark has now established a strong and effective SPI organization, with dedicated SPI groups in each unit and an organizationwide SPI group with representatives from all units. However, none of the design centers—including the Aalborg branch—has been able to measure the benefits of achieving level 2. Despite a long tradition of collecting data, this element of SPI has been overlooked in the attempt to achieve level 2. Ericsson Denmark is therefore unable to document the return on investment of its efforts.

We named this initiative "the correct effort" because, as Table 2.3 shows, it follows the recommendations in the SPI literature quite closely. This was particularly true at the Aalborg branch. However, two SPI ideas were not followed. No metrics program was implemented to document the SPI initiative's actual effect, and there was little emphasis on building competence among software practitioners as part of the CMM initiative. These areas represent important opportunities for improving the SPI initiative at Ericsson Denmark. Similarly, much can be achieved by adapting experiences from the Aalborg branch in other parts of the organization. Correct efforts benefit from SPI ideas. But when they become too focused on following the litera-

Table 2.3 *Mapping the Four SPI Initiatives*

Normative SPI Concerns	Correct Effort	Ambitious Effort	Grassroots Effort	Adolescent Effort
SPI Organization	+			
SPI Plan	+	+		
SPI Feedback			+	
Evolution	+		+	+
Norm	+	+	+	
Commitment	+	+	+	+
SE Process	+	+		
SE Competence		+	+	+
SE Context	+	+		

ture's recommendations, they tend to overlook the actual organizational challenges. Chapter 3 discusses this case in more detail.

The Ambitious Effort

Systematic initiated its SPI project in 1997 with the ambitious goal of achieving CMM level 3 within three years. The company's prior experience with improvement programs was in 1991, when it successfully implemented an ISO-compliant quality system. The SPI initiative was seen as a strategic thrust that would strengthen the company's market position and build directly on the earlier success with the QA system.

In early 1997, Systematic underwent an internal CMM-based assessment to signal the beginning of the SPI journey toward level 3. This initial assessment rated the company as a level 1 organization. The company later performed a Bootstrap assessment to gain further insight into possible improvement areas. Management then combined the recommendations from both assessments into a comprehensive SPI plan that was aimed directly at level 3.

Systematic's approach to SPI reflected its ambition to achieve CMM level 3 in less than three years. Instead of implementing incremental and evolutionary improvements—as recommended by the SPI literature—Systematic's approach was to implement improvements to the software engineering process throughout the company. Competent software engineers created organizationwide processes for level 2's six KPAs. To ensure adoption of the new processes, all project managers participated in a comprehensive project-management course, in which they were educated in good project-management practices based on the new processes. The assumption was that this course, along with a high degree of practitioner commitment and competence, would ensure rapid progress.

Throughout the effort, a central SPI group was the focal point for improvement initiatives. Top management was actively involved in SPI, and practitioners participated in dedicated working groups to develop new processes. The SPI organization at Systematic did not, however, follow the recommendations for a level 1 organization, and thus it was subject to many changes. An attempt to establish metrics to provide the necessary improvement-initiative feedback was stranded because of problems with metrics definition. Another barrier to rapid success was Systematic's strong customer orientation. Working-group members were not given additional resources for SPI participation, and thus, even though practitioners were committed to SPI, they often gave customer-oriented tasks higher priority. Given this, it was difficult to establish a well-functioning balance between SPI and software engineering.

We call this "the ambitious effort" because of the company's high goals, its widespread and high-level commitment to SPI, and its consistent attempts to follow key SPI ideas. However, as Table 2.3 shows, the company failed to follow three key ideas.

Systematic did not implement a metrics program or follow an evolutionary approach to SPI. It also had difficulty institutionalizing a well-functioning SPI organization. Systematic did reach level 2 in 1999 and is now on the way toward level 3. Along the way, it has learned one of the hard lessons of ambitious efforts: There is a limit to how hard you can push SPI at the organizational level. Chapter 4 discusses this case in more detail.

The Grassroots Effort

Danske Data initiated its SPI initiative in 1997 with a combined CMM–Bootstrap assessment. Management formulated and accepted a strategy with prioritized improvement projects, and the overall process followed key SPI ideas in most respects. However, one particular sequence of events came to play an important role in the outcome of this case.

Early on, a decision was made to create Danske Data's own standard for professional project management, using CMM as the inspiration. The Danske Data standard includes and extends CMM level 2's key process areas, adding four additional areas that management considered important. The standard was supported by the Project Management Competence Center, a forum for project managers to learn and share experiences. The standard was also used to create a self-assessment tool that project managers could use as part of their competence development. In this way, Danske Data created a context that supports and enables competence development on the project-management level.

The company's success with SPI can be attributed primarily to grassroots commitment. Competent senior project managers were the drivers of this commitment in that they bypassed the existing bureaucracy and went directly to top management to make things happen. They initiated a grassroots movement among project managers that is now spreading throughout the organization at all levels. Thus, Danske Data focused more on competence development than on defining standard processes that can be consistently implemented throughout the organization.

Early on, in 1997, Danske Data's CEO claimed that the SPI initiative would lead to a 10% increase in productivity within three years. As a result, the initiative gave high priority to establishing a metrics program that could verify this ambition. Despite intensive efforts, this turned out to be a difficult exercise. After three years, a simple metrics program is in place, but still without any organizationwide measure of software volume. However, the organization is now committed to using project statistics to support improvement initiatives and management decisions and will continue to refine the metrics program by including function-point measures.

We call this "the grassroots effort" because a few committed individuals took charge of one of the successful initiatives early in the project, and that led to a bottom-up movement among project managers that slowly spread throughout the organization. As Table 2.3 shows, the initiative had some obvious weaknesses. An overall management strategy for the SPI initiative was difficult to establish because of many changes in the method department's organization. When Danske Data reached level 2 by late 1999, management decided to continue toward level 3. An ongoing process of reorganizing the improvement activities will likely continue for some time. Another weakness is the initiative's rather weak focus on software engineering processes. The new standard for professional project management is defined only at a high level and, as such, does not provide much guidance to software engineering practice. In addition, the context to support the use of an improved process relies on individual project managers' use of the new standard to improve their management behavior. This is due in part to the success of the grassroots initiative and its strong focus on competence building. Grassroots efforts can serve as energizers and can create change—but only for a while. Relating such efforts to formally established SPI initiatives will eventually emerge as a challenge. Chapter 5 discusses this case in more detail.

The Adolescent Effort

Normative SPI models never played a dominating role at Brüel & Kjær. In 1996, the company underwent a Bootstrap assessment without initiating any major improvements based on its results. Instead, in the fall of 1997, a group of project managers was selected to directly identify software process problems and solutions in a series of interviews with the SPI group. Based on the interview findings, the project managers agreed to pilot specific improvement initiatives in their software projects. Improvements were thus implemented in an evolutionary, bottom-up approach, in which each project selected and experimented with one specific improvement area. In this way, projects gradually improved their software engineering practices using new ways of working that were tailored to their specific context and situation.

The problems perceived by the project managers became one important driver of the improvement initiative. Another driver was the organization's problem reports, which documented the types of problems encountered in software projects. A systematic study of these reports led management to rethink how requirements were captured and documented. Again, the project managers were involved in deciding which techniques to adopt, and experiments were initiated in specific projects to improve local practices and to set examples for others to follow.

Pursuing this highly evolutionary approach ensured project managers' commitment to changing practices. However, managing the SPI effort was not easy. It was difficult to create an overall strategic SPI plan with organizational vision and goals, and to create improvement plans for each project with milestones, resources, and goals. The SPI initiative therefore remained disintegrated, with asynchronous improvements.

Without coordinated plans, it was difficult to allocate dedicated resources to specific initiatives. In particular, it was difficult to allocate adequate resources to other types of improvements, such as measuring the overall effect of the SPI initiatives.

Brüel & Kjær now faces the challenge of defining and combining good practices from a few projects to make them available to other projects. However, learning among projects will likely be a cumbersome task, because the new software processes have yet to be defined and stabilized into a coherent context that would permit projects to adapt existing practices or adopt new ones.

We call this "the adolescent effort" because it fails to follow key SPI ideas: Normative models were never used to guide the improvement initiative, there were no attempts to develop metrics programs, developing a shared context for software projects was never given high priority, and the management style of the improvement initiative remained ad hoc. Much can, however, be learned from this case: Unconventional sources for learning about current practices were successfully applied; project managers actively participated, ensuring a high commitment to change; and the basic strategy followed an evolutionary approach, ensuring success at the project level. In its most constructive form, adolescent behavior breaks new ground, but it is always quite uncertain whether the new ideas will be compatible with becoming an adult. At this stage, it remains to be seen how Brüel & Kjær's SPI initiative will play out. Chapter 6 discusses this case in more detail.

Draw Your Own Map

An improvement effort is a complex and risky process of change involving many actors. As we show in this chapter, you can use the MAP to evaluate ongoing SPI initiatives and identify each initiative's strengths and weaknesses. Such a diagnosis can show you which SPI ideas are inconsistently followed and thus need to be carefully reconsidered. Would it be a good idea to implement them in your current improvement practices? If not, what will the consequences be? Are there alternative ideas that you could implement to remedy these consequences?

Mapping your SPI initiative in this way will increase your chances of success and minimize your risk of failure. We recommend conducting your diagnosis as a collaborative workshop with the following agenda:

- ◆ Evaluate current SPI practices.
  - – Which of the nine key ideas are currently followed consistently?
  - – Which of the nine key ideas could be better utilized?
- ◆ Evaluate consequences.
  - – What are the consequences of not following all key ideas?
  - – Which activities might remedy these consequences?

◆ Prioritize and reorganize.
  – Which new activities should be initiated?
  – How could the SPI program be reorganized?

Using the ideas we present in this chapter to map your SPI practice will help you create a shared understanding of the problems and opportunities facing your organization (Lanzara and Mathiassen 1985). As participants map their own improvement practices, they'll be challenged to stop and reflect both on the initiative program and on how it is currently designed and organized. Ideally, they will focus on the strengths of the current setup and problems that might emerge and will be inspired to see alternative paths that can improve the odds of success.

Suggested Reading for the MAP

GENERAL

Today, SPI has become one of the dominant approaches to improve software engineering quality and productivity. Many organizations have committed themselves to long-term improvement programs. However, software organizations need guidance to address questions such as, What are the characteristic features of SPI initiatives? How do SPI initiatives compare to other improvement approaches? What are the key benefits and risks related to SPI initiatives? Further guidance and recommendations can be found in the following literature.

Aaen, I.,et al. 2001.

Grady, R.B. 1997. *Successful Software Process Improvement.* Upper Saddle River, NJ: Prentice Hall.

Humphrey, W. 1989.

McFeeley, B. 1996. *IDEAL: A User's Guide for Software Process Improvement.* Handbook CMU/SEI-96-HB-001. Pittsburgh: Software Engineering Institute.

MANAGEMENT OF SPI

Clearly, not every organization has succeeded in its SPI attempts. SPI is a challenging and complex process of change in which effective change management is key to success. Effective management of SPI initiatives requires that the SPI effort be properly organized and planned and that feedback be collected on the improvement effort's effects. Further guidance and recommendations can be found in the following literature.

Organization

Fowler, P., and S. Rifkin, 1990. *Software Engineering Process Group Guide.* Tech Report CMU/SEI-90-TR-24. Pittsburgh: SEI.

Humphrey 1989.

McFeeley 1996.

Plan

Grady 1997.

McFeeley 1996.

Zahran, S. 1998. *Software Process Improvement: Successful Models and Strategies*. Reading, MA: Addison-Wesley.

Feedback

Carleton, A.D., R.E. Park, W.B. Goethert, W.A. Florac, E.K. Bailey, and S.L. Pfleeger. 1992. *Software Measurement for DoD Systems: Recommendations for Initial Core Measures*. Tech Report CMU/SEI-92-TR-19. Pittsburgh: SEI.

Florac, W.A., R.E. Park, and A.D. Carleton. 1997. *Practical Software Measurement: Measuring for Process Management and Improvement*. Tech Report CMU/SEI-97-HB-003. Pittsburgh: SEI.

Grady, R.B. 1992. *Practical Software Metrics for Project Management and Process Improvement*. Upper Saddle River, NJ: Prentice Hall.

APPROACHES TO SPI

The approach addresses how to change the software process. The approach to intervention in SPI is guided by three ideas: It is evolutionary in nature; it is based on idealized, normative models of software engineering; and careful building and development of commitments between the involved actors are essential to success. Further guidance and recommendations can be found in the following literature.

Evolution

Caputo, K. 1998. *CMM Implementation Guide: Choreographing Software Process Improvement*. SEI Series in Software Engineering. Reading, MA: Addison-Wesley.

Grady 1997.

McFeeley 1996.

Zahran 1998.

Norm

Emam, K.E., J.-N. Drouin, and Melo, W. 1998. *SPICE: The Theory and Practice of Software Process Improvement and Capability Determination*. Los Alamitos, CA: IEEE Computer Society Press.

Kuvaja, P., J. Similä, L. Krzanik, A. Bicego, S. Saukkonen and G.N. Koch, 1994. *Software Process Assessment & Improvement: The Bootstrap Approach*. Oxford, UK: Blackwell Publisher.

Paulk, M.C., C.V. Weber, B. Curtis, and M.B. Chrissis, 1995. *The Capability Maturity Model: Guidelines for Improving the Software Process*. SEI Series in Software Engineering. Reading, MA: Addison-Wesley.

Commitment

Grady 1997.

Humphrey 1989.

PERSPECTIVES OF SPI

SPI offers specific perspectives on the intervention target: software engineering practice. On this level, the entire body of knowledge on software engineering is potentially relevant. Within SPI, the focus is on software processes, the key resource is the software developers' competencies, and the intention is to develop a context for software engineering that is both supportive and sustainable. Further guidance and recommendations can be found in the following literature.

Process

Humphrey, W.S. 1988. "Characterizing the Software Process." *IEEE Software*. 5:2:73-79.

Humphrey 1989.

Raynus, J. 1999. *Software Process Improvement with CMM*. Norwood, NJ: Ablex Publishers.

Competence

Curtis, B., W.E. Hefley, and S. Miller. 1995. *People Capability Maturity Model*. Tech Report CMU/SEI-95-MM-02. Pittsburgh: SEI.

Humphrey, W.S. 1995. *A Discipline for Software Engineering*. First ed., SEI Series in Software Engineering. Peter Freeman and John Musa, eds. Reading, MA: Addison-Wesley.

Humphrey, W.S. 1997. *Managing Technical People: Innovation, Teamwork, and the Software Process*. SEI Series in Software Engineering. Reading, MA: Addison-Wesley.

Hutchings, T., M.G. Hyde, D. Marca, and L. Cohen. 1993. "Process Improvement that Lasts: An Integrated Training and Consulting Method." *Communications of the ACM*. 36:10:104–113.

Context

Humphrey 1989.

Humphrey 1997.

2.5 REFERENCES

Aaen, I., J. Arent, L. Mathiassen, and O. Ngwenyama. 2001. "A Conceptual MAP of Software Process Improvement." *Scandinavian Journal of Information Systems*. 13:1.

Bach, J. 1995. "Enough about Process: What We Need Are Heroes." *IEEE Software*. 12:2:96–98.

Basili, V.R. 1992. *Software Modeling and Measurement: The Goal/Question/Metric Paradigm.* CS-TR-2956. College Park, MD: University of Maryland.

Davenport, T.H. 1993. *Process Innovation: Reengineering Work through Information Technology.* Boston: Harvard Business School Press.

Fuggetta, A., and G.P. Picco. 1994. "An Annotated Bibliography on Software Process Improvement." *ACM SIGSOFT Software Engineering Notes.* 19:3:66–68.

Grady, R.B. 1997. *Successful Software Process Improvement.* Upper Saddle River, NJ: Prentice Hall.

Herbsleb, J., et al. 1997. "Software Quality and the Capability Maturity Model." *Communications of the ACM.* 40:6:30–40.

Humphrey, W. 1989. *Managing the Software Process,* first ed. SEI Series in Software Engineering. Ed. Nico Habermann. Reading, MA: Addison-Wesley.

Jakobsen, A.B. 1998. "Bottom-Up Process Improvement Tricks." *IEEE Software.* 15:1:64–68.

Lanzara, G.F., and L. Mathiassen. 1985. "Mapping Situations within a System Development Project." *Information & Management.* 8:1:3–20.

Paulk, M.C. 1996. "Effective CMM-Based Process Improvement." Sixth International Conference on Software Quality. Ottawa, Canada: ASQC.

Paulk, M.C. 1999. *A Software Process Bibliography.* Pittsburgh: Software Engineering Institute. Available from http://www.sei.cmu.edu/cmm/docs/biblio.html.

Zahran, S. 1998. *Software Process Improvement: Successful Models and Strategies.* SEI Series in Software Engineering. Reading, MA: Addison-Wesley.

PART II

Learning from Experience

Chapter 3

The Correct Effort

Ivan Aaen and Stig Bang

Early in the spring of 1997, Ericsson Denmark adopted an aggressive new approach to our SPI effort in the systems development division. The ambitious goal was to reach CMM level 2 in a single year, even though the organization was undergoing structural changes and experiencing rapid growth. Nonetheless, we achieved this seemingly unrealistic goal, although not in the way we expected and only after many lessons learned. Ultimately, our organization's structure, culture, size, and dynamic proved to be dominant factors in determining which SPI activities actually contributed to success, and which were simply a waste of time and resources.

The SPI literature contains much good advice for planning and managing a *correct* SPI program: Seek active sponsorship, establish clear goals, ensure management commitment, plan activities carefully, and so on (Caputo 1998; Fowler and Rifkin 1990; Herbsleb et al. 1997; Humphrey 1989; Hutchings et al. 1993; McFeeley 1996; and Raynus 1999). We did all that—we thought—and yet our progress was negligible. The SPI program had been carefully designed to follow the SPI textbooks, but somehow it seemed that what we had was yet another massive and well-intentioned investment that produced few results.

We had a hard time identifying the real driving forces of our SPI achievements (and lack of achievements) amid the turmoil of early events. Later, we discovered that a successful SPI program requires more than models, plans, assessments, and the traditional SPI competence areas. Thus, "the correct effort" refers both to how the SPI program was initially perceived and what it actually grew to be following pivotal shifts in our SPI tactics. Achieving CMM level 2 was only a small part of the benefits we gained in carefully working with SPI over a three-year period. The lessons we learned the hard way changed the SPI effort from being "seemingly correct" to being well on its way to truly effective.

Our insight into this effort comes from two perspectives: Stig Bang managed the SPI department at Ericsson Denmark, and Ivan Aaen, an external researcher from Aalborg University, served on the program's steering committee.

3.1 BACKGROUND

The Ericsson Corporation is one of the world's largest suppliers of telecom equipment. Over the past 20 years, the telecom industry has gradually shifted its emphasis from hardware-only products to software-operated products and pure software solutions. Ericsson's major product areas—fixed and wireless switching equipment, mobile phones, telecom management systems, PBX systems, transmission equipment, defense systems, and Internet solutions—are all heavily reliant on software. Early on, Ericsson realized that the industry was changing and also recognized the importance of software in its products. As a result, the company has a long history of improving its software development operations.

In 1992, Ericsson took the first steps to set up a corporatewide SPI program called the Ericsson System Software Initiative (ESSI). From the start, ESSI had a top-down structure that ensured alignment, deployment, and follow-up on corporate goals in its widespread network of software development subsidiaries around the world. The corporate ESSI program originated in Ericsson's largest and most complex software development area—telephone exchanges—aiming to drastically reduce the software's fault density. Management defined an aggressive goal to this end: an annual reduction in fault density of 50%. CMM was part of Ericsson's long-term strategy for improving software development performance. To support this, corporate management created an international corps of trained CMM assessors to assess the company's international software development sites.

By the end of 1996, the corporate ESSI program had been operational for a couple of years, and most of Ericsson's international software development sites had made good progress toward reaching the corporate fault density goals. Moreover, in the first CMM assessment, most sites were rated at level 1; all level 1 sites that were assessed a second time were rated at CMM level 2. However, at Ericsson Denmark we had not yet achieved the fault density goals, and we were coming up for our second CMM assessment.

Inside Ericsson Denmark: Structural Complexity and Growth

In 1996 Ericsson Denmark had a mid-sized systems development division with 233 people working in four product areas. Work on telephone exchanges—the old legacy-system product area—occupied roughly half of the total division employees.

Early in 1996, Ericsson Denmark underwent a major structural change, replacing the traditional line organization with a matrix organization. Under the matrix organization, both our internal division and each of its product areas reported to a corresponding business unit in another country. Typically, this reporting occurred at both the line and the project level because most Ericsson Denmark projects were part of international projects.

This change was motivated by the fact that times were changing and Ericsson had upcoming challenges to meet. Ericsson's "customers" (the business units) required greater flexibility, new skills, increased visibility, and rapid expansion to keep up with demands for new software products. One of the key components in Ericsson's response to business unit demands was the new matrix organization.

The new organization meant that Ericsson Denmark had to form a *resource pool* of programmers and testers so that they could be assigned more flexibly to projects than was the case in the old line organization. The idea behind the resource pool was to allow for more dynamic project staffing across the product areas. There were natural limitations to this end, though, because the Ericsson Denmark organization was geographically distributed between two locations: one in Copenhagen and the other in Aalborg, in the northern part of Denmark. Furthermore, the four product areas differed in technology and scope. To be efficient, moving people between product areas would require careful competence management.

In addition, Ericsson Denmark had to expand to meet business demands. During 1997, we recruited 92 new employees. This 40% increase in the workforce was by itself a massive undertaking; still, management felt confident that we could meet the SPI goals despite this rapid growth. To meet the challenge, management formed a new SPI department to support the division with methods, tools, processes, and quality assurance. The SPI department staff came from staff positions in the old line organizations, and most of them had years of experience within their fields of specialty.

3.2 LAUNCHING THE SEEMINGLY CORRECT EFFORT

Ericsson Denmark had been enrolled in ESSI since 1994 and thus had a few years' experience with SPI, but not with CMM. For systems divisions such as Ericsson Denmark, the corporate office had no stated goals for achieving any particular CMM maturity level, although maturity assessments were expected to take place every other year. Ericsson Denmark was assessed for the first time in May 1995 and—not surprisingly—we were rated at CMM level 1. In the following two years, however, we did not include CMM as part of our improvement strategy because we were trying hard to satisfy the fault density goals.

The ESSI SPI program was the biggest single improvement program ever launched in our division. The previous ESSI programs had been more decentralized and uncoordinated and had significantly fewer resources. The new budget totaled 8,600 person-hours and 1 MDKK (US$125,000)—a total of 3% of the 1997 budget and enough to attract serious management attention to the program. An executive steering committee was formed and consisted of the project-office manager, the SPI department manager, and the division head himself. To the division head, this was an important program, and, given the track record of previous ESSI initiatives, he wanted to be personally involved in managing the program.

SPI Goals

When the ESSI SPI program was initiated in 1997, the overall ESSI program consisted of three corporate goals: the fault density goal, a lead-time precision goal, and a lead-time reduction goal (although not all goals applied to all product areas). Following standard corporate guidelines for goal analysis and breakdown, the goals were transformed into six Vital Few Areas (VFAs), each of which had subgoals. The six VFAs were

- Increased use of reviews and inspections
- Improved testing strategies
- Identification and strengthening of key software competencies
- Improved competence and resource management
- Improved product usability
- Improved teamwork

Ericsson Denmark also set a goal of reaching CMM level 2 by early 1998. The six level 2 KPAs are

- Requirements management
- Software project planning
- Software project tracking and oversight
- Software quality assurance
- Software configuration management
- Software subcontract management

In accordance with the corporate requirement that CMM assessments take place biannually, Ericsson Denmark was scheduled for an assessment in spring of 1997. However, we were granted a one-year extension to achieve process improvements.

SPI Organization and Start-up

For each VFA and KPA, a working group was formed to derive a generic framework—including processes, methods, templates, and tools—that could easily be adapted to fit most Ericsson Denmark projects. The development projects already well under way would then adopt the new techniques as appropriate, whereas new projects were expected to take on most of them (see Figure 3.1).

Most of the people involved in the working groups were either SPI professionals or managers. Because we were in the middle of a period of aggressive recruitment, it was hard to allocate "productive" resources for improvements. Ericsson Denmark's staff recruitment in general could barely keep up with business demands. Furthermore, the most experienced of the existing personnel were heavily involved in training and mentoring new employees.

To put weight behind the CMM level 2 goal, Ericsson organized a daylong Executive CMM Seminar in Stockholm led by Bill Curtis. All of Ericsson Denmark's senior management team attended. After the seminar, they concluded that all personnel

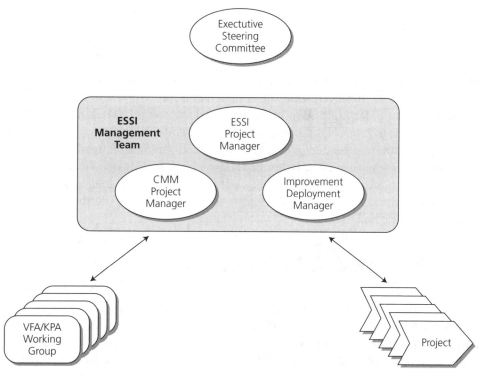

Figure 3.1   *The initial SPI organization*

should receive professional CMM training, and they hired Bill Curtis to train the entire division. Every employee received a half-day course on CMM concepts, and all personnel managers and project managers received three days of basic CMM training.

Our ESSI program was in the hands of an experienced improvement manager. In addition, one project manager coordinated CMM working groups, and another coordinated the deployment of VFAs and KPAs into actual development projects. When all the plans were complete and all working groups formed, Ericsson Denmark held a kick-off meeting to boost team support for the program.

3.3 THE ASSESSMENTS

Everything seemed to be well under way for our 1997 ESSI program, but as time went by, progress proved slower than expected. The improvements depended on the working groups, which were either suffering from lost resources and internal disputes or spending too much time discussing ambition levels and researching concepts and tools. Moreover, when it was time to implement results into projects, the projects had to invest energy in adapting the processes to fit their needs. Without extra resources at their disposal, some projects were reluctant to implement the changes. Moreover, the sheer number of improvement areas was more than most projects could absorb. Even if a project agreed to take on, say, five or six improvement areas, it was difficult to give each area the attention needed to make it work.

The real worry, however, was CMM implementation. The CMM compliance was measured using CMM Light Assessments (Daskalantonakis 1994), a questionnaire-based technique to rate CMM requirement fulfillment at the project and organization levels. Results are represented on a scale from 1 to 10 (total fulfillment). CMM Light Assessments were used every quarter as a status check on Ericsson Denmark's CMM implementation progress. In the third quarter of 1997, KPAs averaged a score of 6; when the exercise was repeated in the fourth quarter, the picture was more or less the same. Something had to be done.

Accelerator Assessment: An Eye-Opener

In November 1997, Ericsson Denmark offered to be a pilot site to run a CMM accelerator assessment—an assessment that evaluates how CMM improvements are run, rather than the actual CMM level. To Ericsson Denmark's senior management, this seemed a welcome opportunity to put the CMM effort back on track, and they accepted the offer. The CMM accelerator assessment proved to be a turning point for our CMM program, leading to a complete change in the program's structure and activities. The results from the assessment sent clear messages to senior management, including the following:

- Way too many improvement goals and activities were going on at once, without any set priorities.
- Management was not demonstrating active leadership or commitment to the improvement work.
- There was too much focus on the working groups and too little focus on implementation.

Faced with the formal corporate CMM assessment in 1998, senior management had to make a tough choice: Postpone the assessment again and still face a likely CMM level 1 score, or drop some other activities and focus on achieving CMM level 2. They chose the latter. All ESSI activities other than CMM level 2 KPAs were put on hold from that moment on, leaving CMM level 2 as the sole improvement goal.

UltraLight Assessments: Getting People Involved

One of the CMM Accelerator Assessment recommendations is to use CMM UltraLight Assessments, a technique that had been used successfully by other Ericsson companies to advance the implementation of CMM in projects (see Chapter 10). UltraLight Assessment is a technique that maps every CMM key practice to the equivalent practice implemented by a project. If the implemented key practice satisfies the CMM clause, it is marked as "green" on a scoreboard. If a practice is partly implemented, it is marked "blue," and otherwise it is considered unfulfilled and marked "red." To demonstrate active leadership and commitment, the entire senior management team (including the product area managers) acted as a steering committee and reserved a full day each month to follow up on projects' progress toward blue and green key practices.

And it worked! In preparation for the formal corporate CMM assessment in June 1998, every project manager had to demonstrate how the project had progressed. If a project needed help in implementing the CMM, SPI staff was called in to assist, but the responsibility for making progress rested solely on the staff of each project. It took a while for the project managers to realize that senior management was just as serious about CMM implementation as it used to be about normal development work. But as soon as the message was clear, the projects started making real progress in CMM implementation.

When the formal corporate CMM assessment resulted in the expected CMM level 2 judgment, the staff at Ericsson Denmark felt pride and a sense of achievement.

However, some practitioners felt that they were unable to benefit from the relatively short and intense CMM implementation because little time remained to reflect on the improvements made. Still, all projects had worked very hard to achieve the goal. Senior managers had stuck their necks out to meet this goal, and naturally they felt relieved when the corporate SPI program congratulated them. Also, many of the practitioners involved in the CMM implementation felt that some much-needed improvements had finally taken place and that they had been able to influence them. When a big party was held to celebrate the assessment result, many practitioners were surprised to learn that "it meant that much to the organization."

3.4 AFTERMATH

The staff at Ericsson Denmark devoted a lot of energy and attention to get to CMM level 2 before the formal assessment. In the final months, signs of fatigue were visible. The ESSI program managers knew that if momentum was going to continue they had to plan for the time after the assessment.

We knew that we could not simply rush toward CMM level 3 without a consolidation phase. The formal CMM assessment had findings at CMM level 2 that needed attention. Also, the strict focus on CMM meant that all other improvement areas were postponed, regardless of their relevance. However, we could not simply revive actions related to the ESSI VFAs and continue with them as we had before the CMM Accelerator Assessment. Clearly, such a strategy would not work because the program was too large and unfocused. Moreover, Ericsson Denmark was planning to change the matrix structure to give more responsibility to the product areas, so we had to find other ways to organize the improvement efforts.

Typically, the recommended approach for companies moving from CMM level 2 to level 3 is to set up a software engineering process group (SEPG) (Fowler and Rifkin 1990) to coordinate efforts. We decided to adopt this approach and set up an SEPG for each product area, with an SPI advisory committee (SPIAC) to facilitate experience sharing among SEPGs (see Figure 3.2). By that time, the flexible resource pool had been abandoned and the product areas had been transformed into regular departments that were relatively independent. The role of the SEPGs was first to help consolidate the CMM level 2 improvement areas and then to coordinate future improvements within the departmental context.

SEPGs were appointed in all four product areas and were staffed by a mix of SPI professionals and practitioners. Soon, however, several SEPGs found that their product area groups lacked commitment to make further improvements. At the same time, the division head left the company and a number of management changes took place. This naturally took some focus away from the SPI program. And, equally prob-

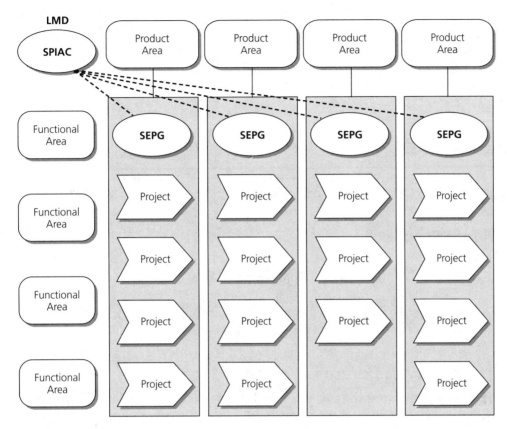

Figure 3.2 *The revised SPI organization*

lematic, the departments did not have a clearly defined goal to pursue other than "consolidate the CMM level 2 improvement areas." The UltraLight Assessments were more or less the only improvement activities that persisted from the days before the formal CMM assessment.

Only in the Aalborg department did the SEPG continue the momentum from before the assessment—albeit after a short "relaxation period." Being a small department of 35 people, situated away from the rest of Ericsson Denmark, Aalborg was accustomed to having to justify its existence and manage all support functions internally. Within the department these circumstances had created an entrepreneurial culture in which people were highly dependent on each other. They knew they had to be better to stay competitive, and, with CMM level 2, they now had an edge over the other software development sites in their respective business unit. Furthermore,

Aalborg's management was largely unaffected by changes in Ericsson Denmark management and thus was able to continue its CMM focus. Because Aalborg's department manager was a strong believer in CMM, he soon announced that his department would aim for CMM level 3 to increase its productivity and thus be more competitive. This new goal initiated a new improvement momentum in the department.

3.5 OUTCOMES

The results of carefully working with SPI over a three-year period go beyond the achievement of CMM level 2. First, we'll examine the successes of our effort.

Rapid Progress

The obvious success is that we moved from CMM level 1 to CMM level 2 in just over a year. Although our basic level of CMM compliance was fairly high to begin with, this is still a rapid advance compared with most companies (Herbsleb et al. 1997). Much of this success can be attributed to management's decision to focus the improvement efforts and their demonstration of strong commitment to achieve CMM level 2.

The CMM Accelerator Assessment

This event was the turning point for our SPI effort, and it pushed the organization in the right direction. Even though staffers at Ericsson Denmark were already aware of many of the problems revealed by the assessment results, management either did not know or did not believe such problems existed. The simple fact that external experts analyzed the organization and rendered conclusions gave the problems credibility and weight in the eyes of senior management. Sometimes you cannot see the forest for the trees. Equally important was the timing of the CMM Accelerator Assessment: It was the last chance to make radical improvements to meet the target.

The CMM UltraLight Assessments

The strongest single driver of the CMM improvements was the use of CMM UltraLight Assessments. These assessments were an excellent tool for management to follow up on progress, and the mapping process itself served as a learning process for assessment participants. The UltraLight Assessments were largely responsible for practitioners' understanding of how to comply with CMM requirements in real life. Given that practitioners were the focus of the formal corporate CMM assessment, it was crucial that all of them understood how CMM was implemented in their respective projects.

Although our successes mostly relate to the time between the CMM Accelerator Assessment and the formal CMM assessment, when we look at the entire 1997–1999 period, two failures emerge.

Lack of Process Performance Measures

It has been difficult to measure the real effects of the CMM level 2 rating. Although we keep a mandatory measurements database for figures on fault density and lead-time precision, the measurements are not actively tracked or used to guide the improvement efforts. We are continuing to perform UltraLight Assessments on both the project and the department level, but measurements of actual process performance have not been institutionalized. CMM level 2 was what everybody wanted, but it is not possible to calculate the return on investment of having achieved the goal.

Loss of Momentum in the SPI Effort

The tremendous external pressure clearly indicated that the CMM level 2 rating was a highly important goal, but the relation between this goal and business goals was not clear. Following the formal CMM assessment, this became obvious when only the Aalborg department continued the improvement efforts. The Aalborg department *needed* the improvements, which were in line with its overall business strategy. This is also why Aalborg consciously chose to go after CMM level 3. The other departments have had a hard time putting the improvements into a business context, although they recognize that the improvements are important and relevant. It seems that the same symptoms that existed before the CMM Accelerator Assessment—lack of prioritization and lack of management commitment—have returned. The departments are struggling to get back on track, but, almost a year after the formal CMM assessment, Ericsson Denmark has yet to establish a new strategic SPI plan that sets overall priorities for the Copenhagen departments.

3.6 REFLECTIONS

Working with multiple SPI goals in a setting characterized by organization complexities and rapid growth proved difficult. Ericsson Denmark's SPI program was assumed to be "correct" in the sense that it was designed to use the best practices available, to involve the most experienced people around, and to be supported by external consultants and assessors. Yet there are many ways in which such an SPI program can go wrong. First, the commitments to SPI must be real. At Ericsson Denmark, there was full, widespread support for improvement activities from the beginning, but when real action was required, the commitment was put to the test. The responsibility for verifying improvement progress had to be given to the practitioners themselves before their actual commitment—or lack thereof—could be revealed (and thus acted upon by management). Even then, practitioners had mixed feelings about improvements when senior management started to push for the CMM implementation. Perhaps the clearest evidence of the difference in commitment levels can be seen after the formal CMM assessment, when the Aalborg department's progress continued far beyond that of the rest of Ericsson Denmark.

It is also important to be aware of the needs of different stakeholders in an organization of this complexity. Initially, both the matrix organization and Ericsson Denmark's relatively large SPI structure made it difficult to identify stakeholders and their influence, especially because the organization was fairly new and growing rapidly. Improvements mean change, and change can either be a benefit or a threat, depending on the perspective of the person or group. Such perspectives need not be static, but if priorities are to influence perspectives they must be clearly communicated to every stakeholder in the organization. In Ericsson Denmark, that setting of priorities came almost a year after the SPI program was initiated, and that made it difficult for the SPI people to "sell" project improvements.

Even when priorities seem clear, they can change without notice. The long history of participation in the corporate ESSI program had created an unspoken assumption among managers and practitioners that fault density reduction was senior management's most important goal for 1997 because it had been the priority in every other year. To drop that target and focus instead on CMM was virtually unthinkable, and when it happened it became obvious to everyone in the organization that CMM was important. Putting the corporate ESSI program on hold for a while marked a healthy move away from the traditional improvement routines of the organization.

In the initial attempt to combine the ESSI and CMM efforts, improvement work was reorganized to prioritize CMM over existing improvement goals. Focusing only on CMM gave practitioners the opportunity to clarify and restructure Ericsson Denmark's initial, overly complex SPI efforts. The number of improvement areas, working groups, and individual negotiations ongoing in all projects was simply too complicated to permit clear management and communication. Furthermore, there were critical dependencies that bottlenecked progress. An SPI program must be simple to understand and must allow organizationwide participation, rather than merely account for every improvement need. An SPI program cannot and should not try to solve every problem in the organization; such an attempt leads easily to overcomplexity.

Finally, improvement efforts need an energy surplus. Concurrent change efforts steal energies from each other, and if an organization engages in other changes—such as those resulting from reorganization, in our case—process improvement efforts typically lose their prominence. An organization can absorb only so much change at one time. The rapid growth in Ericsson Denmark's staff should have been recognized as a challenge in itself.

3.7 LESSONS FOR THE CORRECT EFFORT

We have learned many valuable lessons that can help other organizations design an SPI effort that is truly correct (that is, effective and efficient).

Focus and Simplify

SPI is a practical issue—and a massive challenge to the organization. Everyone involved in the effort must know what is to be achieved and why. In our case, the decision to put the ESSI activities on hold and insist on CMM level 2 as the sole improvement goal was vital to our success. This decision simplified and focused our improvement effort and made the goal highly visible and imminent. Ericsson Denmark was initially engaged in two huge SPI efforts: ESSI's six VFAs and CMM level 2's six KPAs. Despite their seemingly correct design, these efforts were simply more than we could undertake at one time. The problem was one not only of size but also of conflicting content. The VFAs primarily addressed issues from CMM level 3, and these issues were difficult to combine with level 2 improvements. CMM level 2 focuses on the project level, whereas level 3 focuses on the organization; combining the two levels typically shifts improvements from addressing immediate project concerns to designing abstract process definitions. Also, CMM is designed in separate steps, in which proven level 2 processes provide the foundation for moving to level 3, and so on. Management's decision to simplify and focus our efforts on level 2 meant that both short- and long-term improvement goals were consistent with CMM sequencing.

Involve Practitioners

SPI's aim is also practical: to develop software processes that are effective and efficient in daily use. Despite this, it is often difficult to meaningfully engage practitioners in SPI. In many organizations, process design is considered the task of expert groups. Unfortunately, process development isolated from practice tends to aim for universality and generality at the expense of practical concerns.

Initially, Ericsson Denmark's SPI effort took place without significant practitioner involvement. As a result, as the CMM Accelerator Assessment assessors noted, there was too much focus on process design and too little focus on implementation. Introducing CMM UltraLight Assessments made work on KPAs an issue for practitioners, and thus practical concerns and requirements came into focus. Involving practitioners in software process design is more likely to create processes that relate to practitioners' actual work, and thus it increases the likelihood of successful implementation.

Ensure Management Attention and Feedback

Although SPI is practical, there is more to success than using appropriate assessment techniques. If SPI is to be taken seriously by practitioners, management attention and feedback are required. Practitioners are busy with and committed to everyday problems in their projects; SPI will get their attention only if management clearly signals that SPI is important and that it will contribute to easing everyday problems.

Initially, Ericsson Denmark's management was focused on the SPI effort alone. Practitioners did not feel that management considered their participation in SPI important. Thus, the CMM Accelerator Assessment assessors complained that management was not demonstrating active leadership and commitment to the improvement work. In response, management decided to have monthly steering committee meetings. When projects were pressured to improve their UltraLight Assessment scores, these monthly meetings served both to maintain this pressure and make progress visible. It was obvious to everyone that SPI was important and that the projects had no alternative but to improve. The assessments helped management monitor progress and offer assistance in dealing with SPI problems.

Promote Individual Responsibility

SPI relies on people working to achieve SPI goals. Some of these people are process designers, and others are process users. Only when these people individually and collectively define and implement useful processes can the SPI effort's goals be met. This boils down to individual responsibility.

Early in the ESSI program, responsibility for improvements was put on working groups. These groups were not necessarily the people who would implement the processes and use them in their daily work. During the UltraLight Assessments, every project manager was responsible for preparing assessment scores. Thus, managers had to bring up process issues in their project groups and discuss how to comply with the key CMM practices. This strategy turbocharged the implementation of CMM level 2 key practices and process areas.

Keep SPI Local

Part of SPI's practicality is that it aims to produce effective and efficient software processes for practitioners with distinct local commitments. In other words, the software processes are contextual and specific. Such processes might well be based on standards decided by corporate headquarters, but in the end, practitioners at the local level interpret and adapt these processes to their particular setting, and most of the energy spent improving processes originates at the local level. Keeping SPI local is about maintaining the relevance of and energy for SPI.

In our case, the importance of local initiative is evident when we compare how process improvement took place at the two geographical locations. The Aalborg example is remarkable in the resolve to develop software processes locally and the practitioners' pride in being at the leading edge. For many reasons, Aalborg was allowed to develop its processes with greater liberty than were the departments in Copenhagen. This policy most likely contributed markedly not only to the speed of improvements but also to the continued momentum of Aalborg's SPI efforts as they pursue CMM level 3.

3.8   THE FUTURE

Much has happened at Ericsson since the big push toward the formal CMM assessment, and new improvement initiatives have been launched. CMM is no longer the predominant SPI strategy, and fault density reduction is no longer a corporate goal. The telecom business is facing some of the same drivers as the computer business— shorter time to market, sourcing of third-party products, and low-cost volume competition—and thus the value of using a process maturity model originally created for developing defense software is questionable. The new improvement wave focuses on innovation, patents, and "new ways of working," and it has been heavily supported to meet the changing competition. The use of CMM, however, is still encouraged by corporate management as a key best practice for Ericsson's systems development units. Ericsson also plans to embrace the emerging CMMI standard from the Software Engineering Institute, which will have a broader scope, including systems engineering and a system lifecycle view of software development. Most importantly, Ericsson corporate is increasing its emphasis on fitness-for-use and the business contribution of the local SPI programs.

In line with this, Ericsson Denmark launched a new, strategic CMM program during 1999 that aims at having most development departments at level 3 in 2001. The program focuses strongly on individual department efforts, led by local SEPGs and coordinated by a central SEPG council. The SPI program will benefit from another initiative also launched by Ericsson Denmark during 1999—the Balanced Scorecard—which includes measurements related directly to software development performance. Because the Balanced Scorecard initiative will have undivided management attention, it could help drive the SPI efforts forward. However, it could also distract attention from SPI in favor of other business parameters with an urgent need for improvement. Nevertheless, the 1997–1999 CMM program has had a long-term effect on how Ericsson Denmark conducts and relates to SPI. The most important lesson has been that, with the correct effort, SPI can yield near-term results, but the biggest reward will most likely come from long-term perseverance.

3.9 REFERENCES

Caputo, K. 1998. *CMM Implementation Guide: Choreographing Software Process Improvement*. Reading, MA: Addison-Wesley.

Daskalantonakis, M.K. 1994. "Achieving Higher SEI Levels." *IEEE Software*. 11:17–24.

Fowler, P., and S. Rifkin. 1990. *Software Engineering Process Group Guide*. Tech. Report CMU/SEI-90-TR-24. Pittsburgh: Software Engineering Institute.

Herbsleb, J., D. Zubrow, D. Goldenson, W. Hayes, and M. Paulk. 1997. "Software Quality and the Capability Maturity Model." *Communications of the ACM*. 40:30–40.

Humphrey, W. 1989. *Managing the Software Process*, first ed. Reading, MA: Addison-Wesley.

Hutchings, T., M. G. Hyde, D. Marca, and L. Cohen. 1993. "Process Improvement that Lasts: An Integrated Training and Consulting Method." *Communications of the ACM*. 36:104–113.

McFeeley, B. 1996. *IDEAL: A User's Guide for Software Process Improvement*. SEI Handbook CMU/SEI-96-HB-001. Pittsburgh: Software Engineering Institute.

Raynus, J. 1999. *Software Process Improvement with CMM*. Norwood, NJ: Ablex.

Chapter 4

The Ambitious Effort: Stalemates and Insider Solutions

Ivan Aaen, Mads Christiansen,
and Carsten Højmose Kristensen

The ambitious effort took place at Systematic Software Engineering, an organization characterized by highly qualified staff at all levels, strong management and employee commitment, a receptive and peer-oriented culture, previous experience with a highly successful improvement program, and a well-established quality function. At the start of our SPI effort, all indications were that we could expect rapid and impressive results from our improvement effort. Top management thus set the goal of moving the organization from CMM level 1 to level 3 within three years.

These expectations were dashed: Improvements came much slower than expected, and the effort ran into several crises. What caused these crises in such a highly ambitious organization? Were our ambitions in fact part of the problem?

We see ambitious organizations as typically decentralized and flat—having highly educated employees who work in an informal atmosphere and exercise extensive discretion in their work. Employees often have close customer relationships and engage in peer consultations when facing new challenges. Thus, the problems faced by ambitious organizations in their SPI efforts may differ from those encountered by other organizations. In fact, as we found, ambition itself is often a key factor both in the crises and in their solutions.

The story in this chapter zooms in on ambitions. We show how Systematic's management, the overall organization, and the SPI activities were all driven by ambition, and how a schism emerged between ambition and caution. We describe our crises in relation to three project situations, each of which featured a *stalemate*—a deadlock in the improvement effort—and a resolution. We describe these resolutions as *insider solutions,* a term we derived from a statement by Systematic's CEO, who said that "the door to change is opened from the inside." That is, to be effective, change cannot be introduced by force; it must be embraced by the people within the organization.

The normative literature on SPI generally puts heavy emphasis on planning, preparation, and prevention. On the planning and preparation side, the IDEAL model (McFeeley 1996) and reports by Fowler and Rifkin (1990) and Humphrey et al. (1991) point to commitment, management support, employee qualifications, experience, and so on as major factors facilitating SPI. Because we were an ambitious organization, these factors were clearly in place in our case: There was strong management support for the improvement effort, and the SPI manager was highly motivated, qualified, and experienced. Also, the SPI group had a detailed plan from the start, as well as results from two complementary assessments to help establish project goals.

On the prevention side, Herbsleb et al. (1997) identify several critical factors for SPI success, including management supervision, goal formulation, SPI resources, assignment of responsibilities, SPI staffing, and the involvement of technical staff. Again, we generally did well on these factors: Management took an active part in the SPI group's activities, overall goals were clearly stated, resources were formally dedicated to the SPI group, and responsibilities were assigned to key staff members. Also, SPI group members were generally competent, although some were junior staff members at Systematic and one senior member's authority was nominal. Several well-respected members of the technical staff engaged in developing the new software processes. Being an ambitious organization, Systematic had very few problems with factors such as organizational politics or turf guarding, but the junior professional expertise of some SPI group members made it somewhat problematic at times to conclude discussions and roll out new processes.

Our expectations for SPI were high, and it came as a surprise when the SPI effort did not progress as planned despite our achieving many useful results. In this situation, the normative SPI literature provided scant help. Little has been written about how to make expectations and realities meet when all your planning, preparation, and prevention to this end fail. Normative literature is generally good for helping you see where you are going (such as Paulk et al. 1993a and Paulk et al. 1993b), and assessments can help you determine where you are and which problems you face (Dunaway and Masters 1996 and Humphrey 1989). Unfortunately, such knowledge is not enough. You also need help getting out of the quagmire from time to time. Our experiences can offer insight into how and why ambitious organizations can run into stalemates and how insider solutions can facilitate progress in such situations. Our hope is that our experience will help ambitious organizations benefit from their ambitions while also accommodating the difficulties inherent in SPI efforts.

This chapter is organized as follows. We first present the organization and context for the SPI effort and then describe three situations in which stalemates and solutions arose. Finally, we discuss the role of ambitions, the actors in an ambitious organization, and the nature of the stalemates and insider solutions.

4.1 THE SYSTEMATIC CONTEXT

Established in 1985, Systematic focuses on complex IT solutions within information and communications systems. The company's international customers include military institutions and suppliers as well as data communications, transportation, and manufacturing companies and organizations involved in the finance and health care sectors.

As a systems integrator, Systematic has established a special competency in managing and implementing complex software projects requiring high reliability and secure communications 24 hours a day. The company's core competence is delivering products on time and to the quality and budget agreed on with the customer. Systematic's goal is to be an internationally recognized software supplier and systems integrator within our core fields of expertise: (1) communication and interoperability between defense units and (2) electronic integration between applications and systems.

Organization

Three people privately own Systematic, with the CEO as majority shareholder. The management group also includes business managers for each of Systematic's three line-of-business departments, as well as managers of staff functions. In 1997–1999, the company's staff increased significantly. At the end of fiscal year 1999, there were 137 employees in Denmark: 105 software engineers and 32 people working in finance, administration, internal IT, quality assurance, and cleaning or food services.

All software development takes place in project teams led by a project manager. Most managers started as software developers and were later trained and promoted internally, reflecting Systematic's belief in organic growth. Project teams range from 2 to 18 members and last from two months to three years. Typically, team members participate throughout the process, from requirements specification to design, programming, test, documentation, installation, and user training. The company believes that this policy ensures maximum commitment and development of staff competence.

Despite the smaller number of graduates in computer science and systems engineering in Denmark, two-thirds of the employees hold a master's or Ph.D. degree. To attract knowledge about state-of-the-art technologies, high flexibility, and openness toward change, the company hires highly educated people. Such individuals typically have very high personal ambitions and a readiness to improve processes and performance individually and collectively. The average age of employees is 32 years, and 83% of the staff are under 40.

Systematic's culture emphasizes freedom with responsibility. All software development takes place in project teams that give members influence over their own tasks; the team as a whole is responsible for meeting time, budget, and quality requirements. This *peer-based* arrangement is an important feature of Systematic's company culture.

Systematic has a dedicated SPI group with an average staff of two full-time employees. The SPI group gets assistance from work groups, which are convened for specific, short-term tasks as needed. Management oversight and involvement with the SPI group changed frequently over the three-year period we are concerned with here.

Our experience in this effort comes from two perspectives. Two of us served as external researchers in the SPI group: Ivan Aaen from Aalborg University, and Mads Christiansen from Delta. Carsten Højmose Kristensen initially participated in work groups and worked briefly with the SPI group. Later, in June 1998, he was appointed to lead the company's SPI effort, which he did from that point on.

Leadership Principles

Systematic's set of values serve as both the leadership principles that guide our efforts and the norms that we encourage. We expect all managers and employees to practice the following values in their daily work.

- The customer is our partner. We focus on long-term relationships with a limited number of customers, a policy that offers the opportunity for cooperation and mutual benefit.
- Respect for the customer. We show the customer respect and are not reluctant to admit if we cannot complete an assignment satisfactorily.
- Quality over quantity. We work according to the highest standards of quality and learn from our experience and errors.
- Freedom with responsibility. All software development takes place in project teams in which each employee has influence over his or her own tasks, and the team is jointly responsible for meeting requirements on time, budget, and quality.
- Flat organization. There is always a short distance between staff and management, with minimal bureaucracy. Expectations between managers and staff are harmonized through continuous dialogue, performance reviews, and satisfaction surveys.
- Changes are constant. Employees should seek new challenges to strengthen their skills and competence, and we offer a wide range of supplementary education and in-house training.
- Constant innovation. We cooperate actively with research centers and development institutions in developing and introducing technologies and methods into our activities.

The SPI Effort

In 1992, Systematic's quality assurance system was certified in accordance with ISO 9001 and the military standards to become AQAP 110 and 150. The ISO 9001 certified quality management system forms the basis for numerous elements in Systematic's quality assurance procedures. In the long term, however, this standard is insufficient to meet both customers' increasing demands for quality assurance and internal requirements for the efficiency and predictability of the development process. Thus, in 1997, Systematic strengthened its focus on process improvement and joined the SPI Project. Systematic's SPI Project partners were Aalborg University and Delta Software Engineering. Figure 4.1 offers an overview of the three-year project. For market reasons, the objective and major challenge of the SPI effort was to pursue CMM improvements while at the same time maintaining the quality assurance system as compliant with ISO 9001 and AQAP 110/150.

In April 1997, Systematic was assessed using Aalborg University's Questionnaire Based Assessment (QBA) method, which was designed to measure conformance with CMM level 2 (Arent and Iversen 1996). The QBA assessment indicated that Systematic's maturity was just below level 2. In August 1997, DELTA performed a Bootstrap assessment that showed a maturity level of 2 and pointed out the same issues as had the QBA. The Bootstrap assessment included four projects, which were at level 2, and the Software Producing Unit (SPU), which was at level 2.25. Later assessments showed an increase in project maturity levels: 2.25 in 1998 and 2.5 in 1999. The SPU also increased by 0.25 points at each measurement.

The management group's goals for the SPI project were twofold. The first goal was to establish sound software processes that would increase project productivity, quality, and scheduling predictability. The second goal was very specific from the start: to reach CMM level 3. This goal was motivated by the expectation that U.S. defense industry customers would in time require all suppliers to be at CMM level 3 or higher.

In 1992, Systematic had successfully handled a similar challenge when ISO 9000 certification was required for all approved suppliers to the defense industry. Systematic had the certificate within a year, led by a new quality manager who used a minimalist

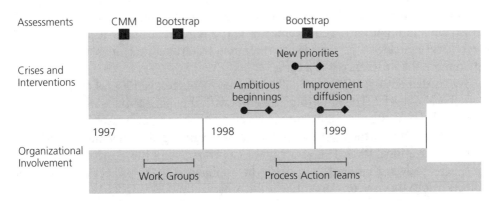

Figure 4.1 *A timeline of the Systematic SPI effort. Bullets and diamonds indicate roughly when project stalemates began and insider solutions emerged*

QA approach that closely followed ISO 9000 requirements. This success created a community spirit that top management expected to benefit from in the SPI project. Thus, they asked the same person—who had since become a business manager—to lead the SPI effort. Management pronounced the SPI effort vitally important to the organization and later said that SPI experience would be mandatory for anyone who wanted to build a career in the company.

At the start of the SPI effort, Systematic's ambitions were high for several reasons.

◆ The organization had previous positive experience with the QA system.

◆ Top management was vocal about commitments.

◆ The educational level throughout the organization was high.

◆ The culture of the employees was open-minded.

◆ There was confidence in the quality of the existing processes.

◆ External partners would contribute with knowledge about SPI and CMM.

Everything pointed to a safe success for the SPI project, which was expected to achieve impressive results using few resources. We now examine why this did not occur, analyzing three project situations and highlighting the major stalemates and solutions in each.

4.2 AMBITIOUS BEGINNINGS

To accelerate the organization's maturation process, top management decided to move directly from CMM level 1 to level 3. The plan was for the organization to simultaneously implement all CMM level 2 KPAs: project planning, project tracking, configuration management, requirements management, quality assurance, and subcontract management. This decision ignored traditional warnings against focusing on more than a few areas at a time.

We carried out the QBA and Bootstrap assessments to diagnose what was needed to reach CMM level 3. The SPI group, together with the management steering group, then decided that the most efficient approach would be to use a level 3 approach to reach level 2. That is, the level 2 KPAs would be developed and implemented directly at the organizational level. This strategy was contrary to SPI literature recommendations, which advise that level 2 processes be established at the project level via pilot projects before they are implemented at the organizational level.

Some participants in the SPI effort were skeptical about bypassing the project level, but their concerns were dismissed. The general attitude was that Systematic was a small and transparent organization and that using pilots would take up valuable time and probably not contribute essential new knowledge. The upside to this strategy was the possibility of rapid progress toward level 3 and less need for re-work—projects would not have to invent their own processes. The disadvantage was that the SPI work would take place on the sidelines and would not be integrated into the projects. Given this, visible results from the SPI effort would take longer to emerge.

The SPI group's goal was to create universal software processes that would be useful as-is for large projects and would easily scale down to smaller projects. Practitioners from ongoing projects would serve as experts and primary designers of the new processes. The SPI group believed that using practitioners in this way would ensure that processes were practical for most projects. It would also create consensus and would positively influence the diffusion and adoption of the new processes across the organization. In essence, practitioners would develop the basic process concepts, and the QA function would implement them.

Part of Systematic's ambition for the project was to succeed using few dedicated resources. The business and, in particular, its customers were not to suffer during the SPI project. Management believed that the project could be staffed with a few permanent members supported by ad hoc experts in process development. If necessary, individuals might acquire needed skills via training. Warnings from the literature—that SPI takes time and requires the dedication of an organization's best people to succeed—were dismissed. In general, such warnings were viewed as relevant to organizations with less knowledge, commitment, and ambition.

Although the project had one full-time employee, the first SPI project manager was assigned to the project part time, and the "part time equals no time" saying soon came true. Top management's commitment to SPI proved to be at odds with the customer orientation that was deeply embedded in the organization's culture. SPI was an internal project without a customer, and thus employees' focus quickly shifted back to product development. This led to a reorganization of the project in the summer of 1997. The SPI project was given a new and dedicated project manager, and two part-time employees replaced the full-time employee.

Given the situation, management decided to form a number of work groups—one for each process area to be improved—and organize the groups according to a charter specifying their responsibilities with respect to deliverables and delivery dates. The groups would be staffed with people who were generally recognized for their expertise in the target process area. The work required for their tasks was considered moderate, and thus group members were given no extra time to fulfill the work-group duties. In short, the approach assumed that shared organizational ambitions would be enough to make the groups act responsibly and in accordance with the spirit of the improvement effort.

The Gold-Plating Stalemate

In August 1997 the SPI group organized five such work groups of seven or eight practitioners—mainly volunteers—from different departments. Their task was to define concepts and implementation plans for the level 2 KPAs. The SPI group did not formally appoint group leaders, and it expected that the groups would work at their own discretion in accordance with their charters. Few constraints were put on the contents of the concepts: As professionals, the work-group members were expected to come up with process concepts that would both honor CMM requirements and be useful to the organization based on the experiences of current and past projects.

The work groups completed their tasks and disbanded by winter 1997. Management reviewed the results and found that none of the concepts was satisfactory and that no implementation plans had been prepared. The SPI group was responsible for amending this situation. At that point, two new full-time members joined the SPI project. Their focus was project management and configuration management. However, they soon left when customers successfully requested that they be appointed to manage projects. Around April 1998, the researchers interviewed people in the organization as a whole about the SPI effort and worked with SPI group members to create an internal status report to capture lessons learned and provide feedback for future SPI change initiatives. The interviews clearly demonstrated that the SPI project had come to a complete standstill: The process concepts were still unacceptable to management, implementation plans had not been prepared, and the project's prestige had reached an all-time low.

The SPI group felt that this situation was not simply a matter of inadequate resources. More time and better staffing in both the SPI group and the work groups would certainly have helped, but the problems were deeply rooted in the work groups' approach. The work groups had been searching for universal software processes that would both comply with CMM requirements and suit any project in the organization. Because work groups were separate from the everyday distractions of ongoing projects, their work became a continuous questing after software processes that would ideally suit any part of the organization. The SPI group assumed that the charters were sufficient to guide the work groups' efforts and thus failed to supervise them to ensure progress and relevance. The result was the *gold-plating* stalemate: The work groups' processes were neither in accordance with these abstract ideals nor ready for practical use.

On several occasions, the management steering group encouraged the business and project managers to strengthen their SPI commitment by implementing the processes being developed. However, the managers knew that they would have trouble in the long run if they relaxed their customer focus. Thus, the SPI project lived a life of its own, with little visibility in the organization and no practical testing of results. Lack of external pressures from ongoing software projects combined with a shortage of resources in the SPI group paved the way for the gold-plating stalemate. For the effort to get back on track, intervention was required.

Insider Solution: Insight

In May 1998, a U.S. specialist facilitated a four-day workshop for Systematic's management and SPI group on "Using the CMM for SPI." The workshop was tailored to the company's needs and had been scheduled for some time; that it occurred when a stalemate had blocked all progress was a fortunate coincidence.

The purpose of the workshop was to offer insight into how an organization is assessed against the CMM level 2 and to provide valuable tips on how to pass the assessment. The workshop succeeded in this, but also—much more importantly—it offered further insights that radically changed the management steering group's perspective on the SPI project.

Initially, the CMM label was the key driver. However, the workshop gave the management steering group and department managers a clearer view of the internal business value of the maturity levels with respect to the software processes. They thus realized that the important benefits come from the evolution of processes themselves; the label is merely something to show the outside world. The insights gained in the workshop created new support and energy for the project. Although the ambition of going directly to CMM level 3 remained intact, management's motivations changed. The new aim of the SPI project was to fundamentally change existing software processes. For everyone connected with the SPI effort, this brought into focus practical concerns for software projects. The SPI effort was now reorganized with respect to resources, tasks, and deliverables. Management also permanently assigned well-respected and competent employees to the SPI project.

A consequence of this deeper understanding of the SPI effort was a widespread and substantial change in the ordering of ambitions. Priority was given to practical solutions that would improve productivity, quality, and predictability, and the achievement of CMM level 3 was seen as a natural extension of this work. The ambition to achieve major results using few resources was abandoned. Similarly, the antagonism between internal and external projects was resolved by giving the SPI project priority and more attention from the management steering group.

In this part of the project, we learned the following lessons:

- Ambitions are a valuable source of energy, but they must be informed by concerns related to everyday working conditions.
- Stalemates can deepen when great ambitions and competing obligations collide. SPI is not a part-time job, and internal and external obligations must be balanced.

◆ Internal solutions depend on insight and understanding from the top down. Insight and understanding are essential for motivation and for developing a common strategic view on SPI.

4.3 NEW PRIORITIES

In August 1998, Process Action Teams (PATs) were deployed, staffed mainly by project managers from different departments. Their task was to develop concepts and processes for specific KPAs within three months, based on charters approved by the management steering group. In September 1998, four PATs were established to create processes for four KPAs: requirements management, configuration management, quality assurance, and subcontractor management. The two remaining level 2 processes—project planning and project tracking—were combined into project management. The SPI group was charged with developing processes for this area.

The SPI group input PAT results into an intranet-based business manual as the results came available. The manual was to serve as a handbook for project managers and others in the organization. It would include process descriptions, procedures, guidelines, a best-practices library, templates, checklists, and other tools to help the projects, making it considerably more comprehensive than the existing QA system. The immediate ambition was to implement all level 2 processes by the end of 1998. The overall goal was still to reach CMM level 3 by 2000.

The PATs delivered their work products (some of which were incomplete) and were adjourned. Management then instructed the SPI group to complete the processes based on the PAT deliverables and guided by the CMM model. Whenever a process was ready, the SPI group would review it and submit it for management approval. Following management approval the plan was to publish the process in the business manual for immediate use across the organization.

The processes from the PATs and the SPI group were ready for approval almost as planned in the period from November 1998 to February 1999. However, the approval process was unexpectedly problematic: The management steering group could not endorse several processes, effectively bringing the SPI project to a new standstill.

The Misalignment Stalemate

The SPI ambitions and the involved parties were once again at odds. Responsibilities for developing process descriptions had been assigned to small, self-regulating expert groups, whose results were incomplete because of lack of focus and prioritization. The PATs had worked autonomously based on the presumption that there would be a tacit understanding of objectives. What had not been taken into account was the inclination of experts to research alternative ways to devise a process and to look for comprehensive solutions. As a consequence, internal disagreements in some PATs over requirements aggravated the misalignment. In the configuration management PAT, for example, one department wanted a universal solution from the start; other departments wanted only basic configuration management procedures. The battle was over an ultimate solution versus a more pragmatic approach. In such "religious wars," people either believe or do not believe. There is nothing to negotiate, and resolution requires management to take a stand.

The business departments were hesitant to release experts to the PATs at the expense of external projects. The result was that some process descriptions were left to the SPI group to finish. The SPI group found it difficult to work on processes that were designed by ambitious experts but had to be completed with a view to pragmatics.

The work in the PATs was controlled by appointed team leaders and PAT charters specifying what the PATs should deliver to the SPI group. Despite this, many people in the organization saw the rejection of the processes as caused primarily by the vague charters that outlined the requirements and expectations for the processes. Thus, the management steering group deemed some processes unacceptable for failing to comply with organizationwide objectives. Had the steering group reviewed draft versions of the process descriptions, the problem might have been recognized earlier.

Insider Solution: Empowerment

An obvious reaction to the rejection would be to rewrite the processes, hold new reviews, and hope for better results. The drawback of this option was that it would delay the benefits to be gained from implementing the new processes and would contribute to an image of the SPI effort as failing. The SPI group was feeling pressure from the organization to produce results, and the rejection of three of the five processes was a major setback.

The SPI group found this option problematic. They felt it would be better to use the rejected versions until better processes had been approved. Not only would this approach offer immediate benefits, but it would also provide a better foundation for improving the processes later based on experiences gained through their early practical use.

The SPI group therefore arranged a meeting with the management steering group and proposed that the business manual be published on the intranet in its present form. Processes that had not been approved would be published as drafts alongside approved parts of the business manual, and the SPI group would encourage departments to use them all. The SPI group would also initiate experiments with rejected processes and invite project managers to participate.

The proposal was consistent with Systematic's espoused value of "freedom with responsibility." The organization wanted competent people to feel empowered to make their own decisions and, in this case, to use unfinished processes at their own discretion hoping that their experiences would be valuable.

The management steering group accepted this proposal and also decided to reverse the producer and customer roles in the SPI project. Initially, the SPI group produced processes for departments, which acted as customers. Now responsibility for producing processes was assigned to the departments, and the SPI group became the customer. The SPI group was responsible for assessing process quality and identifying candidates to include in the business manual. In this way, departments became more involved and committed to using and producing SPI deliverables.

In this part of the project, we learned the following lessons:

* Ambitions cannot serve as a compass when goals are being set. Requirements for new processes must be clarified. An iterative approach to process design can ensure that expectations are aligned throughout the organization.

* Stalemates can emerge when objectives are misaligned. In this case, SPI group members, technical experts, and the management steering group failed to ensure a common view of objectives.

* Insider solutions are rooted in culture, and the organization's culture can be a strong ally in the face of problems. In this case, the standstill caused by rejection of process descriptions was overcome by the established tradition of empowerment.

4.4 IMPROVEMENT DIFFUSION

In January 1999, the management steering group officially adopted the project-management processes in the business manual. Business managers thus had to ensure implementation of the processes in their respective departments, whereas the SPI group was charged with ensuring that the work products would adhere to the business manual processes.

The SPI group devised a three-part rollout plan for the project-management processes. First, they would train project managers in relevant methods and techniques. Second, they would make available on the intranet templates and documents to support practical use of the processes. Third, management would support the effort by asserting that all projects must be managed according to the approved principles. All in all, the plan was viewed as a mainly technical and rational approach to the rollout process.

The plan required different input from various organizational levels. The management steering group was expected to create and sustain the energy and enthusiasm needed to support the rollout. The SPI group would keep them informed about business manual principles, project management in general, and the rollout strategy. The SPI group would offer practitioners whatever support they needed in using the business manual and specific project-management materials.

At the department level, only project managers were mentioned in the rollout plan. The SPI group gave them information about the business manual and offered consulting support in areas such as risk analysis. Project managers were required to prepare implementation plans for their project and to participate in related training activities and workshops. The SPI group assumed that such participation would ensure that project managers would use the project-management processes. Project managers were also expected to create enthusiasm among their teams in support of the rollout. Business managers were not directly involved with the project management and thus had no explicit responsibilities in the rollout.

The Peer Stalemate

Despite the approved plan and the go-ahead from the management steering group, the rollout process failed because project managers did not use the processes. On the surface, this appeared to be because of dissatisfaction with the processes. Some project managers expressed dissatisfaction with particular tools, whereas others "didn't see" processes within a template or felt that their particular projects were "unsuitable" for a proposed process. Such specific dissatisfactions would have been more convincing had the project managers sought workarounds for the problems or employed other new processes whenever the opportunity arose. In reality, however, the voiced dissatisfactions were more of an excuse for projects and departments to remain passive. The likely reason is that business and project managers faced stronger pressures from customers and the management steering group regarding external project deliverables compared with the pressures for implementing new project-management processes. Thus, even though improved project management was expected, project teams did not invest the effort needed to adopt the new processes. Several factors were involved in this outcome.

The organization had limited experience in rollout processes, and not enough people knew how to proceed. Moreover, because it took so long to develop the processes, many people assumed that they would be complex and difficult to put into practical use.

As planned, the management steering group had declared the project-management process a new organizational standard immediately following rollout. Having done so, however, members of the management steering group played no further role in the rollout process. They did not exert pressure on the business managers, who in turn did not exert pressure on their project managers. Projects were basically left to do as they used to do.

Because the SPI group worked in a consulting and facilitating role during rollout, the responsibility for implementation was relegated to departments, which gave higher priority to other issues and limited attention to the rollout processes. One factor here was ownership. The processes were developed for the organization level, and the SPI group did not involve the department level in pilot studies before submitting processes for approval. The departments were thus still somewhat alienated and felt little responsibility for applying the new processes at the project level. Also, because project managers had no experience with the practical relevance of the new processes, they were naturally less appealing.

In ambitious organizations such as Systematic, egalitarian culture is common. Systematic gets its strength by empowering competent people, and this empowerment rests on mutual consideration. However, this strength in the organization's everyday workings can be a weakness when it is attempting change. To respect the egalitarian leanings, changes cannot be issued in the form of edicts, but rather must come through convincing peers that the new way of doing things is better and that change will be worth the effort.

This is one reason the rollout plan contained few directives. Instead, it stressed such things as information, training, and facilitation rather than planning for the SPI group to play a more active role. The basic idea of the rollout plan was to combine the management steering group's recommendation that the processes be used with offers of support to introduce and sustain them. The SPI group assumed that the fact that the management steering group wanted the change was enough to make project managers request support and take personal responsibility for introducing and using the new processes.

However, in Systematic's culture, project managers tended to be both empowered and committed to their customers. They thus balanced internal demands for process improvement against external commitments and gave the latter priority. The peer stalemate was the result: In an egalitarian culture, empowered managers were relatively free to select their priorities, and, given that the company highly values its external commitments, such prioritization was typically unfavorable to internal process improvement. The SPI group's rollout plan was thus flawed. What they needed was a plan that might leverage Systematic's peer-driven culture.

Insider Solution: The Role Model

The peer stalemate lasted for three months. When the management steering group decided to move responsibility from the SPI group to the business departments, the then-leader of the ISO 9000 effort—who had since become a business manager—saw this as a chance to lend the rollout process a much needed hand. Being the hero from the ISO 9000 effort and the former management member of the SPI group, he had expected rapid progress and felt somewhat embarrassed with the slow progress in the SPI effort. Now he saw an opportunity to act as a change agent.

After consulting the SPI group leader, the business manager decided on a two-part plan. First, he would roll out the new processes in his own department. The second step was to provoke other departments to do the same. The strategy underlying both steps was constructive competition.

To get his own department to implement project planning processes, the change agent held out bait: If all projects implemented the processes by a given date, he would have a grill party at his home. The type of inducement was unimportant. What did matter is that everybody in the department felt obliged to comply, lest they be labeled "party killers." The strategy created both group pressure and competition within the department to reach the goal. The department was further motivated by the prospect of being front-runners at Systematic.

The strategy prompted immediate reactions from other business managers, who did not want to be outdone by a peer. One manager in particular, who had for years been in friendly competition with the change agent, fueled the spreading interest by quickly declaring his own department's intention to immediately begin implementing new project management processes.

The strategy took advantage of Systematic's peer culture at two levels. First, our change agent used peer relationships within his department to create social pressure that would commit everybody to the implementation process, and second, he simultaneously provoked his management-level peers to follow suit. To further strengthen the competition, the management steering group introduced regular self-assessments and began to put each project's achievements on public display.

As a result of the change agent's intervention, the rollout process finally got under way, with the departments as main actors. By leveraging the peer culture's inherent susceptibility to group pressures, the strategy changed the departments' stance from passive to highly active. Furthermore, by actively involving project teams in implementation, the processes benefited from adaptation to local conditions. Thus, the process implementation fell more in line with the standard recommendation that level 2 processes be implemented at the project level first before they are introduced at the organizational level.

In this part of the project, we learned the following lessons:

- Ambitious organizations are peer organizations. The desire to maintain peer relations can be a strong motivator of change at the individual level.
- Stalemates can emerge when peers stop challenging each other.
- Insider solutions can employ friendly competition as an instrument. In the ambitious organization, constructive competition can be a driver of change at the individual, project, and department level.
- Insider solutions can rely on heroes. In an organization of more than 100 people, one champion finally set the rollout process in motion.
- Putting achievements on public display makes solutions visible to customers and employees.

4.5 LESSONS FROM THE AMBITIOUS ORGANIZATION

Our experience at Systematic taught us much about SPI efforts and the special challenges ambitious organizations face when it comes to change. In this final section we go beyond the three situations and focus on the roles of ambitions and organizational actors, and on problems and solutions.

The Role of Ambitions

Not surprisingly, ambitions were the source of trouble in all three situations. In the first situation, the ambitious goal of advancing Systematic from CMM level 1 to level 3 meant that CMM level 2 was treated mostly as a milestone under way. One side effect was that the level 2 goals—which should have provided concrete guidelines for the work groups—were out of focus in the quest for universal processes. Rather, the focus was on organization-level processes and abstract quality goals at the expense of everyday utility. Given this, pilot projects were ignored and processes were developed in a setting where practical concerns played a minor role. These ambitions continued to influence the SPI effort in later situations. They were the key factor in the misalignment stalemate, and they also explain the alienation behind the implementation problems that were prevalent in the peer stalemate.

On the other hand, ambitions were also a driving force throughout. When the members of the management steering group radically changed perspective on the SPI project, they did so with the ambition to foster a defined process that was an integrated and useful framework for everyday development and maintenance of software. Also, the decision to develop an organizationwide business manual gave the improvement project an important practical dimension. When combined with pilot projects and beta testing, the manual paved the way for effective diffusion and utilization of the software processes. This suggests that when strategy and strategic ambitions are combined, they can create energy and direction for SPI efforts.

The Role of the Organization

In this chapter, we identify three main actors: the management steering group, the SPI group, and the departments. All three contributed to the problems. The management steering group was first among equals to create high ambitions, and, in part because of these ambitions, it stalled progress by rejecting processes. The SPI group was remarkably passive when SPI goals were formulated and resources allocated, and the group failed to manage the religious wars prevalent in the second situation. The departments were also remarkably passive during the peer stalemate.

On the other hand, all actors also played important positive roles. The management steering group reoriented its view of the SPI project's goals and mobilized the organization accordingly. The SPI group encouraged empowerment during the misalignment stalemate. As for the departments, they played a central role in ensuring progress in the SPI project. Although they served as targets for improvement in both the gold-plating and misalignment stalemates, during the peer stalemate, the departments took over the initiative and ensured that the processes were tested and put to practical use.

All the SPI problems encountered were solved with the departments—typically the target group—playing a key role. This suggests that when departments participate, the SPI effort focuses on local and practical concerns, which are most relevant to success.

The Nature of the Problems and Solutions

All three stalemates were paradoxical: The gold-plating stalemate was basically a conflict between abstract ideals and practical utility; the misalignment stalemate was a clash between requirements for a complete process and a more incremental approach; and the peer stalemate was a dilemma involving traditional competence and change. These paradoxes were all answered by practical solutions such as the business manual, pilots, and beta tests. This suggests that stalemates can be broken by maintaining a focus on the utility of the software process.

The insider solutions have one thing in common: They were never what they seemed to be at first glance. Insight was what came out of a simple demand for straight tips on how to pass an assessment. Empowerment is normally thought of as the ability to act without asking, but in this case empowerment led to role reversal as the process providers became process customers. Peer relationships are normally thought of as providing a basis for mutual respect and camaraderie, but here the peer structure was used to create constructive competition and challenge.

4.6 CONCLUSION

An ambitious organization employs people who are highly qualified, motivated, flexible, and prepared to change. Such competence can lead management to underestimate the effort required to succeed in SPI. Management is challenged to ensure that competing obligations are resolved and that the SPI group is equipped with sufficient resources in terms of quantity and quality. Moreover, management is challenged to ensure that SPI goals are aligned and realistic. Insight into SPI objectives, combined with a pragmatic view on how to balance long- and short-term goals, is required.

The SPI group faces a great challenge when working with highly self-confident people. Staffing the SPI group with the right people and supplying these people with adequate resources is important, but perhaps the most important prerequisite for the SPI group is to know its place. The SPI group must meet the departments where they are and help them on their own terms. The group serves mainly as a support group for the departments and as a coordination tool for management. Ultimately, the success of SPI is determined in and by the departments and projects.

Departments are the key actors in the change process. Essentially, SPI is about changing the behavior of practitioners, and in an ambitious organization people change behavior when they realize that the change is for the better. When peers cease to question their practice, stagnation rules. When peers challenge one another, friendly competition can produce individual and departmental momentum.

All in all, the three situations confirm that in an ambitious organization *the door to change is opened from the inside.* If anything, this case confirms the importance of people taking responsibility for their software processes, maintaining a shared vision, and communicating openly across the organization.

4.7 REFERENCES

Arent, J., and J. Iversen. 1996. "Development of a Method for Maturity Assessments in Software Organizations Based on the Capability Maturity Model." Master's Thesis. Aalborg, Denmark: Aalborg University.

Dunaway, D.K., and S. Masters. 1996. "CMM-Based Appraisal for Internal Process Improvement (CBA IPI): Method Description." Technical Report CMU/SEI-96-TR-007. Pittsburgh: Software Engineering Institute.

Fowler, P. and S. Rifkin. 1990. "Software Engineering Process Group Guide." Technical Report CMU/SEI-90-TR-24. Pittsburgh: Software Engineering Institute.

Herbsleb, J., D. Zubrow, D. Goldenson, W. Hayes, and M. Paulk. 1997. "Software Quality and the Capability Maturity Model." *Communications of the ACM*. 40:6: 30–40.

Humphrey, W. 1989. *Managing the Software Process,* first ed. SEI Series in Software Engineering. Nico Habermann, ed. Reading, MA: Addison-Wesley.

Humphrey, W.S., T.R. Snyder, and R.R. Willis. 1991. "Software Process Improvement at Hughes Aircraft." *IEEE Software*. 8:4: 11–23.

McFeeley, B. 1996. *IDEAL: A User's Guide for Software Process Improvement*. Handbook CMU/SEI-96-HB-001. Pittsburgh: Software Engineering Institute.

Paulk, M.C., B. Curtis, M.B. Chrissis, and C. Weber 1993a. "Capability Maturity Model for Software." Technical Report CMU/SEI-93-TR-24. Pittsburgh: Software Enginering Institute.

Paulk, M.C., C.V. Weber, S.M. Garcia, M.B. Chrissis, and M. Bush. 1993b. "Key Practices of the Capability Maturity Model." Technical Report CMU/SEI-93-TR-25. Pittsburgh: Software Engineering Institute.

Chapter 5

The Grassroots Effort

Carsten Vestergaard Andersen, Flemming Krath,
Lise Krukow, Lars Mathiassen, and Jan Pries-Heje

Conventional wisdom holds that SPI should be organized as a participatory process that eventually leads to an empowered software organization. But it is also well known that long-term, upper-management commitment is a critical factor in success. How do you organize your improvement efforts given these partly contradictory claims? And how do you make improvements happen? Are improvements most effectively driven by management in a top-down fashion, in which people are required to participate? Or are improvements better organized as bottom-up initiatives, in which people willingly participate and take responsibility for their own professional development?

We conducted a successful improvement initiative at Danske Data from 1997 to 1999. Our initiative focused on improving project management. Although it was later integrated with the company's larger improvement project, our initiative started outside the established SPI Project and focused on getting individual project managers involved in making improvements. The initiative later moved up the hierarchy, as higher-level managers asked about the norms and practices emerging from the project-management level. We thus characterize our experience as a bottom-up, grassroots effort.

Although our initiative was ultimately successful, it was far from unproblematic. What at first seemed to be a simple, straightforward strategy to improve Danske Data's project management became a complex change process with many opportunities, surprises, and challenges. We describe our initiative and its challenges here, followed by a discussion of how the initiative moved from the grass roots into the wider organization. We then offer an analysis of our experiences from three complementary perspectives: rational, cultural, and political (Dahlbom and Mathiassen 1993).

5.1 CONTEXT: THE SPI PROJECT

In May 1997, Danske Data carried out a joint Bootstrap–CMM assessment. The purposes were to:

♦ Evaluate the present status of software development in the company
♦ Identify strengths and weaknesses in software development
♦ Suggest actions to improve the process

The assessment result rated Danske Data at level 1.5 on the Bootstrap scale. The assessment also helped to identify seven target areas for improvement actions:

1. Test: Strengthen software testing, especially application and integration testing.
2. Design: Improve the design phase from architectural design to detailed design, including improvements to design methods, procedures, templates, and guidelines.
3. Quality assurance: Strengthen quality management within projects.
4. Development model: Modify the development model to better suit actual needs.
5. Organizational implementation: Improve the organizationwide diffusion of new and existing methods, techniques, and tools and ensure their adoption.
6. Project management: Improve project management, especially estimation.
7. Configuration management: Strengthen configuration management, including requirements management.

According to management, the assessment offered valuable insight into the strengths and weaknesses of the company's software development practice. They also said that the assessment "confirmed many of our suspicions but also revealed problems that we had not expected." Everyone involved with the overall SPI Project agreed with the assessment's results: The problems were real and should be dealt with.

Before the 1997 assessment, Danske Data's CEO had publicly stated the goal of the company's SPI initiative: to reach CMM level 2 and improve efficiency by at least 10% within three years. The SPI Project therefore wanted to improve all seven areas suggested in the assessment *and* be able to prove that the improvements raised efficiency by at least 10%. To that end, a metrics program was planned to measure the efficiency of Danske Data's development process. Thus, the SPI Project faced eight areas needing improvement.

Several initiatives were launched to cope with these target problems. A separate team addressed each of the eight improvement areas; the teams were organized as cross-organizational initiatives within the overall SPI Project, which was anchored in the methodology department. Because of lack of ownership, management focus, and (thus) resources, three of the eight improvement initiatives lost momentum and were suspended in their early stages. The remaining five initiatives were all carried through more or less successfully. Following is a brief overview of four of the initiatives. In this chapter, we discuss the fifth initiative, project management, in more detail.

Danske Data Improvement Initiatives

In addition to the project management initiative, Danske Data teams carried out four other initiatives aimed at specific problems.

QUALITY ASSURANCE

Developing quality meetings was one of the SPI initiatives. Today, all development projects hold as many as seven quality meetings. Two of them are mandatory, and the rest vary according to the project. For example, one quality meeting is held before a contract is signed with the customer. The meeting focuses on the contract and issues surrounding it and is carried out by the methodology department. The meeting's result is a written report to the project manager, his or her senior manager, and the managing director.

DEVELOPMENT MODEL

One of the findings of the May 1997 maturity assessment was that, although they knew it existed, project participants never used the company's paper-based development model. The development model was reviewed thoroughly, and many older guidelines and procedures were taken out. The rest of the model was updated and rewritten using a structured-text concept. Finally, the updated development model was implemented as an open-access Lotus Notes database so that it was always one click away.

PROCESS MEASUREMENT

To measure the company's progress toward the CEO's publicly stated goal of a 10% increase in productivity, a metrics program was established. It included metrics for estimating precision and for measuring productivity, quality, and user and employee satisfaction. However, it took two full years and a lot of frustration to start the metrication and reach a satisfactory data quality. Chapter 17 reports on this experience in detail.

ORGANIZATIONAL IMPLEMENTATION

Another important finding of the May 1997 assessment was the method paradox. On the one hand, Danske Data had several available techniques, tools, procedures, and guidelines, all of which the assessors judged to be of high quality. On the other hand, the assessors were unable to find any evidence that any of the techniques, tools, and procedures had been used in the eight projects they assessed. The methodology department's high-quality work in developing company-tailored techniques and procedures had never been diffused to or adopted by the rest of the organization. To overcome the dilemma, a project called Learning How to Implement was launched. The idea is for a project to arrange an implementation workshop at an early stage in product development. In other words, early on, attention is focused on how to make software developers change their behavior in practice. This early input on methods and tools under development is meant to ensure successful implementation in advance. Chapter 15 reports on this experience in detail.

5.2 ACTION: PROJECT-MANAGEMENT INITIATIVE

In the past, Danske Data's methodology department and top management had tried and failed to strengthen project-management culture and establish project-management education. However, the need and demand among project managers for education and better support were increasing.

Our group—a small team of senior project managers—took formal responsibility for this initiative. At first we thought that educating project managers would be enough to improve project management. But, through discussions, we realized that education alone was insufficient. We thus shifted our strategy from a narrow focus on education to a broader view of competence development that included education. We also wanted to actively involve project managers. In doing so, we hoped to institutionalize project-management competence individually as well as organizationally, and to release and utilize the energy and potential of the project management staff.

When we started the initiative, top management had been discussing the idea of creating competence centers to foster cross-organizational learning and support and thus meet the increased demand for better and quicker IT services. It was natural to merge this idea with our initiative and call it the Project Management Competence Center (PMC Center).

The fundamental idea was to create opportunities for project managers to learn and share their experience. To realize this idea, we focused on four main areas:

- Create a standard for project management that is supported from the bottom up.
- Offer incentives to enhance the visibility of project management and to reward good practice.
- Encourage debate to enhance the visibility of initiatives and to motivate self-organized learning.
- Provide education to train project managers and to develop and maintain project management culture.

With this focus in mind, we shaped the building blocks for the PMC Center.

Creating a Standard

The cornerstone of the PMC Center is the Danske Data Standard for Professional Project Management. We developed this standard as a vision of good and competent project management within the organization. Our idea was to set new standards that everyone could relate to and use as inspiration for continuous improvements. The idea for a visionary standard was new to Danske Data. Rather than mandate a standard to be followed, we wanted to create a foundation that would support project managers in taking responsibility for their own development. Consequently, it was important that project managers be able to assess themselves in relation to the standard and thus to identify and prioritize areas that needed improvement. To this end, we developed the self-assessment tool described in Chapter 10.

Before presenting the project-management standard to the organization, we needed commitment to it. We thus held a workshop to discuss the founding of the PMC Center and invited representatives from all organizational levels, including the CEO. The event lasted two days, during which we discussed and completed the standard, with commitment from all participants. The resulting standard can be seen as a major amendment to CMM level 2, extended from the usual 6 KPAs to 10, with the added KPAs tailored to company-specific needs. The four new KPSs developed were called partnership, teambuilding, business innovation, and competence. In Table 5.1 an example of one new KPA is shown.

Using CMM as inspiration proved advantageous. It made development relatively easy and inexpensive because we were able to reuse much of the model's structure and content. Furthermore, using CMM as a starting point created consistency between the CEO's visions and our own visions for the PMC Center. Consequently, our new standard enjoys a natural commitment from top management.

Table 5.1 *The Business Innovation KPA*

Key Process Area	Purpose	Goals
Business Innovation	Contribute to the effective and durable integration of the delivered IT systems into the customers' day-to-day business and overall IT strategy.	The customers' IT strategy is stated and realized, with active contribution from the project team.
		The project team actively contributes to creating a plan for implementing the IT system into the customers' day-to-day business.

A vision that is not deeply rooted in the organization dies. Vision diffusion and adoption are thus crucial to success. To introduce our standard, we created a road show that toured all parts of Danske Data. Project managers reacted positively, and we believed that the seeds of the grass roots were sown. However, a year after the road show, we concluded that only a small group of project managers and even fewer software developers were familiar with the standard. As we learned, diffusion does not automatically ensure adoption.

When we launched the standard-based project-manager education program (described later in the section Providing Education) and self-assessment tool (see Chapter 10), the standard was revived as a platform for improvement. The idea was that, through self-assessment and education, project managers could learn how to relate their practice to the standard and how to meet its expectations. Through this process, we hope that project managers will adopt and even become ambassadors for the standard. Our experience thus far has taught us that a vision alone is difficult for people to adopt. They need accompanying initiatives that relate the vision to practice.

Finally, we created our standard to be dynamic, developing continuously based on practitioners' experiences with using it. The project-manager education provides an excellent forum for debating the standard. Also, we wrote the standard to leave room for interpretation and variation. Although there is no prescribed way to meet the standard's expectations, it does provide a shared vision that all project managers can relate to. Whether or not they will all adopt it remains to be seen.

Offering Incentives, Creating Debate

Our goal with incentives was to get project managers actively engaged in the change process. We also wanted to provoke a debate about the new standard and the PMC Center. After several discussions, we decided to launch a Project Manager of the Year initiative. The idea was simple. Each of the four development centers would select its top project manager, and from the four the CEO would select Danske Data's overall project manager of the year.

In keeping with our grassroots philosophy, each center would design its own nomination process using two basic criteria. First, candidates should actively use the standard to promote better practices. Second, candidates should be active in the PMC Center, helping to improve project-management practices across the organization. Our hope was that this initiative would stimulate local debate as well as discussions across the organization.

Top management liked the idea. We launched the initiative with a reward of $4,000 for each of the four local project managers, and an additional $8,000 for the overall winner. We knew that this incentive scheme would be considered rather controversial in a Scandinavian context, where collaboration, equality, and social responsibility are primary values. Nonetheless, we made the scheme an integral part of our initiative and hoped for both support and debate.

We definitely succeeded in creating debate. Most upper-level managers were in favor of the scheme, but project managers and systems developers had mixed opinions. Those in favor saw the reward initiative as a means to promote project management as an important discipline. Proponents also thought it would strengthen project managers' position in the organization and facilitate the improvement of project-management practices. Opponents of the idea viewed good project-management practices as the result of a team effort and thus thought it was wrong to reward individuals. Some also believed that it would be impossible to create fair and transparent procedures for selecting the project manager of the year.

The year after the launch, the Project Manager of the Year initiative went forward as planned, although debate about the scheme continued. Introducing this reward mechanism definitely helped us make the organization and its members focus on the project-management initiative and, in particular, on the standard. It also led to more general discussions of incentive schemes within the organization. How this reward initiative will develop in the future remains an open question.

Another way we attempted to create discussion about the standard was by creating a *task pool*. The task pool contained different tasks that project managers could volunteer for through an electronic news board. Over eight months, we announced many opportunities, including organizing study groups, coordinating groups for exchanging experience with other companies, establishing local libraries of project-management literature, creating customized local initiatives within a fixed budget, and developing a new performance evaluation based on the standard. However, the response was not overwhelming. We were disappointed to realize that, by itself, offering new possibilities was not enough to release energy for change.

Consequently, we shifted our focus to establishing an education program that would enable project managers to meet the new standard's expectations. Our first task was to decide whether to buy education or create it ourselves.

Providing Education

Before establishing the PMC Center, we had many discussions with the methodology department's official SPI staff. A central topic was whether to buy or develop our own standard and project-manager education program. Members of the methodology department had ongoing contacts with various agencies that offered project-management education, and they favored an outsourcing approach.

However, our goal was to create an education program that would enable project managers to meet the new standard's expectations. Because we wanted to ensure coherence between education, the development model, and the standard, as well as with

Danske Data's processes and culture, we felt that we *had* to develop our own project-manager education program. We thus argued strongly for—and got—permission to develop the program in-house.

Our program draws on Danske Data's knowledge and resources wherever possible, and we buy external expertise only when it is unavailable in-house. There are several advantages to this do-it-yourself approach.

- Coherence is assured. We created coherence between the education, the standard, the development model, and the company's processes and culture. Had we chosen CMM as our norm and decided to outsource project-manager education, achieving this cohesion would have been highly unlikely.

- Results are customized and flexible. We created a dynamic platform for improvement that is customized to fit the company's needs. If these needs change or if top management alters its vision, we can modify both the standard and the education program. This flexibility would have been impossible using CMM as the norm. Also, the flexibility of external teachers is limited.

- Energy and morale increase. A widespread result of doing it ourselves was pride. As change agents, we are proud to have succeeded in implementing an improvement platform. In addition, the internal teachers are proud to educate their colleagues, and top management is proud that Danske Data has its own standard and project-management education program. Pride should not be underestimated as an outcome; it creates energy and boosts morale.

The question of whether to do it yourself depends on various organizational factors, such as the organization's experience with project management, the maturity of existing best practices, and the organization's size. In the case of Danske Data, we are confident that it was the right decision and that the combination of coherent factors will create a synergetic effect that will diffuse existing best practices, create increased focus on available methods and techniques, and stimulate learning. Finally, we have gotten very positive feedback from project managers who have completed the education program.

5.3 UP FROM THE GRASS ROOTS

From the beginning, the PMC Center was supported by top management, primarily in the form of resources and economics rather than in active involvement in the change process. This approach worked initially, given our primary focus on project managers and efforts to improve their work. Nonetheless, we knew that sustainable changes in project management require commitment and involvement on all levels.

We had many discussions early on as to when and how to ensure upper-management commitment and involvement in the PMC Center. Should senior management participate in the education program along with project managers, or would it be better to create a somewhat separate education program? The pros and cons were not evident. And given that our energy and resources were focused on establishing the main education program, we neglected this discussion for some time.

Danske Data has approximately 150 project managers, and we knew that educating all of them would take a long time. We decided to speed up the education plan as much as possible, aiming to educate approximately one-third within the first year. The project-management education turned out to be very successful.

When we announced the first project-management class, we had a hard time getting the most qualified project managers to sign up. After the first class, this situation changed dramatically. We found ourselves in the middle of a highly political management negotiation over which organizational units would get their project managers in on the next classes.

After completing the second class, we saw project managers beginning to network and use common terminology and project-management disciplines. We were seeing the first vague signs of a new cross-organizational coalition among project managers, based on shared beliefs and practices.

Following the third class, another significant change emerged. Project managers began requiring senior management to use the standard as a basis for providing support and defining the scope of project management. Most senior managers were unfamiliar with terminology from the standard, the education program, and the development model. They thus found themselves in a vacuum and demanded action from top management.

Project management was now on the organizational agenda. Top management actively participated in designing a two-day management conference that included the content and outcome of the education program. Selected project managers who had completed the education presented their personal experiences of both the content and usability of the program. External teachers provided a management summary of their contribution. In addition, we discussed management-related views on project management. The conference was very successful. We are now confident that management at all levels of Danske Data has made a full and active commitment to the standard, the education program, and continuous improvement of project management.

In retrospect, we were lucky that we lacked the resources to involve senior management earlier in the process. Instead of meeting resistance to change, we incidentally created a situation in which curiosity and need were positive driving forces. At this point, the change process is speeding up. Responsibility for the PMC Center has been transferred to top management and a few senior managers. Also, project managers have put forth several initiatives aimed at making their lives easier; these are now in the works.

5.4 REFLECTION: THREE PERSPECTIVES

The process of change in project management at Danske Data was a complicated one, and a single perspective on change is insufficient to capture the richness of our experience. We began the process with a rational perspective but soon found it inadequate to contend with the challenges at hand. We thus examined cultural and political issues, attempting to gain a deeper understanding of the organization so that we could better implement changes.

Change: A Rational View

The rational viewpoint on organizational design and change originates in work by three key figures at the close of the nineteenth century: Frederick Taylor, Henri Fayol, and Max Weber. Taylor invented scientific management, including the key belief that "it is possible and desirable to establish, through methodological study and the application of scientific principles, the one best way of carrying out any job" (cited from Burnes 1996, p. 28).

Although more than a century old, this perspective persists and influences our practices as change agents in SPI. The rational view includes the following principles:

- Organizations are rational entities that can be designed based on explicit goals.
- People behave in optimizing ways and have rational decision-making capacities.
- Improvement is about the efficiency and effectiveness of the production process.

At Danske Data, we initiated process improvement by taking a rational approach. Our rationale was classic: *If you don't know where you stand, any map will do.* Consequently, our focus was on assessing the existing software development practice and on designing and planning an improvement strategy accordingly. Our belief was that if we got this right, we would succeed in creating the necessary foundation for improving Danske Data and that implementing the actual improvements would be simply a matter of carrying out the plans.

In October 1999, a new Bootstrap assessment was carried out, finding an overall increase in the maturity level of 0.50 since the first assessment. The independent assessors stated that improvement activities between the two assessments "had a widespread effect," including in the area of project management. From a rational point of view, then, the SPI effort looked like a success. Weaknesses were identified, initiatives were launched, and results—in the form of measured improvements—were achieved.

However, a rational perspective does not explain why our grassroots approach was successful. Nor does it explain why a simple training program in project management became the core of the improvement. Furthermore, a rational perspective would assume that the cash prize for project manager of the year would create motivation rather than a lot of discussion. To explain these things, we must look at our effort from other viewpoints.

Change as a Cultural Process

Organizational change, and in particular SPI, is far from a fully rational enterprise. To understand the grassroots effort, we must complement rationalism with a cultural perspective, which was born in the 1930s and 1940s. The cultural view focuses on human relations and an organization's norms and traditions (Borum 1995 and Burnes 1996). It includes the following principles:

- Organizations are cooperative social systems that can be designed only in part.
- People behave in self-sacrificing or self-satisfying ways and seek to meet emotional needs.
- Improvement requires communication and interaction among groups and individuals.

From a cultural perspective, we can explain the project-management initiative's success by examining how we involved project managers and addressed their subcultures. For example, we invited important project managers and senior project managers to participate in the workshop that initiated both the standard and the PMC Center. The workshop gave valuable inspiration to the design of the standard and served as an initial handshake between some of the key actors involved. We can also explain, from a cultural perspective, why the Project Manager of the Year award created so much discussion. For this explanation, we turn to the work of Hofstede (1980).

From 1967 to 1978, Hofstede investigated the cultural values within IBM in 40 countries. He collected more than 100,000 questionnaires. Based on the answers, Hofstede identified four cultural dimensions along which he could place the 40 countries. "The concept of national culture or national character has suffered from vagueness," he wrote. "For a set of forty independent nations, I have tried to determine empirically the main criteria by which their national cultures differed." Hofstede found four such criteria: power distance, uncertainty avoidance, individualism-collectivism, and masculinity-femininity.

Hofstede characterized Denmark—along with the other Scandinavian countries—as having the most feminine culture in the world, whereas the United States, for example, has a very masculine culture. Hofstede also offers several examples of typical assumptions and behaviors of feminine and masculine cultures:

- ◆ Feminine cultures value assertive and nurturing behavior in both men and women, whereas masculine cultures prescribe more polarized roles, in which men are typically assertive and women nurturing.
- ◆ Feminine cultures emphasize quality of life and view work as something that supports life, whereas masculine cultures stress performance and see work as the center of life.
- ◆ Feminine cultures value people and environment and see beauty in the small and slow; masculine cultures value money and things and see beauty in the big and fast.

What does this difference mean? Hofstede says that in Scandinavian countries, the feminine cultural characteristics play out in the use of intuition and a concern for consensus that are "well embedded in the total texture of these societies." Contrasting this, the emphasis on the masculine in U.S. culture stresses "facts" and "clear responsibilities." According to Hofstede, however, "In complex decision-making situations, 'facts' no longer exist independently from the people who define them, so 'fact-based management' becomes a misleading slogan."

In our initiative, the masculine focus on performance and individualism inherent in naming a "best" project manager is probably what repulsed some at Danske Data, thereby provoking debate and raising doubts about whether we should continue the program.

The Politics of Change

Digging deeper in our understanding of organizational change in general and SPI in particular, we find power and politics to be the next prevalent issue. However much their leaders might desire otherwise, organizations are not machines. Rather, they are "communities of people, and therefore behave just like other communities. They compete amongst themselves for power and resources, there are differences of opinion and of values, conflicts of priorities and of goals" (Handy 1993). The political view of organizations includes the following principles (Borum 1995 and Burnes 1996):

- ◆ Organizations are shaped through interests and power relations.
- ◆ People commit themselves to different interests.
- ◆ Improvement happens through power struggles between groups or coalitions.

The philosophy of our project-management initiative is captured very well by Peter Senge (1990): "In an increasingly dynamic, interdependent, and unpredictable world, it is simply no longer possible for anyone 'to figure it all out at the top.' The old model 'the top thinks and the local acts,' must now give way to integrating thinking and acting at all levels." As Senge suggests, developers and project managers are key resources who should be actively involved in setting the SPI agenda, and SPI efforts should be organized to accommodate their active participation.

In our case, however, improvement efforts had traditionally been developed and diffused from the centralized methodology department, which had the overall responsibility for the SPI Project. Because of political interests, geographic subcultures, and our differing opinions on such things as how to develop the education program, a competition developed between our team and the established SPI staff. In the wake of our successful campaign to develop the education program in-house, the conflict reached its peak and the PMC Center was seen as an open threat to the Methodology Department. However, less than six months later, we established a political and personal alliance with the SPI Project's leader at what we later called "the Aalborg meeting." At that meeting, we decided to join forces, agreeing to focus on our standard while also ensuring coherence with the improved development model that was the result of other SPI Project initiatives. This agreement changed our situation from one of opposition to cooperation, and it turned out to be fundamental to the project-management initiative's success.

Table 5.2 summarizes our analysis of the project-management initiative from all three perspectives.

Table 5.2 *Three Perspectives on the Project-Management Initiative*

Initiative Element	Rational Process	Cultivation Process	Political Process
SPI Context	A production system in which you optimize output based on rigorous analysis	A social system with communication and co-operation among people	A political system with stakeholders defending their self-interest
Actors in SPI	A formal SPI organization	A coherent network of SPI actors	Competing SPI initiatives
Strategy for SPI	• Assess process to identify weaknesses • Address weaknesses through a targeted SPI initiative • Measure results	• Get the commitment of involved groups • Address culture • Focus on communication	• Formulate initiatives based on interests • Allow initiatives to grow and merge • Emphasize negotiation
Examples from Danske Data	• Improved process measurement • Improved implementation	• PMC Center • The project-management standard • Project Manager of the Year award	• Do-it-yourself approach • Integration with SPI effort

5.5 *LESSONS LEARNED*

Taking a grassroots approach to SPI has been both rewarding and demanding. And although it is no panacea for the myriad challenges involved in complex organizational change, the grassroots approach was a success and taught us valuable lessons. We present those lessons here, in the hope that they might inspire and inform your own improvement efforts. The six lessons are ordered in relation to the three perspectives described in the preceding section: starting from a rational perspective, continuing with the cultural, and concluding with the political.

◆ **Know the Terrain and Involve Key Players**

Our approach was grassroots efforts in two ways: Our improvement team was composed of senior project managers, and we involved other project managers in the initiative. As senior project managers, we had a good sense of current practices and knew their strengths and weaknesses, and we also knew—from experience—the opportunities and threats facing our initiative. Actively involving other project managers gave us important input on new initiatives and helped us diffuse our ideas across the organization. But, most importantly, having project managers involved helped us to create an environment in which everyone was working to improve project management.

◆ **Create Synergy with Related Initiatives**

Our initiative benefited enormously from being part of a group of related improvement efforts. The synergy that emerged among the initiatives helped each effort succeed. Among the key related initiatives we worked with were those focused on establishing a new electronic development model, implementing a software metrics program, and introducing a self-assessment tool that was related to the new standard. A grassroots effort completely detached from conventional improvement efforts would be quite different and probably both harder and less successful overall.

◆ **Establish and Maintain a Shared Vision**

A grassroots initiative is a loosely coupled system in which all actors have other primary activities that compete with their engagement in the change process. The energy and coherence of such an initiative stem from shared beliefs and a personal interest in making things better. We thus spent considerable time discussing possible initiatives and launched them only when there was mutual agreement among participants. If individuals do not continue to identify with an initiative's goals, the effort can be seriously jeopardized.

◆ Remember Your Customers

The most serious threat to our initiative was, in some sense, our interest in it. We found in our discussions a kind of sanctuary for sharing common interests and challenging each other's understandings of project management and SPI. However, we soon realized that even grassroots efforts have customers—in our case, the project managers, systems developers, and higher-level managers in the organization. Discussion and debate are essential, but they are only a first step. You must translate your ideas into tangible action and initiatives and disseminate your work into the wider organization.

◆ Expect and Utilize Conflict

Because grassroots efforts are not as integrated in the management process as more conventional initiatives, questions naturally arise about who is in charge, what the goals are, and how the goals will be achieved. The answers to such questions are not established at the start; rather, they emerge as part of the process. Thus, it is not surprising that we experienced conflicts as we went along. Such conflicts occurred both between individuals and among people in different parts of the organization who opposed our ideas and initiatives. Clearly, such conflicts can constitute a serious threat to the effort. However, realizing that conflicts are merely expressions of the organizational culture that you are in the process of transforming can help you listen, debate ideas, and sometimes change direction. The conflicts created by grassroots efforts are risky, but they also offer unique opportunities for learning.

◆ Think Long-Term

Grassroots efforts are ephemeral. Eventually, they die. For your grassroots initiatives to have a lasting effect on your organization, you must move your effort's obligations and practices to other parts of the organization. This is not a trivial task; many people view participants in a grassroots effort as an exclusive, special-interest group detached from more troublesome daily routines. In our case, it was not until the PMC Center, the standard, and the education program were successfully launched that we realized this was a problem. At that point, we had to endure a number of political games to actively persuade others to become involved and take responsibility for the initiative's continued development. We strongly recommend that in your own efforts, you consider these long-term concerns early in the process.

5.6 *CONCLUSION*

In our experiences improving Danske Data's project management, we gained insight both into the company as the subject of change and into ourselves as change agents. In the end, we also learned more about the mechanisms of organizational change than we initially expected. Going into the project, we conceived SPI at Danske Data from a rational point of view, but during the process we learned that the mechanisms of organizational change work in different layers and that you must understand each layer to master the process of change.

5.7 *REFERENCES*

Borum, Finn. 1995. *Strategier for Organisationsændring*. Copenhagen: Handelshøjskolens Forlag. Distributed through Munksgaard Int'l.

Burnes, Bernard. 1996. *Managing Change*, second ed. London: Pitman Publishing.

Dahlbom, Bo, and Lars Mathiassen. 1993. *Computers in Context: The Philosophy and Practice of Systems Design*. Oxford, UK: Blackwell Publishers.

Handy, Charles. 1993. *Understanding Organizations,* fourth ed. New York: Penguin Books.

Hofstede, G. 1980. "Motivation, Leadership and Organization: Do American Theories Apply Abroad?" *Organizational Dynamics*. Summer.

Humphrey, Watts. 1997. *Managing Technical People*. Reading, MA: Addison-Wesley.

Senge, Peter. 1990. "The Leader's New Work: Building Learning Organizations." *Sloan Management Review*. Fall:7–23.

Chapter 6

The Adolescent Effort

Peter Axel Nielsen, Jakob H. Iversen, Jørn Johansen,
and Lars Birger Nielsen

At Brüel & Kjær, traditional SPI ideas are often met with skepticism by software developers and project managers. To succeed in our efforts, we needed a different approach to SPI—one that was tailored to both the company's unique character and its overall business climate.

Brüel & Kjær engineers sophisticated electronic products for measuring and monitoring sound and vibration. Before our SPI effort, market turbulence resulted in a painful downsizing, and the company sold several divisions. When we began the SPI effort, the company was facing serious challenges, including a decreasing traditional market and a tremendous need for new products, coupled with management's desire to develop a common platform for its numerous software products. Given the situation, the SPI effort got little management attention.

Our SPI group at the time consisted of a large part-time staff, including one of Brüel & Kjær's two technical directors, the SPI project manager, three SPI practitioners, two consultants, and three researchers. The group's experiences and perspectives were diverse. The technical director was convinced that nothing would happen without project managers' active participation. The consultants, who had previously done a Bootstrap assessment of Brüel & Kjær, believed that the improvement areas were already clearly identified. The researchers knew very little about the company and needed to learn about how its software processes were actually performed. These and other factors eventually coalesced into our adolescent strategy.

We call our strategy "adolescent" because it abandons most of the established SPI ideas. It is also pragmatic and focuses on finding practical, workable solutions to SPI problems. We put little effort into making improvement plans, getting the commitment of top management, or using maturity models such as CMM or improvement models such as IDEAL. All our effort was directed at *influencing* the right people at the right time.

In this chapter, we explain the adolescent strategy in more detail and offer an overview of how the strategy played out in our SPI initiatives. We then discuss what went right in our adolescent effort and analyze the point at which things began to go wrong.

Product Profile

Brüel & Kjær's customers are research and development labs in the automotive and communication industries as well as private and public institutions in the environmental and occupational health industries. Brüel & Kjær's headquarters for product development, marketing, logistics, and manufacturing is in Nærum, Denmark.

Before performing sound or vibration measurements, researchers must set up the measurement and perform all the required operations in the entire measurement chain, which covers the conversion of the analog sound or vibration signal using either a microphone or an accelerometer, electrical conditioning, A/D conversion, real-time signal analysis, advanced post-processing, and, finally, presentation and documentation of the measurement. The software is built into products and guides customers through this complex setup process.

6.1 THE ADOLESCENT STRATEGY

As Table 6.1 shows, our adolescent strategy had three primary elements: It focused strongly on project-manager involvement, based software process assessments on problem diagnosis, and used support teams to disseminate ideas and techniques.

Table 6.1 *The Adolescent Strategy's Three Key Elements*

1. Focus on project managers
   - Select problem and solution.
   - Implement solutions in a project.
   - Evaluate improvement process.

2. Problem diagnosis
   - Interview project manager.
   - Classify problem.
   - Define areas for improvement.

3. Support teams
   - Supply solution and knowledge.
   - Follow up on implementation of solution.
   - Evaluate and adjust solution.

Focus on Project Managers

Successful change requires that change agents clearly articulate both what must be changed and the basic objectives for the change. Another critical success factor is getting key actors in the organization to commit to change. In the case of Brüel & Kjær, the basic objective was to change the software processes. However, identifying key actors and determining how to implement change were less obvious.

Within the SPI group, our perception of the situation was as follows.

- Management supported the SPI project by allocating resources, and they expected that resources alone would enable the SPI group to change the software processes.

- Top management expected project managers to develop new and innovative products that would make the company profitable.

- Project managers were confident that they could fulfill management expectations. This confidence was based on the fact that all project managers had met performance expectations in the past. Given this past performance, project managers were in a position to decide how they would conduct their individual projects.

- Despite extensive organizational changes at Brüel & Kjær from 1993 to 1996, project managers had maintained and even extended their influential position.

Given this situation, we knew that to succeed with the SPI initiative, we would have to directly involve project managers in the research and development department.

Problem Diagnosis

In October 1996, before the SPI project, Brüel & Kjær had its first Bootstrap assessment. However, because of reorganization, the recommendations from the assessment were largely ignored. In March 1997, our SPI group held its first meeting. In the six months since the Bootstrap assessment, much of the organization's SPI focus had been lost. We realized that we had to revitalize this focus, but simply conducting another Bootstrap assessment would yield the same result as the previous one and would therefore waste resources. To succeed, we had to focus on project managers and get their support for SPI initiatives. We therefore decided to perform a problem diagnosis with the following goals:

- Identify the problems in software processes as perceived by the project managers.
- Understand what is causing the problems.
- Support the development of a specific improvement strategy.

- Involve the project managers actively in both the assessment and subsequent improvement initiatives.
- Ensure that the entire SPI group—including the outside consultants and researchers—gained a deep understanding of the organization.

Chapter 9 describes the problem diagnosis in greater detail.

Support Teams

After we identified the problematic software processes, we selected seven specific processes to improve. We then organized seven support teams to help focus and facilitate each improvement initiative (see Figure 6.1). All but one of the seven improvement initiatives were assigned to projects.

The goal of support teams was to support, mentor, and train development project participants. The support teams also had to ensure the effective kick-off of initiatives and ensure that knowledge about software processes and SPI was transferred to the projects. To guarantee competence and experience, support teams were made up mostly of SPI group members.

There were several phases in the support of teamwork over the course of an initiative. In the first phase, the team focused on finding a development project team that wanted to improve its processes and whose project manager was also willing to get involved. The support team would then engage in logistical activities, such as arranging the first meeting, producing introductory material, and writing minutes and other documentation.

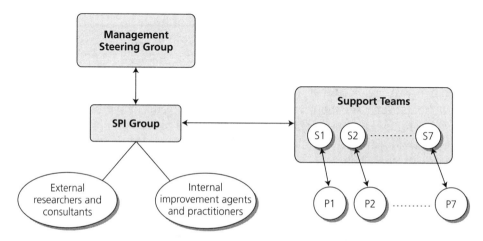

Figure 6.1 *Organization of the SPI project*

In the second phase, members of the support team conveyed their knowledge of methods, techniques, theory, and practice by inspiring, training, and mentoring the project teams. Although we never intended the support teams to teach courses, some did. In the final phase, the support team documented the improvement experience. This was important; one of our main goals was to collect and communicate the knowledge and insight gained through these projects.

6.2 IMPROVEMENT INITIATIVES

Using the October 1996 Bootstrap assessment (see Chapter 7), the problem diagnosis technique (see Chapter 9), and the error detection technique (see Chapter 8), we identified seven potential improvement areas. We decided to form five support teams addressing six of the potential improvement areas:

1. Development model initiative, combining two potential improvement areas, namely to have a prescriptive process model, and to experiment with prototypes.

2. Requirements specification initiative, addressing the potential improvements related to software requirements specification and requirements management.

3. Reuse initiative, addressing the potential improvement related to software reuse.

4. Project tracking initiative, addressing the improvement need for better project tracking and control.

5. Configuration management initiative, addressing the improvement need for both requirements, configuration and change management.

The potential improvement area of risk management was not addressed by any initiative.

We decided to give priority to five support teams to encompass six of the improvement initiatives: development model (1, 3), requirements specification (4), reuse (7), project tracking (5), and configuration and change management (4, 6).

Of the five SPI project initiatives we started, some were successful and others were not (see Figure 6.2). In our view, an initiative's success strongly depended on how closely it adhered to the adolescent strategy: Successful initiatives were targeted at specific needs in specific development projects, whereas unsuccessful ones attempted more general process improvements. We now describe the five improvement initiatives and their relative success in more detail.

Development Model Initiative

The goal of the development model initiative was to create a new development model for the company and test it in a single project (Nørbjerg and Vinter 1999). The initiative's support team consisted of a researcher and two SPI practitioners.

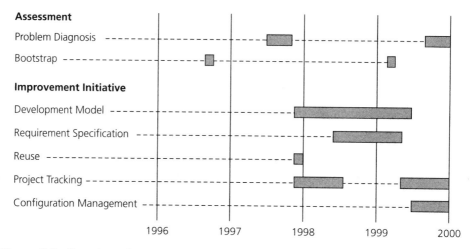

Figure 6.2 Overview of assessments and improvement initiatives

Implementation

From December 1997 to May 1999, the support team met with the development team once or twice a month to discuss status, progress, and plans. The group designed the new development model based on the following principles:

- Project tracking based on time rather than functionality
- Incremental development
- Risk management
- Flexible planning

The new development model consisted of three phases:

- Clarification: Identify and resolve the technical risks related to developers' inexperience with the domain and its requirements.
- Construction: Develop several running code increments in one- to two-month intervals. Each code increment implements a vertical cross section of the total functionality but is not yet "release quality."
- Stabilization: Integrate code increments and quality assurance to release quality.

Developers must also build early working prototypes for later integration and stabilization to release quality. The prototypes are developed using *time-boxes*, which contain a group of related, prioritized tasks carried out within a limited time interval. Each time-box has a clear focus and a business objective that must be fulfilled within a clearly defined deadline. If developers cannot meet the objectives in time, they must reorganize the task to meet the deadline. Developers use time-boxes in the construction phase as basic building blocks for project planning and tracking. The result is a concrete, ready-to-use product.

Conclusion

The main lesson we learned from this initiative was that it is possible to carry out an incremental development process and still maintain a project and its visibility. The new development model gives project teams an overview of their status and progress and consequently increases their confidence in meeting deadlines. However, there are some drawbacks. For example, developers continuously redesign and replan projects, practices that considerably increase complexity in managing personnel resources.

The development project went well, and its target project team was pleased with the progress and the new way of working. However, during March 1999, it gradually became clear that management had to cancel the project for strategic reasons. We were therefore unable to make a final evaluation of the new model's benefits.

Requirements Specification Initiative

Before our improvement initiative, Brüel & Kjær's error reports were studied and it was found that many errors were introduced during requirements specification (see Chapter 8). We began our initiative by conducting two pilot experiments using new requirements specification techniques. Our experiments were very promising: The techniques enhanced product usability, and fewer errors were reported after product release. The company therefore decided to roll out the new techniques in several projects.

Implementation

We first conducted a workshop for three projects that focused on scenarios, prototyping, and usability. During workshop exercises, project teams worked with the new techniques using their own projects as examples. Following the workshop, the three project teams used the techniques to complete the requirements specification. Throughout this process, our support team regularly monitored and assisted the project teams and met with them to discuss status and plans. Status reporting focused on progress in requirements specification and on the teams' experience with the new techniques. Planning focused on the project teams' near-term plans for the requirements specification and ways that our support team might help with these plans.

Conclusion

Applying scenarios and usability techniques is an effective and efficient way to make better products. The new techniques let project teams better identify their customers' needs, facilitate knowledge transfer between customers and project teams, and support cooperation within project teams. In the wake of this success, the new techniques were widely adopted throughout Brüel & Kjær, and the quality assurance department incorporated the techniques into a new development model.

Reuse Initiative

Neither the problem diagnosis nor the Bootstrap assessment recommended reuse as an improvement area. However, we decided to add a reuse initiative because top management had previously decided to develop a common platform for several products. We started this initiative with the approval of top management and project managers.

Implementation

Management established a working group at the development department level that was responsible for the new platform, its architecture, and reuse. The working group held a few meetings, including two meetings with the support team. After that, it stopped its work. No resources were used to support the group, and no further support was requested. Thus, the support team had nothing to support.

Conclusion

Reuse was never a stated vision for Brüel & Kjær. There was no direction to improve in and no commitment to improve, and hence the area could not be improved. The SPI group concluded that improvement activities not based on the adolescent strategy were a waste of time and resources at that time.

Project Tracking Initiative

We chose this improvement area based on the problem diagnosis, the Bootstrap recommendations, and a need expressed by the technical director to the SPI group. He perceived this area to be so important that he wanted to handle it personally.

Implementation

The technical director hired an external consultancy to develop a new project planning tool. The tool was based on MS Project, with added support for estimation based on historical data, for resource planning based on human resource data, and for tracking against time and progress. As part of the deliverable, the consultancy held a training course for all project managers on how to use the tool.

The consultancy delivered the tool late and with several usability problems. Project managers started using the tool, but only for planning. Although a few project managers used most of the tool's advanced features, none used it to its full potential. In short, the tool was never fully adopted by project managers. It functioned neither as a basis for status reporting to the technical director nor as a common basis for project tracking, especially because projects did not share tool-generated data.

Eighteen months after the tool was rolled out, the technical director asked our SPI group to establish a tool support team. We did this and held five meetings with project managers, but attendance was not required and some relevant project managers did not attend. We then decided to develop a project-planning workshop with the goals of improving project planning and increasing knowledge about the tool, and hence increase its use. After we achieved this, we would focus on strengthening status reporting about projects to management.

Conclusion

We completed the workshop material and twice planned to present the workshop, but each time we had to cancel because of time pressures within the organization. Clearly, this improvement initiative suffered several major setbacks. A reasonable explanation is that project plans are important political instruments in the organization. This fact works against the tool's goal, which is to have open, transparent, and shared project plans across projects. Without strong incentives, most project managers were unwilling to surrender the political benefits of keeping project plans confidential.

Configuration Management Initiative

The 1997 problem diagnosis identified project conclusion as a problem area. In essence, projects were having problems handling complex software configurations under the pressure of deadlines. At that time, there were insufficient resources to launch an improvement initiative directed at configuration management. After the spring 1999 Bootstrap assessment identified configuration management as a top priority, the configuration management initiative was launched.

Implementation

It was obvious from the beginning that configuration management cuts across several projects. In contrast to previous initiatives, we could not experiment with one project and a support team. However, it took the support team some time to realize that this area was different from previous initiatives in others ways as well.

Our support team assembled a group of developers interested in configuration management problems and held a few meetings. At the first meeting, the technical director announced that he wanted the support team to write a configuration management procedure that all projects would have to use. In subsequent meetings, the support team worked with the developer group to determine the main configuration management problems. Based on the understanding gained in these meetings, the support team developed three models: The first described configuration management as a private study room, the second described it as warehouse management, and the third described it as coordination at a building site.

The support team then designed a one-day workshop to take a project group through the three models. The goal was to facilitate a process wherein the project group would find its own solutions to problems based on explanations offered by the different models. The workshop's result would be the organized configuration management for that project. Although the first project would work almost from scratch, later workshops would be based on previous results. Thus, within a few months, we could reach a stable configuration management process.

Conclusion

In August 1999, the technical director ordered the support team to stop the work on the workshop and write a procedure right away. As of December 1999, the procedure had not been produced and the workshop had not been held.

6.3 STRENGTHS AND WEAKNESSES OF THE ADOLESCENT STRATEGY

At Brüel & Kjær, the adolescent strategy for SPI improvement had strengths and weaknesses, all of which relate in some way to our project-manager focus. Such a focus requires that project managers be fully committed to implementing improvements and that improvements make sense for each project. The benefit is that whenever improvements are implemented, they are likely to stick because implementation itself implies that project managers are highly committed.

To illustrate particular aspects of the adolescent strategy, we consider two examples from our experience: requirements specification and reuse.

The problem diagnosis identified problems with requirements specification in several of the interviews. It was thus considered a problem by project managers. Requirements specification was also an area in which the SPI group had considerable experience. For example, one internal SPI practitioner had helped to design a facilitated process to help projects to develop better requirements specifications. When the projects started using the requirements specification techniques, they quickly adopted them in daily practice.

The problem diagnosis did not identify problems with reuse. It was nevertheless added as a finding to the problem diagnosis report, and a support team was established. After a few meetings with project managers, however, it was clear that there was no real interest in reuse and the meetings stopped.

The two examples differ in many ways that help illuminate when and in what situations an adolescent strategy is appropriate. First, the target problem must be acknowledged by relevant actors. If no one perceives a problem, there is no motivation to improve. In our case, we relied heavily on project managers, and any initiative that did not have their full support was unlikely to succeed.

Second, the SPI group had a very high knowledge-transfer capability with requirements specification. We had a set of concepts and techniques that were ready to implement. There was no need for experiments to gain new knowledge, and thus projects could benefit from the improvement immediately. On the other hand, the SPI group had little experience with reuse. As a result, it required a substantial effort for us to simply understand and scope the problem and determine possible solutions. We had to do this work before any improvement activities could start.

Third, each application of the requirements specification techniques addressed the specific problems of a specific project and assisted the project in doing things that needed to be done anyway. It was thus very easy for the project managers to see the benefits. Reuse by nature involves more projects, and this meant that each project manager would not immediately see the direct benefits of participating. To effectively implement such improvements, management must play an active role.

Our experience led us to derive a list of the adolescent strategy's strengths and weaknesses, which are shown in Table 6.2.

Table 6.2 *Strengths and Weaknesses of the Adolescent Approach*

Strengths	Weaknesses
• Focus is on project managers, who have the power to effectively implement improvements. • Implementation is a collaboration between projects and support teams. • Improvements last. • The SPI group gains considerable knowledge about the organization. • When the SPI group is knowledgeable in a given area, implementing initiatives is easy.	• Because the support and focus of top management are lacking, it is difficult to make cross-organizational improvements. • Prioritizing improvement initiatives is left to the project managers and the SPI group. • Project managers do not have all the power to initiate change. • The SPI group can change only those practices that project participants want changed; if few improvements are requested, the SPI group has little to do. • If the SPI group lacks knowledge in an improvement area, it must take the time to learn before improvements can begin, and thus project benefits are delayed.

6.4 CONCLUSION: NOTHING IS STABLE

The adolescent strategy worked well for a long time. It matched our situation, which was characterized by

- Top management's focus on the projects
- Project managers' confidence in their own performance
- A history of powerful project managers

When the new technical director was appointed in late 1998, our situation began a gradual but radical change. The new technical director was a powerful manager with a firm grip on the projects and their resources, tasks, and deadlines. Another major change was that the R&D department formed a new strategy that required that all future products be based on the same technical software platform. As a result, a significant amount of software development became dependent on deliverables from other projects. To deliver products on time, projects had to coordinate and share software processes.

A final and significant change was that many of the project-oriented improvement initiatives were successful. Not surprisingly, a new Bootstrap assessment identified few problematic project-oriented software processes. The assessment rated Brüel & Kjær at 2.5. Although the Bootstrap rating is not directly equivalent to CMM, many CMM level 2 problems had been resolved. The focus thus shifted to improving organization-wide processes such as reuse, project tracking, and configuration management.

As the situation at Brüel & Kjær began to change, our adolescent strategy met increasing obstacles. The reuse improvement initiative never took off, for example, and the new technical director reframed the configuration management initiative. As the lists in Table 6.2 show, the new situation undermined the strengths of the adolescent strategy and played to its weaknesses. The adolescent strategy cannot cope effectively with organizationwide software processes because they require top management involvement to succeed.

Early in autumn 1999, our SPI group gradually realized this misfit. We were helped in part by the technical director's dismay with the SPI group, a reaction that was not easily ignored. Another aid to our understanding was that the new Bootstrap assessment identified organizationwide processes as problematic—although we did not realize the implications of this right away. Only later, when it was clear that the configuration management improvement had failed, did we finally fully realize that our once-successful strategy had turned sour.

With hindsight, it is easy to see that we should have adopted a new strategy sooner. That we did not see this was devastating to our efforts. The SPI group had gone from being marginalized in 1997 to being a central force in 1998. In 1999, the group was marginalized once again. Our own slow interpretation of the changes in the situation seemed to have itself become an obstacle to further improvement initiatives. At the time, the basic attitude among SPI group members was, "We like what we are doing and the way we do it, and we will stick to this approach." However, this attitude conflicts with the essential requirement in any type of improvement: You must be prepared to change the way you work.

To change the way we work, we must take into account our own experiences and recent changes at Brüel & Kjær. As we have learned, the software practitioners and project managers will ignore SPI efforts that are not oriented to their specific, practical problems. On the other hand, top management will not allow SPI efforts unless they are organizationwide. To succeed, our new strategy must account for these factors as well as for Brüel & Kjær's current situation:

- Increased dependency among projects: The concurrent development of the common Brüel & Kjær PC-based analyzer platform and new applications requires project managers to coordinate and schedule internal releases of software components. Without this coordination, application projects will not be released on time with the specified functionality.

- Increased understanding of software processes among project managers: During the past two years, each project manager has completed at least two projects. This has increased the project managers' experience in project management as well as software processes in general.

- Increased focus on developing technology competence: The new technical director's increased focus on technology competence requires a change in how product development is organized. In this new organization, the responsibilities of project managers have changed. Project managers are now responsible only for developing the new product's software or hardware, and competence managers are responsible for developing practitioners' competencies in different technology areas.

Given this, our new strategy will consist of three parts. First, software practitioners and project managers must realize that, from now on, software processes must be organizationwide. Simply telling them this is unlikely to be sufficient. However, recent events will likely help. Many of the project managers who were so powerful in early 1997 have now either left Brüel & Kjær or have moved into other jobs within the company. A plausible explanation for this is that being one of the old-time project managers under the new technical director has not been easy.

Second, forums must be created where the relevant software practitioners can meet to create the new software processes. These forums might well be organized as projects with goals, resources, and deadlines. In such a setting, SPI group members would not function as support team but rather as project managers for the process forums.

Third, the SPI group must work closely with the new technology competence managers. For example, the SPI group could be reorganized and staffed in part by the technology competence managers, something that would re-create the problem-oriented focus.

This strategy is much more complex than the adolescent strategy. Still, that fact doesn't explain why we didn't choose this new strategy early in 1999, when the situation had obviously changed. The unfortunate explanation is that we simply assumed that the situation was stable. It wasn't. And it never is.

6.5 REFERENCE

Nørbjerg, J., and O. Vinter. 1999. *Report from Improvement Activity: Development Model* (in Danish). Nærum, Denmark: Brüel & Kjær.

PART III

Initiating Learning

Chapter 7

Learning from Assessments

Anne Mette Jonassen Hass and Jørn Johansen

In his book *Fragments of a Forthright Message,* Danish philosopher Søren Kierkegaard wrote that to really help a person you must know where that person is in his or her life. The same principle applies to organizations involved in SPI. When you set out to improve your organization's software development processes, you must know the starting point as well as the goal. You also need to know whether you've reached your goals when the planned SPI activities are complete.

There are many ways to define your organization's starting point, such as relying on gut feelings, interviews, or the opinion of the majority or some specialized group. However, many organizations prefer more formal methods, such as assessments. The benefit of formal assessments is that they can give an organization a defined starting point and goal as well as enable you to visibly track progress toward that goal.

One formal assessment tool is Bootstrap, which includes both a model and a method for assessing the maturity of software-producing organizations. As part of the SPI Project, we used Bootstrap to assess three organizations over a two- to three-year period. Through this experience, we realized that assessments have as much to teach assessors as they do the target organizations. Here, we discuss lessons learned from both an organizational and an assessor perspective. First, however, we describe our Bootstrap tool and analyze the results from our assessments of the organizations.

7.1 THE BOOTSTRAP TOOL

Bootstrap version 2.3 (Kuvaja 1994 and Hass et al. 1996) consists of an assessment method and a model for software development activities, which is shown in Figure 7.1. The Bootstrap method consists of a preliminary meeting, an assessment week, and delivery of an assessment report.

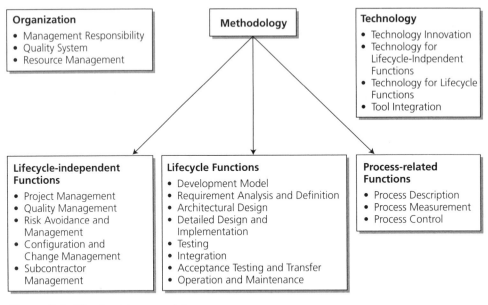

Organization
- Management Responsibility
- Quality System
- Resource Management

Methodology

Technology
- Technology Innovation
- Technology for Lifecycle-Indpendent Functions
- Technology for Lifecycle Functions
- Tool Integration

Lifecycle-independent Functions
- Project Management
- Quality Management
- Risk Avoidance and Management
- Configuration and Change Management
- Subcontractor Management

Lifecycle Functions
- Development Model
- Requirement Analysis and Definition
- Architectural Design
- Detailed Design and Implementation
- Testing
- Integration
- Acceptance Testing and Transfer
- Operation and Maintenance

Process-related Functions
- Process Description
- Process Measurement
- Process Control

Figure 7.1 *The Bootstrap model*

The aim of the preliminary meeting is to give assessors an overview of the organization and to ensure management commitment to the assessment and the SPI activities that will follow. During the assessment week, the assessment team—consisting of at least two certified assessors—spends three to four days interviewing key people in the organization. Although we call it a "week," the actual length of this assessment period varies depending on how many projects we're assessing. On average, we assess four projects, but we might do more or less depending on the nature of an organization's typical projects.

The assessment week starts with an opening meeting that offers assessment participants a general introduction to the Bootstrap model and method. The goal of the meeting is to give all participants the same starting point. We then begin the interviews. We base our detailed assessments on two questionnaires: one for the Software Producing Unit, or SPU (typically the organization's management); and one for the project teams. The first part of a questionnaire asks general questions, and the second part covers the Bootstrap model and includes about 200 detailed questions. We use the questionnaires both as a guide for interviews and as a tool for scoring assessment results.

The assessment week concludes with a meeting in which we present the preliminary results of the assessment. We then further analyze the results and deliver a final report.

The Bootstrap method includes an algorithm for generating detailed maturity profiles from the completed questionnaires. The result is a set of profiles that rates the maturity on a scale from 1 to 5, with a precision of 0.25 for each of the areas defined in the model. We produce a set of profiles for the SPU and for each of the assessed projects. The SPU set profiles management and analyzes management's support for the projects that they are ultimately responsible for. The second set profiles the projects and analyzes organizational practices. Using these maturity profiles, we can identify strengths and weaknesses for the overall organization, as well as areas that most urgently need improvement. Our suggestions for improvement areas are also based on additional information such as benchmarking against similar organizations and the nature of the target organization, its products, and the market. The final assessment report contains a list of the top four to seven improvement areas and a preliminary plan for implementing improvements in the organization.

The Bootstrap assessment tool is relevant only for software development; it does not cover hardware development, production, marketing, and so on. In conducting the Bootstrap assessments, we took care to ensure that the second assessment was as independent of the first assessment as possible so that we could get a true picture of the new state (the ending point) unbiased by knowledge of the starting point. To accomplish this, we ensured that different assessors carried out the first and second assessments and that the second assessors did not consult results from the first assessment before performing the second.

7.2 OVERVIEW OF THE RESULTS

Three of the four organizations in the SPI Project decided to use Bootstrap as their assessment tool: Brüel & Kjær, Systematic, and Danske Data. We performed one Bootstrap assessment at each organization before it started its SPI activities, and another after it had implemented some software process improvements. We performed the assessments as follows:

- At Brüel & Kjær, we performed the first assessment in 1996; the company subsequently divided, and we performed follow-up assessments at both B&K CMS and B&K S&V in 1999.
- At Systematic, we performed the first assessment in 1997 and the second in 1998.
- At Danske Data, we performed the first assessment in 1997 and the second in 1999.

Table 7.1 shows the changes in overall maturity for SPU management and projects in each of the three organizations.

The results look negligible. Presented with these results, the organizations initially reacted with despondency over the numbers, followed by reluctant agreement.

Table 7.1 Changes in Overall Maturity from First to Second Assessment

	SPU	Projects
B&K	0.0	0.0
B&K CMS	0.0	0.0
Systematic	0.25	0.25
Danske Data	0.25	0.25

The organizations knew that they had improved in some areas but also understood that the overall results were not dramatic.

We calculate the overall maturity level based on a consolidation of much more detailed data. Figure 7.2 shows the results in Table 7.1 in more detail, highlighting

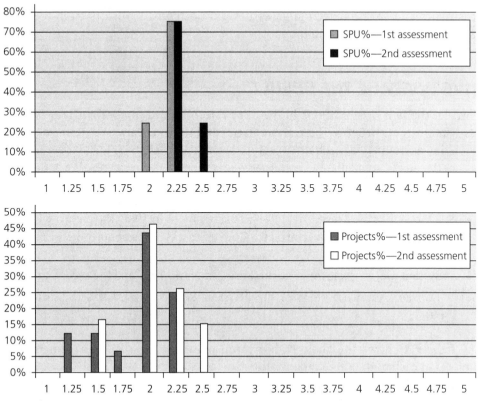

Figure 7.2 The maturity distribution in the first and second assessments

changes in the distribution of the measured maturity levels for the SPUs and the projects. These illustrations clearly show an overall improvement in both cases.

Based on our second assessments, we reached one general conclusion: The second assessments showed that the organizations are much more solidly positioned at level 2 than they were at the first assessment.

The assessment results include sets of detailed profiles for the SPU and projects in each organization. Figures 7.3 and 7.4 show an example of a profile set for one organization. These profiles present the maturity levels for each area at the first and second assessments, and thus the increase or decrease in maturity for each area. We produced four such sets of comparison profiles for each organization, creating a large amount of data, which forms the basis for our discussion and conclusions.

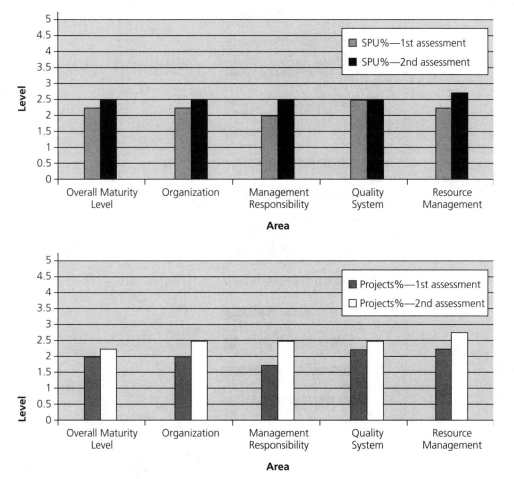

Figure 7.3   *Assessment profiles (1) from the first and second assessments*

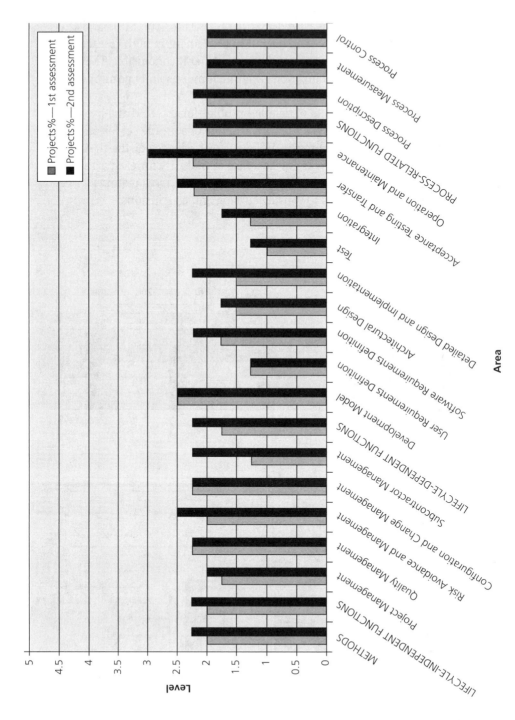

Figure 7.4a   Assessment profiles (2) for projects from the first and second assessments

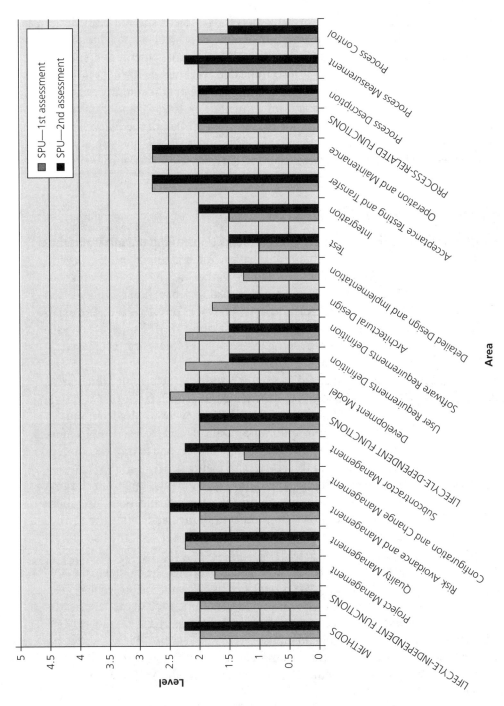

Figure 7.4b   *Assessment profiles (2) for SPU from the first and second assessments*

As the figures show, the sample organization's assessment showed marked improvement in lifecycle-independent functions, such as project management, risk avoidance and management, configuration and change management, and subcontractor management. The assessment also indicated weaknesses in lifecycle functions, including user requirement definition, software requirement definition, architectural design, detailed design and implementation, testing, and integration. Curiously, the maturity level decreased for SPU in the first half of the lifecycle-independent areas. At the second assessment, the SPU's and projects' understanding of these processes and how they are practiced are much more closely aligned.

7.3 ORGANIZATIONAL LEARNING

Assessment profiles are the basis for our recommendations to the organizations, but this is only part of the Bootstrap method. We also use information about the organization's needs and business objectives—which we gather during the assessment—and combine it with the Bootstrap model's built-in roadmap, benchmark information about the organization's business sector, and the assessment profiles to create a set of recommended improvement areas. We validate these areas through a risk analysis. Although our discussion here focuses on the assessment profiles, our recommendations are informed by this additional information.

For each organization, we analyzed the set of profiles to determine which areas defined in the Bootstrap model showed maturity increases, decreases, or no change between the two assessments. Figures 7.5, 7.6, and 7.7 show examples from our assessment of Brüel & Kjær, Systematic, and Danske Data. They are described in more detail later in the chapter. The figures include the first and second lists of recommendations, the activities performed, and the changes in maturity.

The leftmost column in each figure shows our recommendations from the first Bootstrap assessment, numbered according to priority. The organizations also chose to work on other areas; these are shown unnumbered immediately after the recommended areas. The areas that were the focus of SPI activities between the two assessments are shown in ***bold italic***.

The column to the right of the recommendation list shows the changes in maturity level from the first to the second assessment for the SPU and the projects, respectively. Maturity-level changes are shown for all recommended areas, as are the additional areas the organization chose to work on and areas that subsequently appeared on the second list of recommendations.

The rightmost column shows the recommendation list from the second assessment. The areas that the organization planned to work on after this assessment are shown in ***bold italic.***

The arrows indicate developments between the two assessments as follows:

 An arrow pointing to the star indicates that the area has improved so much that it does not appear on the recommended improvement list.

An arrow pointing to the second list of recommendations indicates that the area reappears on the list after the second assessment.

 An arrow pointing to the shaded circle indicates that the organization has not worked on the area, and it does not appear on the second list of recommended improvements.

 An arrow pointing away from the shaded circle indicates areas that are new on the second list of recommendations.

A dotted arrow indicates a potential improvement area that might be removed or substituted with a related and more relevant improvement area.

Brüel & Kjær

As Figure 7.5 shows, Brüel & Kjær is a relatively focused organization. We gave Brüel & Kjær seven recommendations based on the first Bootstrap assessment, and they added reuse as an improvement area on their own initiative. Brüel & Kjær's actual improvement focused on three areas: development model, user requirement specification, and

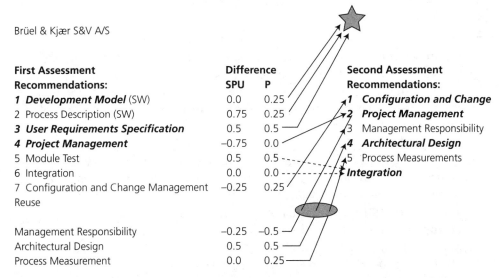

Brüel & Kjær S&V A/S

First Assessment Recommendations:	Difference SPU	P	Second Assessment Recommendations:
1 Development Model (SW)	0.0	0.25	*1 Configuration and Change*
2 Process Description (SW)	0.75	0.25	*2 Project Management*
3 User Requirements Specification	0.5	0.5	3 Management Responsibility
4 Project Management	−0.75	0.0	*4 Architectural Design*
5 Module Test	0.5	0.5	5 Process Measurements
6 Integration	0.0	0.0	*Integration*
7 Configuration and Change Management	−0.25	0.25	
Reuse			
Management Responsibility	−0.25	−0.5	
Architectural Design	0.5	0.5	
Process Measurement	0.0	0.25	

Figure 7.5 *Work and changes between the first and second assessments at Brüel & Kjær*

project management. It met with success in all three areas, and particularly in user requirement specification, primarily because it had initiated related SPI activities before the first assessment.

As Figure 7.5 shows, project management and configuration and change management reappeared as improvement recommendations. Module test was improved but also reappeared on the list. The organization neglected integration and canceled reuse. Although module test and integration remained improvement areas, we did not recommend them because the improvement actions needed focus. Brüel & Kjær's management was convinced of the importance of these improvement areas and chose to continue improving them after the second assessment, especially the integration area. Because of organizational changes, management responsibility decreased and thus became a natural improvement area. Demand for process measurement has increased—particularly in relation to the need to strengthen the visibility of improvements in general and project management in particular. Design documentation and methods were generally scarce and, given the organization's goal of creating a common project platform, we selected architectural design—which is also related to integration—as the most relevant improvement area.

The Brüel & Kjær experience shows that improved areas disappear and unimproved areas reappear, sometimes in a related area, such as when module test and integration reappeared as integration. It also shows that trying to improve reuse was premature because the organization lacked the necessary maturity.

Systematic

As Figure 7.6 shows, Systematic is an ambitious and focused organization; we offered seven recommended improvement areas at the first assessment, and they added three more of their own. The organization primarily focused on five areas: detailed design and implementation, subcontractor management, project management, and process description from our recommendations, and risk management, which was one of the areas they chose of their own initiative. The organization succeeded in all areas except process description. They also put some effort into improving process measurement by introducing self-assessments at the project level, but the initiative on its own was insufficient to fulfill Bootstrap requirements. Systematic focused some effort on configuration and change management (which includes requirement management in the Bootstrap model). In fact, this effort did not introduce significant changes; the area is comprehensive and includes many disciplines. Systematic put this area on standby. We recommended the consolidating area at the second assessment to ensure diffusion and adoption of the implemented improvements.

The Systematic experience shows that targeted improvement efforts were beneficial, and unimproved areas reappeared at the next assessment. This experience also

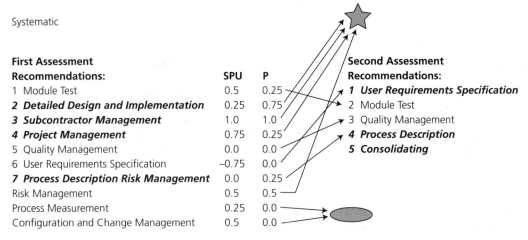

Systematic

First Assessment Recommendations:	SPU	P	Second Assessment Recommendations:
1 Module Test	0.5	0.25	**1 User Requirements Specification**
2 Detailed Design and Implementation	0.25	0.75	2 Module Test
3 Subcontractor Management	1.0	1.0	3 Quality Management
4 Project Management	0.75	0.25	**4 Process Description**
5 Quality Management	0.0	0.0	**5 Consolidating**
6 User Requirements Specification	−0.75	0.0	
7 Process Description Risk Management	0.0	0.25	
Risk Management	0.5	0.5	
Process Measurement	0.25	0.0	
Configuration and Change Management	0.5	0.0	

Figure 7.6 *Changes between the first and second assessments at Systematic*

shows that improvement areas chosen by the organization are just as viable as those recommended in the assessment, particularly when the organization perceives an important need and thus has added will to make improvements.

Danske Data

After the first assessment, Danske Data was very ambitious and chose many improvement areas. After the second assessment, they realized the value of focusing on only a few. The organization focused primarily on five areas: development model, diffusion and adoption, and project management, which we recommended, and their own added areas of process description and process measurement. In the areas we recommended, they succeeded only in project management, but they also showed some improvement in both of their selected areas. Although diffusion and adoption is not a specific Bootstrap improvement area, we recommended it to ensure success with the organization's improvement work. Danske Data has put a lot of effort into improving diffusion and adoption, and, although it is not yet completely implemented, this area looks as if it will be successful.

At Danske Data, unimproved recommended areas from the first assessment reappear as recommended improvement areas at the second assessment. As this example shows, areas chosen by the organization itself can be successfully improved, and areas can disappear or reappear as related improvement areas either because of organizational changes or because the organization realizes the need to focus its improvement work.

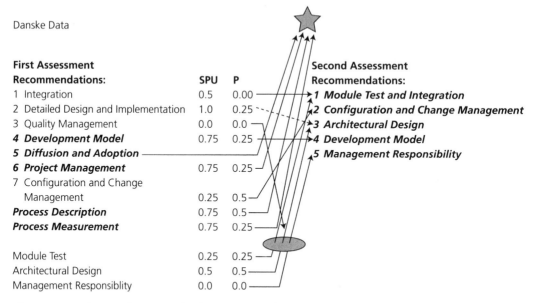

Danske Data

First Assessment Recommendations:	SPU	P	Second Assessment Recommendations:
1 Integration	0.5	0.00	*1 Module Test and Integration*
2 Detailed Design and Implementation	1.0	0.25	*2 Configuration and Change Management*
3 Quality Management	0.0	0.0	*3 Architectural Design*
4 Development Model	0.75	0.25	*4 Development Model*
5 Diffusion and Adoption			*5 Management Responsibility*
6 Project Management	0.75	0.25	
7 Configuration and Change Management	0.25	0.5	
Process Description	0.75	0.5	
Process Measurement	0.75	0.25	
Module Test	0.25	0.25	
Architectural Design	0.5	0.5	
Management Responsiblity	0.0	0.0	

Figure 7.7 *Changes between the first and second assessments at Danske Data*

General Lessons

We followed each organization's SPI activities between the two assessments very closely and were also directly involved in some of the improvement work. We also collected supplemental information from discussions with project managers and top managers. We substantiated our documentation through workshops, minutes from organization meetings, and the detailed reports from the Bootstrap assessments (Pries-Heje and Johansen 1997; Jonassen Hass et al. 1999; Nielsen and Johansen 1997; Nielsen and Johansen 1998; Jonassen Hass and Johansen 1996; Jonassen Hass and Johansen 1999a; Jonassen Hass and Johansen 1996b). Each company also continued its SPI work after the second assessment, and we have tracked this work to see how they will sustain their SPI efforts.

In the period between assessments, all the companies changed the way their SPI projects were organized. Although this may have influenced the assessment results, it is also a fact of life and something most organizations experience when they undertake SPI activities.

Although organizations can learn from a single assessment, they learn even more from subsequent assessments. In this case, the three organizations learned many lessons—both positive and negative—from participating in our project. They discussed the following lessons learned during Center for Software Processing Improvement workshops.

Participants mentioned several positive results and realizations from the assessment project, including the following:

- Rather than simply remain static, recommended areas that are not worked on can lose ground and will reappear on the recommendation list at the next assessment.
- For the overall maturity to increase, an organization must sustain maturity in all areas.
- Improvement areas addressed by Bootstrap are also addressed by other assessment methods.
- Metrics and assessment results increase management involvement and focus on improvements, and improvement debates are more constructive when they are based on such facts rather than gut feelings and personal opinions.
- To support the decision to improve particular areas, assessment recommendations typically must be supported by additional assessments or evaluations.
- Publishing goals ensures that people will pay attention to them.

Participants also mentioned negative results and realizations, including the following:

- To increase an area's maturity from one assessment to the next, formal and focused improvement activities are required.
- Improvement activities were too controlled by the CMM model's roadmap rather than by the total picture of the organization offered by the assessment.
- Bootstrap's assessment model criteria and questionnaire were too confidential.
- When companies undergo major changes, such as reorganization, the assessment results are more difficult to use.
- Although it does address them, the Bootstrap method must pay even more attention to how the organization conducts business, including its market position, competitors, and overall goals.
- If an organization regards an assessment as an examination, it increases the risk of producing misleading results.

The positive experiences they discussed primarily address the usefulness and reliability of the assessment results. Such results let the organizations track improvements from one assessment to the next and thereby gave them the opportunity to document the benefits of their improvement work. The results also let them hold more focused and fact-based discussions about SPI work and clearly state improvement goals and track progress toward them.

Other assessment methods reached the same conclusions as our Bootstrap assessment. This helped the staff members sell the results and improvement plans within their organizations. The results were further validated by the fact that unimproved areas reappeared on the recommendation list (except when unrelated organizational changes eliminated the improvement areas or changed the focus).

The organizations' negative experiences are primarily related to the fact that the details of the Bootstrap model are necessarily secretive because of licensing agreements. This will change with the next version of Bootstrap, which is very similar to SPICE, the ISO standard for assessments. Participants also felt that Bootstrap was still too restrictive, even though it offers much more freedom than the CMM. Bootstrap's model and method must offer more consideration for an organization's particular situation and business parameters. Finally, there was a general tendency among project participants to regard an assessment as an examination. The negative side effect here is that training and improvements initiated before assessments tended to disappear after the assessment was over.

Overall, participants from all three organizations regarded the assessments as a very useful tool. Before the first assessments, some participants expressed reservations, but we did not hear any such reservations before the second assessments. Organizations were also more focused on the recommendations for the second assessments, and we take this as an indication of increasing trust in the method based on experience with the assessments and SPI activities over time.

7.4 ASSESSOR EXPERIENCES

Assessors learn from assessments at two levels. They learn from performing assessments in general as well as from performing more than one assessment in the same organization. In this project, we learned several lessons. Based on the results, we formed several general conclusions. We also learned how assessments can provide a valid picture of an organization, how overall results can disguise important details, and that we can trust the validity of assessment results and recommendations.

General Conclusions

The main reason that the organizations' maturity increase was less than expected after the first assessment is that the organizations chose not to work on some of the recommended areas. The neglected areas were generally the ones with the lowest maturity and thus had a big effect on the overall maturity of the organization.

In some cases, the organizations used additional methods to help them identify target areas for SPI work. Most of these target areas corresponded to our Bootstrap recommendations, although some did not. Work in these other areas may have contributed to the neglect of some of the areas recommended by the assessments. As our results show, maturity increases in the independently selected areas did not have much effect on an organization's overall maturity, and these improvements certainly did not compensate for the negative impact of ignoring the Bootstrap-recommended areas.

When we compared maturity changes in management with that in projects, we found that management's maturity increased slightly less and even decreased in some cases. Management's maturity thus got closer to project maturity from the first to the second assessment. We conclude from this that management's general understanding of what software production actually entails in each organization fell more into line with the realities that projects face. The assessment of management itself can contribute to such increased understanding, as can management's active involvement in SPI activities. In these cases, it is not easy to tell which of these had a greater impact, but there is no doubt that the assessment itself had a significant effect.

As might be expected, in all cases, work on target areas increased their maturity and thus they were no longer in urgent need of improvement. Thus, recommended improvement areas that were targeted for work did not reappear in the second assessment, whereas those that were neglected did. Although there might be some knock-on effect from other improvements, in general, areas do not significantly mature without focused improvement activities.

Following the second assessment, all three organizations planned further improvement work. In all cases, the planned improvements follow the assessment recommendations more closely than they did following the first assessment. We take this as a sign of a rising confidence in the assessment results.

Sample or Overview?

One of the primary objections to assessments is that they provide only sporadic samples from assessed organizations rather than a valid picture of overall operations. We agree that assessments use samples, and, taken on their own, such samples are not sufficient to meet the goal of assessment, which is to provide an organizational overview that includes both management and projects. For this reason, the Bootstrap method does not rely solely on the Bootstrap model; the organization's particular situation is always taken into account in identifying target improvement areas.

Suppose you find a boy lying on the ground beside his bicycle and immediately seek to help him. Depending on his condition, you might call an ambulance, drive him home, or help him up and onto the bicycle again. To provide efficient help that will also prevent later trouble, you need more information. For example, was he hit by a car? Was he learning how to use the bicycle's brakes? Did he hit a rock on the path? Or is he just taking a rest? To help the boy properly, you must understand the entire situation. If you rely on some generalized advice (such as "If you see a boy who appears to have fallen, help him up") you can do more harm than good (for example, he might have a broken bone that requires stabilization). Generalized advice (the model) is not enough for effective intervention. You also need a method to help you understand the entire situation. Based upon both, you can act or offer recommendations accordingly.

In working with the three organizations, we became even more convinced of the importance of understanding an organization's entire picture when preparing a practical and usable list of recommendations. Thus, as we discussed earlier, we chose or changed recommendations several times based on an organization's particular situation.

Revealing Details

Another lesson we learned was that it is important to base conclusions on more than averaged data. Using mathematical functions to reduce information hides information. For example, if we look solely at the maturity results in Table 7.1, it appears that little or nothing has changed in the three organizations. However, when we examine their maturity profiles in detail, we see that many things have changed: Some areas have improved, others have stabilized, and still others are unchanged.

Assessment Validity

We have closely followed the ongoing discussion surrounding the validity of assessments. The focus of discussion has primarily been on software capability evaluations, but the validity of SEI assessments has also been discussed (Bollinger and McGowan 1991; Humphrey and Curtis 1991; O'Connell and Saiedian 2000).

Based on our experience in this project, as well as that in the 44 other Bootstrap assessments, we are increasingly convinced that many of the discussions and analogies about assessment validity are weak and in some cases wrong. For example, assessments are often compared to evaluating a car's overall paint job by looking at a few spots: Companies can display their best areas and thus give a false impression. However, a good assessment does not simply look for spots that were nicely painted, badly painted, or not painted at all. Instead, it questions the entire painting process. In our experience, it is very difficult to cheat in the assessment.

Assessments are often described as being like an exam for evaluating a student. However, an examination and the mark or grade it earns is not in itself sufficient to offer a detailed picture of a student's capabilities. In addition, the results are not always clear. For example, say a student is assigned an essay on the topic of laziness and turns in a paper with only his name and a single word: *laziness*. Is the student a genius and thus deserving of a high mark, or lazy and deserving of a low mark?

Our experiences show that, rather than view an organization as one student and the assessment as an exam, it is much more useful to view an organization as a class. The aim of the assessment is to determine the organization's level: Is it a preschool class? Is it in the middle or upper grades? Or is it at a college or university level? Assessors base their determination of maturity level on multiple factors, making it easier to assign levels and difficult for organizations to cheat. Among the factors we look at are how managers and project teams communicate, cooperate, and focus, and also how they discuss processes, both in terms of the language they use and how they articulate their methods, disciplines, tools, procedures, and capabilities.

As with students in a class, there can be some differences in maturity between an organization's SPU management and its projects. Some projects or the management (or both) are past the graduation mark, others just meet it, and still others are below the mark. Only when the organization as a whole passes the mark does it graduate to the next level. This process affects our recommendations. If the organization as a whole—management and projects—has not passed the exam in an area, the area stays on the list of recommendations. When the organization passes, it graduates in this area and the area disappears from the recommendations list. New areas, belonging to the next grade, then appear.

As our perspectives here indicate, simply basing recommendations on the model-related assessment data is insufficient. The organization's actual situation—the total picture—must be considered. This broader view helps assessors produce a much more realistic and usable list of recommendations. Our experiences also indicate that an organization's overall maturity level is of little importance to the actual improvement work; the detailed profiles are what inspire and educate management and project participants.

7.5 CONCLUSION

As our experiences show, assessments are a useful tool for identifying the starting point for SPI activities. We also recommend using the same tool for further assessments because this lets you compare the two sets of results, track projects, and plan future activities in a consistent way.

Returning to Kierkegaard, to help an organization you must know where that organization is, just as to help a class, you must know the level at which the students are learning. Although it is not difficult to establish an organization's maturity level, it is difficult to effectively explain its implications. In this effort, having a model is indispensable. Using a consistent model helps participants visualize the curriculum, and using a consistent method helps them understand their state as compared to the model's requirements. Together, the model and method create a full and accurate picture of the organization's situation. When you have that, you are ready to help the organization define a relevant and successful improvement program.

7.6 REFERENCES

Bollinger, T.B., and C. McGowan. 1991. "A Critical Look at Software Capability Evaluations." *IEEE Software*. July.

Humphrey, W., and B. Curtis. 1991. "Comments on 'A Critical Look.'" *IEEE Software*. July.

Jonassen Hass, A.M. and J. Johansen. 1996. "Bruel & Kjaer A/S: BOOTSTRAP Assessment Report." DELTA (Confidential).

Jonassen Hass, A.M. and J. Johansen. 1999a. Bruel & Kjaer, Schenck A/S, Condition Monitoring Systems: BOOTSTRAP Assessment Report." DELTA (Confidential).

Jonassen Hass, A.M. and J. Johansen. 1999b. "Bruel & Kjaer Sound & Vibration Measurement A/S: BOOTSTRAP Assessment Report." DELTA (Confidential).

Jonassen Haas, A.M., J. Johansen, and O. Anderson. 1996. "Softwareudvikling I Elektronikindustrien." DELTA Rapport, D-260.

Jonassen Hass, A.M., J. Pries-Heje, and J. Johansen. 1999. "Danske Data: BOOTSTRAP Assessment Report." DELTA (Confidential).

Kuvaja, Pasi, J. Simila, L. Krzanik, A. Bicego, S. Saukkonen, and G. Koch. 1994. *Software Process Assessment and Improvement: the BOOTSTRAP Approach*. Blackwell Publishers, Oxford, UK.

Nielsen, C.T., and J. Johansen. 1997. "Systematic Software Engineering A/S: BOOTSTRAP Assessment report." DELTA (Confidential).

Nielsen, C.T., and J. Johansen. 1998. "Systematic Software Engineering A/S: BOOTSTRAP Assessment Report." DELTA (Confidential).

O'Connell, E., and H. Saiedian. 2000. "Can You Trust Software Capability Evaluations?" *Computer*. February.

Pries-Heje, J., and J. Johansen. 1997. "Danske Data: BOOTSTRAP Assessment Report. DELTA (Confidential).

Chapter 8

From Problem Reports to Better Products

Otto Vinter

Organizations typically base their SPI efforts on well-known models of software process maturity such as the Software Engineering Institute's CMM (Paulk et al. 1993) and the European counterpart, Bootstrap (Bicego et al. 1998). Assessing current practices using such normative models is generally considered the proper way to identify and prioritize improvement initiatives. However, some researchers claim that these models offer a rigid and limited view of the software development process and fail to consider the variety among and complexity within software producing organizations (Bollinger and McGowan 1991). Many organizations find it difficult to translate their assessment results into concrete improvement actions. Furthermore, almost all SPI practitioners in organizations at the lower maturity levels (1–2) have encountered severe resistance to their improvement initiatives. Taken together, these factors indicate a need for alternative or complementary assessment approaches.

At Brüel & Kjær, we developed one such approach, which focuses on defect analysis. Although our projects were funded by the Commission of the European Communities (CEC) and started before the SPI Project, our experience and results provided a foundation for diffusion and adoption actions.

Our approach to defect-analysis was born from our improvement process. Brüel & Kjær management did not want to invest in a comprehensive SPI program because the company had just been through a major reorganization and downsizing. Thus, rather than start our improvement program with a traditional maturity-model assessment, we had to develop an incremental strategy based on experience and available information and to focus our approach on major process issues.

The result was an approach to defect-analysis that uses problem reports from past projects to help SPI practitioners identify specific, frequently occurring problems. These problems then serve as the focus of improvement actions. In our case, we performed analyses in the context of two SPI projects. The first project—the Prevention of Errors through Experience-Driven Test Efforts, or PET—focused on analyzing bug distributions for the purpose of improving the test and release process. In the second project—the Methodology for Preventing Requirements Issues from Becoming Defects, or PRIDE—we took our analysis a step further, focusing on specific issues related to requirements engineering. These defect analyses put us in a better position to determine how such problems might be prevented and thus to implement focused solutions. Here, I offer an overview of our efforts; detailed information on both projects is also available in our final project reports (Vinter et al. 1996a, 1996b, 1999).

Brüel & Kjær's Development Process

When we began our work, Brüel & Kjær's software development process was considered unsatisfactory. Too many projects had schedule overruns, and products were often shipped with bugs. Even when task forces were formed to improve the quality, bugs were still found in the field. The general opinion was that these bugs were caused by inadequate product testing before release.

Brüel & Kjær's development process is based on a waterfall model, centered on the problems of controlling the hardware development and production process. Although Brüel & Kjær is ISO 9001 certified (International Organization for Standardization 1994), the company has few procedures specifically aimed at software development.

All product development is organized around projects, which are led by project managers. Most developers have engineering degrees of various types, including software engineering. Project managers are often technically brilliant but lacking in formal management background or training.

Although Brüel & Kjær products were for many years based on embedded real-time software, a shift in market demand over the past couple of years changed this, and the majority of applications are now standard PC applications in MS Windows NT.

Specifications are traditionally technology-driven: They take full advantage of the hardware's capabilities. We typically develop applications based on a traditional written requirements specification. However, we have also tried to develop applications based on a minimal requirements specification combined with rapid prototyping of complex domain areas.

Both approaches have resulted in ambiguous and incomplete requirements specifications, which have led to predictable problems during development: new or altered requirements stemming from marketing input late in the development process. This has created rework, more bugs, and schedule slippage.

We typically sketch a software system's design early in the process and do detailed design in the coding phase.

Each programmer does *unit testing* on his or her own unit by linking to the other available (and often untested) units. Such tests thus act more as an integration test. In the real integration test (which is actually a system test), all programmers test everything—often without an overall plan. A small group of people with domain knowledge perform the acceptance testing; such testing is often unsystematic and is given few resources.

8.1 THE DEFECT-ANALYSIS APPROACH

A problem report at Brüel & Kjær can contain anything from a serious defect to a suggested improvement. To reflect such distinctions, we label issues raised by reports "bugs" rather than "defects." Problem reporting typically starts when individual developers have debugged their own software unit—that is, when they have integrated their unit with the other units in the system. Reporting continues until product support ends.

Sample Problem Reports

- D1: When a 3-D picture is rotated or zoomed, the annotations on coordinate axes, grid surfaces, and soon are also rotated and zoomed. This problem can make the annotations unreadable.
  - Explanation: The 3-D package works on bitmaps when it moves and zooms. Defining the picture, however, is performed with separate commands for axes and annotations. The problem stems from a mistaken expectation of the third-party software specification. From a quality factor viewpoint, this is a usability problem.

- D137: The measurement sequence should be Z shaped, S shaped, or Free shaped. However, I cannot find a "Free shape" button; there are two buttons, one labeled "Z shape" and the other "S shape."
  - Explanation: When both buttons are out, it means Free shape. From a quality factor viewpoint, this is a question of usability. Although the developer understood the tacit requirement for choosing between the alternatives, he guessed wrong about how to deal with it.

Most projects had numerous problem reports, so we analyzed an equally spaced sample (such as every fourth report). In this way, we could maintain the correct distribution of issues over time. All samples consisted of at least 100 reports.

The bug analysis was a cooperative effort between our SPI group and developers who had inside knowledge about the issues raised in the problem reports. Without this developer participation, we could never have reached correct conclusions.

We sorted the problem reports according to the specific developer related to them (typically, the one who had fixed the bugs) and analyzed the reports in an interview with that developer. In some cases, we interviewed more than one person about the report, but we never interviewed in groups of more than two developers. Two to three people from the SPI group were present for each interview, and we made sure that the same group participated throughout the product's analysis to maintain consistency of results. Even though the analysis took place more than a year after problem reports were issued, when prompted, developers remembered the bugs and were able to discuss them in detail.

To classify bugs, we chose a taxonomy proposed by Boris Beizer (1990). This taxonomy suited our purposes surprisingly well, considering that it was developed in the mid-1980s and therefore contains some categories that are irrelevant to modern programming languages and tools. Also, we extended the taxonomy with a few new categories, the most significant being a subcategory for problems with third-party software (subcategory 78).

Our SPI group had studied Beizer's taxonomy and knew it well. Developers learned about the taxonomy in the interviews as we classified their problem reports. When everyone was familiar with the taxonomy, categorizing each bug took about five minutes.

Beizer's Bug Taxonomy

There are several taxonomies for bug classification (Chillarege et al. 1992; IEEE 1995), but the most detailed one is by Boris Beizer (1990). Beizer's taxonomy splits bugs into nine main categories, which are further detailed in as many as four levels. For example, under category 1 (Requirements and Features), category 16 covers changes to requirements, category 162 indicates a feature has changed, and category 1621 indicates that the change was that a feature was added.

The taxonomy is complemented with extensive statistical material on bug distribution in the different categories. The statistics are based on 16,209 bugs from projects with a total of 6,877 million lines of code.

The main categories are as follows:

1. Requirements and Features: Bugs related to requirements as specified or as implemented.
2. Functionality as Implemented: Requirements are (assumed) correct, but implementation is wrong.
3. Structural Bugs: Bugs related to the component's structure (the code).
4. Data: Bugs in the definition, structure, or use of data.
5. Implementation: Typographical bugs, standards violations, and bugs in the documentation.
6. Integration: Bugs related to interfaces between components or to external interfaces.
7. System and Software Architecture: Bugs affecting the entire software system (such as the architecture or system generation).
8. Test Definition or Execution Bugs: Bugs in the definition, design, and execution of tests or test data.
9. Other Bugs, Unspecified.

In interviews, developers were initially inclined to blame most problems on either lack of precise requirements (category 1) or to blame themselves for a "simple coding error" (category 3). However, throughout the interviews we challenged these opinions, continually pressing the developers for more information and offering other suggestions as to what may have caused the problem. This technique quickly triggered a deeper look; developers uncovered more information, which typically changed the bug category and identified the real underlying cause.

At the end of the interview, we reviewed Beizer's description of the selected category to ensure that developers agreed that it was the most probable cause of the bug. We did this because we found it extremely important to categorize the bug down to the last digit in Beizer's taxonomy. Initially, to avoid going into the details of the taxonomy, we used only the nine main categories. However, after a small pilot study, we were unsure that we had arrived at the correct result. We thus ran another pilot in which we used all levels of the taxonomy. The two samples did not match. We concluded that when only the main categories were used, it was too easy for developers to jump to conclusions about the cause of a bug.

As a final step in our analysis of a bug, we asked developers to speculate about what might have prevented the bug during testing. In the first analysis (PET), we asked developers only whether and how the bug could have been found in testing. In the second analysis (PRIDE), we expanded the analysis with additional classifications and created a comprehensive list of prevention techniques for requirements-related problems. This extended analysis required approximately 30 additional minutes per bug.

8.2   DEFECT-ANALYSIS RESULTS

We analyzed reports from seven typical Brüel & Kjær software development projects, which included both embedded real-time projects and applications in MS Windows NT. The project sizes averaged seven person-years, with a 12–18 month development time and code at 50–100 thousand lines of noncommented source statements (KNCSS). The programming languages we covered were Pascal, C, and C++.

In all, we analyzed approximately 1,000 problem reports from seven different products, totaling approximately 600 KNCSS. The product was released to customers 3–18 months before our analysis. This allowed us the opportunity to study problem reports based on actual product use.

Bug-Distribution Analysis

During the PET project, we examined problem reports from several embedded systems software products. Figure 8.1 shows a typical result of our bug categorization

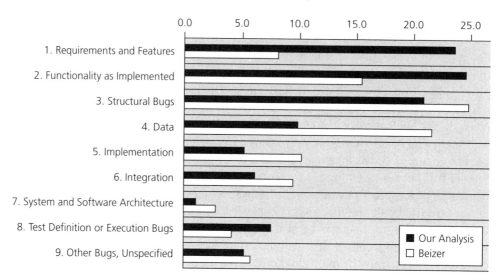

Figure 8.1 *Problem report categories from a typical product compared to Beizer's statistics*

compared with Beizer's statistics. As the figure shows, we found major differences between our results and Beizer's. We now explain some of these variations.

Clearly, our results showed a far greater problem with requirements than the Beizer reports. This difference can be attributed partially to the fact that Beizer's statistics are gathered primarily from large companies that deliver software on U.S. government contracts. In such circumstances, requirements must be stable and precisely defined.

In examining the requirements' subcategories, we found that many of our problems were caused by missing or incomplete requirements (subcategory 13: Completeness). This subcategory accounted for 12.1% of our problems compared with 1.4% of Beizer's. Another major subcategory was related to requirements changing during implementation or use (subcategory 16: Requirements Changes). This subcategory accounted for 8.7% of our problems compared with 1.7% of Beizer's.

We also saw a higher percentage of problems related to functionality as implemented (category 2). Looking deeper into this, we found that the problems stemmed from developers misinterpreting the requirements in one way or another (subcategory 211: Feature Misunderstood, Wrong; subcategory 241: Domain Misunderstood). These subcategories accounted for 14.7% of our bugs compared with 2.3% of Beizer's. The pattern repeated in category 8 (Test Definition or Execution Bugs), where bugs were caused by testers misinterpreting the requirements (subcategory

811: Requirements Misunderstood). This subcategory accounted for 6.9% of our problems compared with 0.02% of Beizer's.

On the other hand, we apparently had significantly fewer problems than Beizer reports in defining, structuring, and using data (category 4). The explanation here is straightforward: Data structures in embedded real-time applications are much simpler than in the applications that Beizer reports on, and we also use less default information. Therefore, fewer bugs would be expected.

We also had fewer bugs in category 5 (Implementation). This is because bugs related to standards violations, typographical problems in the code, and so on are not reported in our company. Consequently our analysis covers only documentation problems (subcategory 53), which in Beizer's statistics account for 5.9%. This number is quite close to our own.

From our bug-distribution analysis, we concluded that most of our bugs were related to problems with requirements. When we added the "misunderstood" subcategories (subcategories 211, 241, and 811) to Beizer's Requirements and Features category (category 1), we found that requirements-related problems accounted for 45.2% of all bugs. The primary issues seemed not to be in what is actually written in the requirements specification document, but rather in what people either do not know or tacitly assume about the requirements. We demonstrate this in Figure 8.2, grouping the issues into missing (subcategory 13), changed (subcategory 16), misunderstood (subcategories 211, 241, 811), and other (other subcategories of category 1).

We also concluded that the problem reports from embedded real-time projects showed the same pattern as for other types of software. Thus, our major problems were related to flaws in the development process rather than to the software's embedded real-time nature. This conclusion was quite surprising. Developers of embedded real-time software typically claim that their applications are very difficult to develop

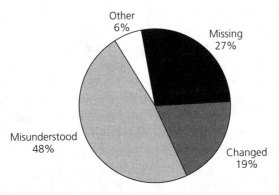

Figure 8.2 *Major subcategories of requirements-related problems*

because of problems related to timing, multitasking, and so on, and because of a lack of efficient development tools. One possible explanation for this could be that Brüel & Kjær uses highly skilled people with engineering degrees to build these applications, rather than programmers with less education and experience.

Requirements-Related Analysis

In our PRIDE project analysis, we included problem reports from both embedded software and PC applications for MS Windows NT. Our goal in the second analysis was to find the root causes of the requirements-related problems.

To make sure that we covered all requirements problems, we first went through each of the categories in Beizer's taxonomy and decided whether it indicated a requirements issue. Using this set of requirements-related categories (Vinter et al. 1999), we found that 51% of all problem reports were requirements-related.

We then expanded our defect analysis to include classifications specifically aimed at characterizing requirements-related bugs. We classified the problem reports by

- ◆ Quality factor: Functionality, reliability, usability, performance, and so on
- ◆ Interface where the bug occurred: User interface, third-party software, front-end system, and so on
- ◆ Error source: Change in user needs, wrong use of specification, tacit requirement, and so on

We based the quality factors on McCall's classification. They are similar to the quality characteristics stated in ISO 9126 (International Organization for Standardization 1991), and can be easily mapped to them (for future analyses, we will use ISO 9126 quality characteristics). Our classification demonstrated clearly that usability issues dominated in requirements-related problem reports (64%). This, too, was something of a surprise. In the requirements engineering community, it is widely assumed that functionality issues are the major requirements problem, but our analysis showed that they represent only 22% of errors.

Our interface classification was a simple list of all software and hardware that the application interfaced with. As expected, the interface classification confirmed that most problems were related to the user interface. However, we also found frequent problems (28%) in understanding and cooperating with third-party software packages and circumventing their bugs. This was the second largest requirements issue in the problem reports.

We developed and redefined the error-source classification while we were classifying the problem reports. The classification confirmed our previous results: Most requirements-related bugs were caused by missing or misunderstood requirements. In 57% of reports, for example, the error source was "tacit requirement."

Given these results, we focused our improvement action on usability problems and on early verification and validation techniques rather than on correctness and completeness of requirements documents.

Bug Distribution over Time

At the start of our defect analysis on a set of problem reports, we analyzed the distribution of the reports over time—that is, the point at which the bugs were reported. Figure 8.3 shows the distribution of a product's problem report. The problem reporting starts when a developer begins integrating the unit. When in-house testing is completed, a trial version of the product is released for use by sales companies and select customers. Usually a product is released when field use has generated sufficient experience and confidence in the product.

Figure 8.3 shows an extreme case, but it illustrates clearly an insufficient testing and release process. The first wave of bugs represents the development team's efforts to test and integrate the system's components; a less intensive bug-finding period follows. What's missing is the expected wave of bugs in the intensive testing phase before the trial release. When we interviewed the project manager, he admitted that "too few resources were assigned in this phase, and testing was not planned and structured properly."

Shortly after the trial version is released, we see a wave of bug reports resulting from practical use of the product. Later, after production release, far fewer bugs are

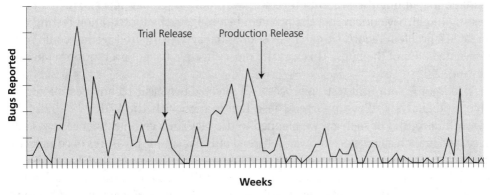

Figure 8.3   *An error-prone product's problem-report distribution over time*

reported. In fact, the spikes in Figure 8.3 following the production release correspond to testing at incremental releases of new product functionality.

Capers Jones (1996) reports that companies with little or no control over the testing process tend to have a defect-removal efficiency rate of only 53%–64% before release. In the product in Figure 8.3, 61% of the bugs were found before the trial release. Jones also reports that simply introducing well-known testing stages can increase a team's defect-removal efficiency to 74%–87%. To get higher efficiency than this requires that a company make dedicated improvements in its testing process.

A distribution over time like that in Figure 8.3 focuses management attention on the company's testing and release processes. It clearly demonstrates that testing needs to improve before trial release. Problem-report distributions over time can easily demonstrate the effectiveness of testing process improvements on each product. Also, the defect-removal efficiency gives a direct indication of the quality of released products.

Finally, the distribution over time normalized by testing effort can also be a dynamic tool for supporting decisions about when to release a product. For example, one might decide to release a product when the number of bugs per testing hour drops below a certain threshold.

8.3 IDENTIFYING PREVENTION TECHNIQUES

Classifying problem reports is one thing. Preventing common problems from reappearing is another. We spent considerable effort trying to find the optimum set of prevention techniques in each case.

When we interviewed developers during the PET analysis, we were not very systematic in defining the prevention issues; we simply asked developers which type of testing might have uncovered the problem before it reached integration testing and created a problem report. Our analysis shows that systematic unit testing could have prevented 20% of the bugs. This was the most effective type of prevention related to testing.

To improve our unit testing process, we selected two basic techniques: static and dynamic analysis. We supported these techniques with the LDRA Testbed tool (www.ldra.com). For metrics, we planned to use McCabe's complexity measure, code size, and branch coverage. However, it turned out that simple measures of complexity and size are not very useful when you're trying to plan efficient testing; being able to visualize and thus review code structure is better. We also found that measuring the coverage using test cases of code branches represents a very efficient way of defining and controlling the prerelease testing level.

Test Improvement Techniques

Based on our findings from analyzing problem reports, we selected the following basic set of techniques to improve the unit testing process (the final PET report contains more detail on each).

- *Static analysis* highlights semantic problems in the source code related to misuse of types and variables. Structural metrics are calculated to indicate the code structure's quality, and the code structure can be visualized for review or inspection.

- *Dynamic analysis* quantifies the test coverage of a software system. It also highlights those parts of the code that test cases have not exercised. Cross references to code help identify new test cases, something that leads to higher code coverage.

During our PRIDE analysis, we asked developers more questions aimed at finding prevention techniques for requirements-related problems. We began the PRIDE analysis with a list of known prevention techniques and added to it when no existing technique seemed capable of preventing the bug in question. Later, when we discussed the effectiveness (*hit rate*) of each technique, we further improved and specified each technique.

We considered and later dropped many well-known techniques because they were useless in relation to the actual bugs. Initially, for example, we thought that argument-based techniques could be useful, but the problem reports did not show a need for them. Others, such as formal (mathematical) specifications, also seemed of little value. Techniques that focused on early experiments with different kinds of prototypes seemed much better suited to preventing real-life bugs. Many of the proposed techniques are commonsense techniques that are moved up from the design phase to the requirements phase and formalized. Used in this context, they can contribute significantly to ensuring a quality product.

Through this process, we produced a list of some 40 prevention techniques grouped into eight categories:

- 1xx: Demand analysis (including scenarios)
- 2xx: Usability techniques (including prototypes)
- 3xx: Validation and testing of external software
- 4xx: Requirements tracing
- 5xx: Risk analysis
- 6xx: Improved specification techniques (such as formal or mathematical)
- 7xx: Checking techniques (including formal inspections)
- 8xx: Other techniques (including performance specifications)

When we had our final list, we estimated a hit rate for each technique on each problem report; then we calculated the technique's overall effectiveness across all problem reports. We also assigned a benefit for preventing each problem report; we could thus calculate the cost/benefit ratio of each technique. Based on these estimates, we selected an optimum set of prevention techniques.

Figure 8.4 shows the results for the top seven techniques with respect to savings. The hit rates are shown as a percentage of the total number of bugs in the project. The savings are shown as a percentage of the total development effort. The numbers in parentheses are those we used to identify each technique. Figure 8.4 shows only the top scorers with respect to savings; because of high costs, other techniques had comparable hit rates but lower savings (in some cases, the costs outweighed the benefits).

When you use more than one technique at the same time, the hit rates do not simply add up. The reason is that the first technique filters out some problems, leaving fewer problems for the second technique to detect. This has an obvious impact on savings. In general, it is best to combine techniques that find different kinds of problems.

In our case, we applied the principle of dynamic programming to calculate combined hit rates and savings, and we found the best combination of techniques with re-

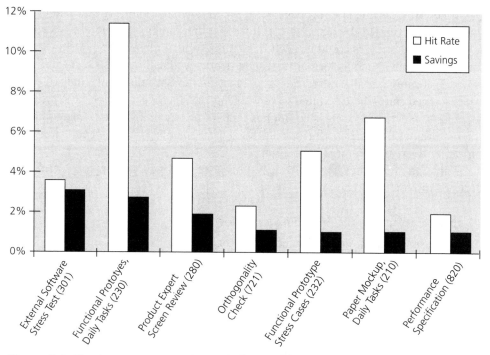

Figure 8.4   *The top seven prevention techniques with respect to savings*

spect to savings. For example, the best combination of four techniques from Figure 8.4 would result in a combined hit rate of 19% of all problem reports (37% of all the requirements-related bugs) and a combined saving of 6% on the total development effort. This would have saved us approximately one month on the 18-month schedule of the analyzed project.

The Experience-Based Requirements Engineering Methodology

Based on our findings from analyzing problem reports, we selected an optimum set of techniques to improve the requirements engineering process. Here is an overview of these techniques. The final PRIDE report (Vinter et al. 1999) contains more detail on each.

REQUIREMENTS ELICITATION AND VALIDATION

- Scenarios: Relate demands to use situations. Describe the essential tasks in each scenario.
- Navigational prototype usability test, daily tasks: Ensure that users can use the system for daily tasks based on a prototype of the user interface with dynamic navigation and static screens.

VERIFICATION OF THE REQUIREMENTS SPECIFICATION

- Expert screen reviews: Have a product expert check screens for deviations from earlier product styles.
- External software stress test: Test to ensure that external software fulfills expectations in requirements specification, with special emphasis on extreme cases.
- Orthogonality check: Ensure that the requirements specification lets users apply an operation or feature whenever it is useful.
- Performance specifications: Check the requirements specification to ensure that it contains performance goals for the requirements.

The set of techniques we selected for application on a new development project was not based solely on the best combination with regard to savings. In our analysis, for example, we did not find scenarios to be effective on their own. However, we included them for two reasons. First, usability is an important issue and scenarios help define the tasks users should perform during usability testing. Second, other sources indicated that scenarios were effective in improving developers' understanding of the domain.

We also decided to include the navigational prototype technique in our optimum set even though it was estimated to have only half the hit rate and much lower savings than a functional prototype. Our SPI group was worried that developing a functional prototype would take too long, and thus usability tests would be delayed until it was too late to make the requirements changes indicated by the tests. On the other hand, developers focused on creating a functional prototype for the usability tests because they were worried that a paper mockup or navigational prototype would be insufficient.

However, after they had described the scenarios, the developers could not wait for a functional prototype to be developed. Instead they developed a prototype with navigational capabilities in only two weeks. They used both Visual Basic and Word 6's Bookmark feature to develop further prototypes. Developers immediately subjected these navigational prototypes to usability tests involving real users, and the number of issues that they found and corrected convinced them that a navigational prototype would be sufficient.

Since we completed our improvement action, other projects have used paper mockups for usability tests and have found them just as effective as navigational prototypes. However, again, they did not believe that paper mockups would work until they tried them and compared the results with their PC-based prototypes. We now recommend that all projects use paper mockups to achieve faster results from usability tests.

8.4 IMPROVEMENTS OBTAINED

Based on our defect analysis and proposed prevention techniques, we performed two full-scale improvement projects. The first project (PET) improved the testing process, and the second (PRIDE) improved the requirements engineering process. For both projects, we selected a baseline product development project. We then trained the development team in the new techniques, which they used as part of their usual development process.

We monitored both projects and, following product release, analyzed the problem reports and compared them with similar products developed by the same teams. The results demonstrate the success of our prevention techniques.

In the improvement phase of the PET project, we introduced the unit testing techniques on a completed product ready for trial release. Of course, this approach meant that we were not using static and dynamic analysis in the unit testing phase of a development process. On the other hand, it gave us an excellent environment for performing our experiment. Without changing any code, we were able to perform an analysis on the product, correct the bugs that we found, issue a new (production) version, and then measure the impact of static and dynamic analysis on the bugs reported from the field on both versions.

We experienced a 46% improvement in testing efficiency (bugs found per person-hour) and raised the branch coverage of all units to more than 85%.

On the production release, the team received 75% fewer problem reports than on the trial version. Of those error reports, 70% were related to requirements—bugs that could not have been found through static and dynamic analysis. Again, this confirmed the need to improve the requirements process.

If the bugs revealed by our static and dynamic analysis had instead been reported from the field, we would have incurred a cost equal to 75% of the resources we spent on the tool and staff training on the baseline project. Thus, companies can expect an almost immediate return on their investment when the techniques are used throughout the testing process.

The overall result of the test improvement action is that we now have the ability to introduce products to the market with remarkably fewer bugs. Given this, the company's reputation for quality will increase and our time to market will be reduced because of lower maintenance.

In the improvement phase of the PRIDE project, we first tried to introduce five of the prevention techniques from our requirements engineering methodology, but this was more than the development team could handle. In the end, the baseline team used two techniques: scenarios and navigational prototype usability tests.

In all, the team described 11 scenarios, although some were less detailed and others were overlapping. They developed three distinct generations of prototypes (and several patches). On average, three people tested each prototype for usability. Initially, the developers used in-house application experts for the usability tests and later ran tests with potential product users. The requirements specification was then written and approved in the conventional way. Product development and release also followed existing practices.

The result was an overall reduction in error reports of 27%. We also found a 72% reduction in usability issues per new screen and a threefold increase in productivity in user-interface design and development.

We were also surprised to find that the techniques reduced not only requirements-related bugs but other categories of bugs as well. Our explanation is that developing scenarios and taking part in the usability tests gave most developers a deep understanding of the domain. This understanding invariably reduced their uncertainty and indecision about which features to include, how they should work, and how they should be implemented and tested. In the team's previous projects, new screens were constantly changing throughout the project.

However, the impact of these techniques was not limited to bug prevention; the users' perception of product quality also significantly increased. Describing scenarios enabled the team to understand important user needs at a very early stage in the requirements engineering process. Developers thus got a clear vision of the product before the requirements were fixed. Subsequent usability tests on early prototypes verified that the concepts derived from the scenario descriptions matched user needs and could be readily understood by users in daily use situations.

The product has now been on the market for more than 18 months and sells more than twice as much as the team's earlier product—this despite the fact that the new product is more expensive than a comparable product and is aimed at a much smaller market niche.

Given this improvement action, we are now in a position to create products that better meet user expectations without increasing our development effort or time to market.

8.5 DISCUSSION

As our results show, defect analysis is a simple and effective approach that can solve major problems in a company's software development process. However, we did face several challenges in our improvement effort, some of which we have yet to solve.

Management Support

Analyzing bugs changed the way we see our software development process and gave us a starting point for improving it. Rather than wait for management to agree to a formal assessment of the development process, our SPI group used readily available information in the problem reports to initiate immediate improvements.

However, the drawback of initiating SPI "from the ground floor" was that we never really got management commitment to the improvement actions. We conducted all SPI activities at the project level. At first, this was an advantage because Brüel & Kjær had a very strong project culture (maturity level 2), and thus improvements could be introduced only through individual project managers.

Now, however, we need higher-level management commitment and involvement to ensure that our improvements are widely adopted. Furthermore, some improvement actions (such as reuse) can be introduced only on an organizational level. Management support is therefore very much needed if we are to continue our SPI program.

Without management commitment, it is also difficult to demonstrate the effects of improvements, because validation takes a long time. Each of our improvement actions followed projects over the full life cycle (12–18 months) and required additional time for analysis and evaluation. The total time for each action was thus 21–27 months.

Typically, management does not have the patience for this; our projects succeeded because we had outside funding from the CEC.

Finally, without a clear indication of purpose backed by management, project managers naturally tend to adopt only those practices that they consider interesting to work with. Without management insistence, important changes in the development process are likely to be ignored.

Taxonomy Limits

Beizer's bug taxonomy is an excellent starting point for defect analysis. However, because it was never intended for this use, it must be complemented with other techniques to be a comprehensive root cause and prevention analysis. Our experience shows that the nature of these additions depends on specific problem-report findings.

Beizer initially intended his taxonomy to be used only by testers to record their findings. We used the taxonomy in a much broader scope. To be fully effective, we had to further subdivide some of the taxonomy's original categories and introduce new ones. Also, some taxonomy categories are no longer relevant with current programming languages, tools, and techniques. All these factors affect the relevance of Beizer's statistics, at least at the detailed level. However, the defect-analysis process was far more important than statistical accuracy.

Measurement Limits

We have validated two improvement cases; in both cases we used problem reports as the measure of success. Improvements made late in the development cycle have an immediate, recognizable effect: a decreased number of problem reports. However, when we introduced improvements early in the development cycle, the decrease in problem reports from these phases was less dramatic. During the design and development stages, the many interactions of people and processes evidently prevented us from establishing a direct relationship.

Clearly, we must expand our defect-analysis approach by introducing other types of defect measurements to find and validate improvements in earlier development phases. We also need to adjust it for use in improvement efforts that are not aimed at reducing problem reports.

Maturity Impact

When we presented management with the results of the first defect analysis, they were convinced that a more formal assessment of our software development processes was needed. We thus underwent a Bootstrap assessment, with the Danish company DELTA serving as assessors. Among its top five recommendations was the need to improve unit testing and requirements.

When we finished both improvement actions, a second Bootstrap assessment was performed (by the same external assessors) to assess our results and further the improvement program. In the second assessment, testing and requirements issues were no longer among the top five recommendations.

We thus conclude that traditional assessments can identify the need for the same improvements identified through defect analysis and also that traditional assessments can record the effect of improvements based on defect analysis. However, we believe that the formal, traditional assessments do not inspire as much drive and motivation to improve. In our case, for example, the first Bootstrap assessment initiated no specific improvement actions.

Normative SPI models such as CMM and Bootstrap should not be discarded. They represent a comprehensive framework for improvement actions and have established a principle for measuring (assessing) the existence and use of software processes in an organization. However, the notion of maturity levels gives rise to recommendations aimed at improving all processes on a specific level to move an organization from one level to the next. For many organizations, these recommendations seem difficult to follow. The required effort and the lack of visible product improvements can discourage some organizations from improving their processes at all.

Alternative approaches to SPI, such as the one we developed, tend to be hot-spot solutions to specific problems. They have a high motivational effect because of the direct contact with and close involvement of developers and project managers. Also, their results tend to be directly visible, such as in our immediate reduction in problem reports.

8.6 SUMMARY AND CONCLUSIONS

Given our experience, we conclude that our defect analysis approach to SPI is an effective and valid alternative to formal assessments. Analyzing problem reports is a simple and easy way to identify important issues in your organization's software development processes. Such an analysis triggers focused improvement actions that can solve major problems in your organization.

You can also use our defect-analysis approach to establish a starting point for your organization's improvement activities. Problem reports contain readily available information, and that lets people within your organization initiate improvements rather than having to wait for management to hire an external company to formally assess all the development processes.

Furthermore, improvements based on defect analysis are highly motivating because they directly involve developers and project managers. Such improvements are visible immediately in the organization through such things as reduced problem reports.

Finally, defect analysis lets you conduct SPI activities at the project level. This is an advantage for organizations with a strong project culture (maturity level 2), in which improvements can be introduced only through individual project managers.

We validated two cases of improvements; in each, we used problem reports as the measure for success. In both cases, the improvements inspired by defect analysis led to better products, both in terms of fewer defects after release and higher customer satisfaction and sales. Such results have encouraged us to pursue continuous improvements that are in keeping with the key process improvement areas of the normative models.

8.7 ACKNOWLEDGMENTS

The PET and PRIDE projects were funded by the Commission of the European Communities under the European System and Software Initiative: ESSI projects 10438 (Vinter et al. 1996a, 1996b) and 21167 (Vinter et al. 1999), respectively. Prof. Søren Lauesen of Copenhagen Business School acted as consultant for Brüel & Kjær on defect analysis for the PRIDE project. He defined the specific classifications for requirements issues, was heavily involved in defining prevention techniques, designed the cost/benefit model, and participated in all project evaluations.

8.8 REFERENCES

Beizer, B. 1990. *Software Testing Techniques*, second ed. New York: Van Nostrand Reinhold.

Bicego, A., M. Khurana, and P. Kuvaja. 1998. *BOOTSTRAP 3.0: Software process Assessment Methodology*. Proceedings of the SQM '98.

Bollinger, T.B., and C. McGowan. 1991. "A Critical Look at Software Capability Evaluation." *IEEE Software*. 8:4:25–41.

Chillarege, R., I. Bhandari, J. Chaar, M. Halliday, D. Moebus, B. Ray, and M. Wong. 1992. Orthogonal Defect Classification. A Concept for In-process Measurement." *IEEE Transactions on Software Engineering*. 18:11:943–956.

IEEE Standards. 1995. *Guide to Classification for Software Anomalies*. IEEE Std. 1044.1–1995 (Unapproved Draft).

International Organizations for Standardization. 1991. *Information Technology— Software Product Evaluation—Quality Characteristics and Guidelines for Their Use*. ISO 9126.

International Organization for Standardization. 1994. *Quality Systems—Model for Quality Assurance in Design, Development, Production, Installation, and Servicing*. ISO 9001:1994 Revised Edition.

Jones, C. 1996. *Quantifying Software Process Improvements*. Proceedings of the SP '96.

Paulk, M.C., B. Curtis, M.B. Chrissis, and C.V. Weber. 1993. *Capability Maturity Model for Software, Version 1.1*. 93-TR-024. Pittsburgh, PA: Software Engineering Institute.

Vinter, O., P.-M. Poulsen, K. Nissen, and J.M. Thomsen. 1996. *The Prevention of Errors through Experience-Driven Test Efforts*. ESSI Project 10438. Final Report, Brüel & Kjær a/S, DK-2850 Naerum, Denmark; http://www.esi.es/ESSI/report/All/ 10438.

Vinter O., P.-M. Poulsen, K. Nissen, J.M. Thomsen, and O. Andersen 1996b. *The Prevention of Errors through Experience-Driven Test Efforts*. DLT Report D-259, DELTA, DK-2970 Horsholm, Denmark.

Vinter O., S. Lauesen, and J. Pries-Heje. 1999. *A Methodology for Preventing Requirements Issues from Becoming Defects*. ESSI Project 21167. Final report, Brüel & Kjær Sound & Vibration Measurement A/S, DK-2850 Naerum, Denmark. http://www.esi.es/ ESSI/Reports/All/21167.

Chapter 9

Problem Diagnosis in SPI

Jakob Iversen, Peter Axel Nielsen,
and Jacob Nørbjerg

To launch a focused SPI project, you must first understand your organization's current situation and most troublesome problems and then identify the areas that most profoundly need improvement. Typically, organizations obtain this understanding by assessing their maturity using a normative maturity model such as CMM or Bootstrap. They subsequently perform assessments at regular intervals to drive their SPI projects forward.

However, this traditional assessment approach can be inadequate for several reasons. First, because formal assessments are based on a maturity model, they are unlikely to identify problems that the model fails to cover. Second, formal assessments are relatively expensive. For example, using the CMM-Based Appraisal for Internal Process Improvement (CBA IPI) to assess four representative projects and interview 40 function-area representatives requires an estimated 200 person-days of effort (Dunaway and Masters 1996). Third, traditional assessments might not adequately address key stakeholders' opinions and beliefs about what constitutes good software practice.

We have developed and tested the *problem diagnosis method*, a new type of assessment that alleviates some of the problems with maturity-based approaches. Problem diagnosis targets the organization's key actors—the people with the greatest influence on the development process. Without their commitment and involvement, software processes are unlikely to change. Thus, rather than rely on formal maturity models, problem diagnosis elicits and systematizes the problems that key actors perceive in the organization's software process.

We developed the problem diagnosis method as part of Brüel & Kjær's SPI project (see Chapter 6). Brüel & Kjær had performed an assessment six months before our project began but had done nothing with the results and thus had lost commitment for improvement (Iversen et al. 1999). Problem diagnosis helped "revive" the results, renew enthusiasm, and get the organization back on track with its improvement efforts. Our method can also be used for identifying improvement areas that fall outside traditional assessments or in place of such assessments if your organization is skeptical about maturity models.

Maturity Assessments

SPI is strongly associated with maturity assessments, which organizations typically use to drive the change process (Humphrey 1989; McFeeley 1996). The main purpose of maturity assessments is to determine the state of an organization's software development process relative to a maturity model such as CMM. In addition, maturity assessment results often serve as the SPI program's kick-off event, in which management announces the weak processes identified by the assessment and commits its support to the improvement process. The assessment results typically include an outline of an improvement strategy and perhaps even a draft of an improvement plan. Subsequent assessments evaluate SPI progress and focus and revitalize the effort at regular intervals.

All maturity assessment methods are based on an underlying model of "good" software practice and a model of the improvement process itself (see also Dunaway and Masters 1996, Kuvaja et al. 1994, Rout 1995, Arent and Iversen 1996, and Daskalantonakis 1994). CMM and its derivative models describe five levels of maturity—from the initial, chaotic level 1 to level 5, which is characterized by extensive use of metrics to monitor and improve process and product quality. Each level is described by a set of KPAs, which are further described by goals and key practices; an organization that fulfills all goals at a certain level and those below is said to be at that level.

Maturity models also provide a roadmap for the improvement process, recommending that organizations ascend from one well-defined level to the next. Thus, an organization at level 1 would address level 2 issues before adopting more advanced practices belonging to higher levels.

Maturity models and their associated assessment methods have the potential to be supportive of the assessment and improvement processes. The organization is evaluated against known and stable criteria, and the levels provide a framework to prioritize improvements. Assessment can thus be carried out systematically, ensuring the reliability of findings.

However, maturity models and assessment methods are not lacking in critics, particularly in relation to validity and reliability. Some argue that the models' underlying assumptions about software processes and software producing organizations might not be applicable in all cases (Bollinger and McGowan 1991, Mathiassen and Sørensen 1996). Such criticisms might be particularly true for CMM because it was developed in close cooperation with large American software organizations (Bollinger and McGowan 1991, Pries-Heje and Baskerville 1998).

9.1 THE PROBLEM DIAGNOSIS METHOD

The problem diagnosis method helps you gather detailed information about how key actors in your organization perceive software process practices, problems, and solutions. Using our method, you first collect the information by interviewing key actors. You then systematize and synthesize the interview results into a diagnosis of your organization's software problems and a strategy for solving them. Next, you meet with key actors to discuss the diagnosis and strategy. The goal is to get key actors to agree on a solution that they believe will solve the problems they perceive.

The problem diagnosis method consists of seven steps:

1. Define your scope.
2. Prepare for interviews.
3. Organize interviews.
4. Conduct interviews.
5. Analyze immediate results.
6. Synthesize problems.
7. Offer feedback and obtain validation.

Step 1: Define Your Scope

The first step in problem diagnosis is to define your scope: Which part of the organization will you cover? Who are the key actors? How can you get them involved?

For your problem diagnosis to succeed, you must include influential individuals. Your target actors should include people with formal authority and those whose authority is based on expertise or the respect of their peers. It is important to include people with formal power in the organization because collectively they determine whether change efforts of any sort succeed or fail; this is particularly true of SPI. In some cases, key actors are easy to identify. For example, a typical group might include a project manager, a software developer from Project XYZ, and a middle manager or senior manager. In other cases, the key actors are less obvious and you'll need to analyze the organization and its power structure to find them.

After you have identified the key actors, you must decide how to involve them. Most of them will participate in the interviews (step 4) and the validation (step 7). However, you might also want to include some of them in the interpretation of the interviews (steps 5 and 6).

Senior managers are particularly interesting key actors and should play a special role in the diagnosis—at least during feedback and validation (step 7). Involving them in this process helps them understand both software practice and SPI efforts. Their involvement in problem diagnosis can have significant impact on subsequent improvement efforts.

Finally, before you begin, you must understand your organization's rationale both for the SPI effort in general and for the problem diagnosis in particular. If the SPI project does not yet have an explicitly stated purpose, this is a good time to formulate one. A defined purpose is important to helping you to properly prepare for the interviews.

Step 2: Prepare for Interviews

Before you hold the interviews, you must produce an interview guide and ensure that your interviewers are well prepared.

The interview guide leads interviewers through the interview and ensures that they cover all relevant issues. In our experience, precisely worded questions can help interviewers understand the goal of the question, but interviewers don't need to use the exact wording during interviews. They should feel free to modify the questions and ask follow-up questions, depending on how each interview goes.

Interview guides can take many forms to suit the content and the SPI group's style. Patton's work (1990) inspired us in this regard. Regardless of the form you choose, your guide should contain questions in two categories that reflect the goals of problem diagnosis:

◆ Questions about a specific project: These questions yield a rich picture of software practices and problems. They aim to elicit details and experiences rather than only opinion.

◆ General questions about strengths and weaknesses in the organization's software processes: These questions help you identify other issues that the interviewee finds relevant and important.

Following is a generic checklist for an interview guide aimed at project managers. Such a guide should include the following:

◆ A description of a specific software development project
◆ Critical events and problems in the project
◆ Software processes and associated problems and suggestions
◆ Strengths and weaknesses in the organization's software processes
◆ Validation of previous assessment results

To tailor the generic guide to your specific purposes, follow these steps:

1. Develop a preliminary interview guide as a list of cues and topics.
2. Conduct a pilot interview. During the pilot interview, the interviewer and observers should systematically note strengths and weaknesses in how the interview progresses.
3. Develop a final interview guide based on the pilot interview. The final interview guide should include
   - Complete phrasing of questions
   - An introduction that explains the purpose of the interview
   - As final section that leaves room for the interviewee to offer his or her impression of the interview and any thoughts on topics not covered

To prepare the interviewers, you can hold formal SPI group training sessions or let interviewers prepare on their own by studying and practicing interviewing skills. In either case, we recommend Patton's book as a resource. Although knowledge about the topic is important, the most important trait in a good interviewer is the ability to listen and a willingness to ask questions, whether they be pleasant, critical, curious, or even "stupid."

Step 3: Organize Interviews

After you have prepared for the interviews, you're ready to allocate roles and produce a timetable for the diagnosis.

We recommend that you use two interviewers, who alternate between acting as primary interviewer and supporting interviewer. Also, you might consider choosing one interviewer from inside the organization or target unit and one from the outside. Your inside interviewer might be a project manager, a middle manager, someone from the QA department, or anyone else with useful and detailed knowledge about the organization. The "insider" is typically good at understanding and following up on complex issues but might be biased. The outside interviewer is typically less biased and might come from a different part of the company or from an outside consultancy or research organization.

Aside from the two interviewers, you should assign at least one person to take notes and transcribe the interview (the results of which are important input to the analysis and synthesis, steps 5 and 6). Others present at the interview (such as other

SPI group members) should act primarily as observers, although you might let them ask follow-up questions.

SPI group members are responsible for results analysis (step 5) and problem synthesis (step 6), although they might also play a key part in implementing improvements. The whole group should therefore be present at the interviews as either formal interviewers, observers, or transcribers. You can distribute the interviews among the SPI group members, but no matter who conducts the interviews, the notes must be transcribed immediately to prepare for analysis (step 5).

It is important to plan each interview, specifying whom to interview and which SPI group members will play which roles. You should also plan when to meet for immediate analysis, problem synthesis, and validation. An interview and follow-up typically take two to three hours.

Step 4: Conduct Interviews

In each interview, the interviewers are responsible for completely covering all the topics in the interview guide, although the question sequence and depth may vary. The interviewers should be aware of why they are conducting interviews: to gain an understanding of the strengths and weaknesses of the organization's software processes. With this understanding, the SPI team members can later frame problems in a way that helps the key actors to realize alternative ways of doing things, something that helps to create a commitment to change.

During interviews, observers should be somehow separated from the process, either sitting in the back of the room or at a separate table. This arrangement helps to avoid crowding the interviewee and also creates a relaxed, informal atmosphere.

Step 5: Analyze Immediate Results

Immediately after each interview, the interviewers and observers discuss their initial observations and reactions to the interview. This analysis evaluates

- The interview: For example, was too much time spent on some questions at the expense of others?
- The interview results: Did interesting problems or solutions surface?

Your analysis should also include any issues that need further discussion, such as topics that emerged that were not included in the guide or were not explored in enough depth. You should include the results from this analysis as a separate section in the interview minutes. You can then use them to prepare for subsequent interviews and the final problem synthesis.

Step 6: Synthesize Problems

When all the interviews are complete, the SPI group synthesizes the findings to create a common understanding of the problems, issues, and opportunities in the organization's software processes. The problem synthesis is a two-step process. First, each member of the SPI group uses the interview minutes and his or her notes to prepare a list of four or five significant problems identified in each interview. The SPI group then meets and discusses the individual lists. The goal of this discussion is to produce a common understanding within the group of the major problems raised in each interview. If the group cannot reach this understanding through an open discussion, you can use more formalized techniques such as voting.

Next, group members again review notes from each interview, this time creating a list of strengths and weaknesses in the organization's software process. This list is informed both by the group members' general understanding and the previously created problem lists.

Based on these analyses, you create a synthesis report that documents what you learned in the interviews and your recommended improvements. You then distribute this report to the interviewees, senior management, and other stakeholders in the diagnosis and SPI processes.

Step 7: Offer Feedback and Obtain Validation

Problem diagnosis concludes with a meeting between the SPI group, interviewees, senior management, and other stakeholders. The meeting's purpose is to provide feedback to the organization—and, in particular, to interviewees—and to get everyone involved in validating the findings.

We recommend that you structure the concluding meeting as a workshop, in which smaller groups discuss the findings and proposed improvements. The goal is to get each participant to commit to actively assisting with improvements in one or more areas.

Your workshop might be organized as follows:

- The opening, which includes introduction of participants and the workshop's purpose
- A plenary (whole group) presentation of your main results
- Break-out sessions, in which smaller groups discuss the results' validity and negotiate individual commitments to improvement actions
- A plenary discussion of the organizational and individual commitments to improvement actions

9.2 USING PROBLEM DIAGNOSIS

We developed the problem diagnosis technique during Brüel & Kjær's SPI project. Six months before the SPI project, Brüel & Kjær had carried out a Bootstrap assessment but had yet to act on the results. Also, our SPI group included several outside researchers and consultants who knew nothing about the organization's software processes (see Chapter 6). Our SPI group therefore faced three challenges:

- To obtain current and valid information about software processes and problems
- To recreate motivation and enthusiasm for process improvements
- To get commitment to the effort from the company's powerful project managers, whose support was essential to success

After developing an interview guide (see Figure 9.1), we interviewed seven project managers. We audiotaped the interviews and took detailed notes. We then presented the interview minutes to the interviewees for comments and immediate feedback.

Through problem synthesis, we came up with a list of six improvement areas. A seventh area—software reuse—was added at the request of internal SPI group members, although it was not identified in the interviews per se. The seven areas are

- Descriptive process model
- Risk management
- Experiments with prototypes
- Software requirements specification and requirements management
- Project tracking and control
- Project conclusion
- Software reuse

We then held a workshop to present our results to the interviewed project managers and the company's technical director. At the start of the workshop, one of the external SPI group members presented the synthesis report. After a short discussion of the identified problems, participants broke into three working groups to discuss why these were problems, what could be done about them, and who was interested in working on solutions. By the end of the workshop, six of the seven project managers had committed to improving their practice in one of the problem areas. The technical director also announced that he would personally take responsibility for the project tracking and control area because he had already invested in a new project-management tool for Brüel & Kjær.

---

1. The software development project

Can you tell us, in your own words, about the project you are currently running?

(The following questions ensure coverage of several areas; use them only when project managers do not cover them in their response to the question above.)

- What is the purpose of the project? What is the proposed functionality of the software?
- How large is the project (budget, resources, calendar time, product size, etc.)? How is the project staffed (number of people, qualifications, etc.)? How is the project organized?
- What conditions is the project subject to (deadlines, marketing, agreements with management, contracts, etc.)?
- What is the planned chronological course of the project? Are there phases, iterations etc.? Any delays so far? When? Why?

---

2. Key events in the project

What critical events (both positive and negative) have had a major impact on the project so far?

- What happened? What were the consequences? How might they have been avoided or further exploited?

---

3. Strengths and weaknesses in the development process

What do you think are the most prominent strengths and weaknesses in the way that your company develops software?

Figure 9.1 *Excerpts from Brüel & Kjær's Interview Guide*

Our workshop discussions confirmed that the project managers viewed the problems we identified as both important and relevant. There was, however, some debate over software reuse. None of the project managers saw the lack of reuse as a significant problem. Most viewed it as something that they knew was important and something that would be "nice to have"; everyone knew that management wanted it. Given this, it was accepted as a problem area, but never on equal terms with the other six areas.

9.3 DISCUSSION

Based on several observations, we have concluded that our problem diagnosis method was useful at Brüel & Kjær. First, at the workshop, project managers expressed surprisingly strong commitment to improving the problem areas. We are confident that we could not have achieved this level of commitment without listening carefully to what they perceived as the relevant issues and problems. Second, project managers were the key actors at Brüel & Kjær; without their support, we would have encountered considerable resistance to change. Third, before the workshop, the technical director was unaware of the problems raised. Finally, using this method helped us gain a thorough understanding of software practices and problems that would help us implement improvements.

Our experiences also gave rise to further observations about how the problem diagnosis method relates to other assessment methods, and how and when our method might be applied.

Is Problem Diagnosis Better Than Model-Based Assessments?

The goal of an assessment is to help practitioners collect valid information about current software practices and problems so that they can use this information to produce recommendations for future improvement initiatives.

Table 9.1 compares recommendations from our problem diagnosis with those of the previous Bootstrap assessment. The two assessments produced corresponding results. The differences are in grouping and level of detail: The Bootstrap recommendations address general areas, whereas our problem diagnosis findings are more specific. For example, whereas Bootstrap identified the general improvement area

Table 9.1 *Recommendations from Problem Diagnosis and Bootstrap Assessment*

Problem Diagnosis	Bootstrap Assessment
• Descriptive process model	• Software development model
• Risk management	• Software processes
• Experiments with prototypes	• Requirements specification
• Software requirements specification and requirements management	• Project management
• Project tracking and control	• Module and integration testing
• Project conclusion	• Configuration management
• Software reuse	

"software process model," our method offered the more specific issues "descriptive process model," "risk management," and "experiments with prototypes." Similarly, our method's recommendation "project conclusion" addresses particular "configuration management" and "testing" issues during the final stages of the project.

Even more interesting, however, is how SPI practitioners can use the information gathered through the assessments to support actual improvements. Our method gave the SPI group a deep and rich understanding of how key organizational actors perceive software process practices and problems, and this understanding provided a valid and useful foundation for subsequent improvement efforts.

The interviews gave SPI group members insight into the software processes as well as exposed us to the project managers' practices, anecdotes, and jargon. This exchange of information revealed problems and helped us better understand the problems and the proposed solutions. Given this information, we were able to point to solutions and implementation strategies that were acceptable to the project managers.

However, we also relied on traditional maturity models at times. They inspired us in producing the interview guide and helped us to identify and structure the problems we uncovered in interviews. Nonetheless, we believe that an SPI group should attempt to frame problems and recommendations in ways that organizational actors recognize and identify with. This approach increases the likelihood that the actors will accept and commit to SPI. In essence, our problem diagnosis method considers the interviewees' viewpoints and suggestions to be more important than abstract model categories.

When Should You Use Problem Diagnosis?

Problem diagnosis is most useful when the success of your SPI effort rests on the involvement and commitment of project managers or other key software professionals. Identifying these key actors is an important part of the method. At Brüel & Kjær, the project managers were obviously both powerful and crucial for SPI success, but in other settings the key actors might not be so obvious. If that is the case, you must analyze your organization and its formal and informal power structures to determine the key actors. If this is not immediately possible, your best move is to expand the scope of your diagnosis so that you can interview more organizational actors.

Who Should Perform Problem Diagnosis?

Knowledge of software practices and the problems revealed by the problem diagnosis is an important asset in subsequent improvement initiatives. Thus, the people performing the problem diagnosis should be the same people who are directly responsible for the improvement projects. In our case, this was the SPI group.

Our method also requires that you have specific skills. First, you must have substantial knowledge of software engineering in general and SPI in particular. You need this knowledge to prepare the interview guide, to meaningfully synthesize interview results, and to suggest solutions. If you aren't familiar with many alternative software development models, it is difficult to suggest a useful model in a given situation.

Second, problem diagnosis requires that you use skilled interviewers, that they have a well-structured interview guide, and that you have plans for and commitments to processing and interpreting interview data.

How Should You Prioritize Findings?

Our technique contains no inherent mechanism to prioritize findings or resolve conflicting views on the software process. If your interviewees are a fairly homogenous group—like the project managers at Brüel & Kjær—it might not be a problem. However, in other cases, conflicting views or pressure from management or other parts of the organization can make it more or less impossible for you to choose and prioritize an acceptable set of recommendations. In such cases, your SPI group can use our technique to identify the conflicting issues and then leave it to the organizational actors themselves to find resolutions.

What Organizational Resources Does Problem Diagnosis Require?

Problem diagnosis requires relatively few resources: Only one person is interviewed at a time, and you can get by with two or three people to interview and take notes. However, as we noted, we recommend that the entire SPI group be present to ensure maximum sharing of information. To save resources, you can conduct interviews over several months, a technique that exacts far less organizational strain than the relatively intense and time-consuming Bootstrap or CMM-based assessments. However, this low impact is also a potential pitfall: It could render the entire SPI project invisible. Thus, you might want to plan other activities to keep your project and its progress visible during a prolonged interview process.

9.4 SUMMARY AND CONCLUSION

Problem diagnosis aims to assist SPI groups in identifying software problems and solutions based on the opinions and insights of key organizational actors. Having successfully applied the method, we subsequently launched several improvement projects at Brüel & Kjær. Wider application is now needed to further validate and refine the problem diagnosis method.

Based on our experiences thus far, we believe that problem diagnosis is particularly useful when an SPI project's success depends on the support of powerful actors, or when a stalled SPI project needs to be revived without too much effort and strain. Both conditions are fairly common.

However, problem diagnosis is not an easy or straightforward technique. As with any SPI initiative, using it requires careful planning and preparation, and you must first select and train the appropriate personnel.

Finally, problem diagnosis does not necessarily preclude more traditional model-based assessments, but we are not yet clear on how our method precisely relates to such assessments. Our experiences indicate that the two approaches can supplement each other, but we must conduct further research, of a more theoretical nature, to determine how and when they might best support each other.

9.5 REFERENCES

Arent, J., and J. Iversen. 1996. *Development of a Method for Maturity Assessments in Software Organizations Based on the Capability Maturity Model* (in Danish). Master's Thesis. Aalborg University.

Bollinger, T.B., and C. McGowan. 1991. "A Critical Look at Software Capability Evaluations." *IEEE Software.* 8:4:25–41.

Daskalantonakis, M.K. 1994. "Achieving Higher SEI Levels." *IEEE Software* 11:4:17–24.

Dunaway, D.K., and S. Masters. 1996. *CMM-Based Appraisal for Internal Process Improvement (CBA IPI): Method Description.* Tech. Report CMU/SEI-96-TR-007. Pittsburgh: Software Engineering Institute.

Humphrey, W.S. 1989. *Managing the Software Process.* Reading, MA: Addison-Wesley.

Iversen, J. H., P. A. Nielsen, and J. Nørbjerg. 1999. "Problem Diagnosis in Software Process Improvement." *The DATABASE for Advances in Information Systems.* 30:2:66–81.

Kuvaja, P. et al. 1994. *Software Process Assessment and Improvement: The BOOTSTRAP Approach.* Oxford, UK: Blackwell Publishers.

Mathiassen, L., and C. Sørensen. 1996. "The Capability Maturity Model and CASE." *Information Systems Journal.* 6:195–208.

McFeeley, B. 1996. *IDEAL: A User's Guide for Software Process Improvement.* Tech Report CMU/SEI-96-HB-001. Pittsburgh: Software Engineering Institute.

Patton, M. Q. 1990. *Qualitative Evaluation and Research Methods.* London: Sage Publications.

Pries-Heje, J., and R. Baskerville. 1998. "Managing Knowledge Capability and Maturity." T. J. Larsen and J. L. DeGross, eds. *Information Systems: Current Issues and Future Changes,* pp. 175–196. Norwell, MA: Kluwer Academic Publishers.

Rout, T.P. 1995. "SPICE: A Framework for Software Process Assessment." *Software Process—Improvement and Practice.* 1:57–66.

Chapter 10

Project Assessments

Carsten V. Andersen, Jesper Arent, Stig Bang,
and Jakob Iversen

Standard maturity assessments play an important role in improvement efforts. An organization often uses them to initiate SPI efforts, and their results typically form the foundation of an organization's understanding of its current software development situation. Also, such assessments are typically performed at regular intervals to check the progress of overall improvement efforts. They can drive the improvement process forward, rate the organization's maturity relative to a maturity model, indicate which processes need improvement, and motivate and commit people to the SPI effort.

However, standard maturity assessments require substantial effort, both within the organization and on the part of assessors who typically help perform them. Thus, it is impractical to use such assessment to regularly check the progress of projects themselves. What is needed instead are methods that are far easier, can be conducted by project staff with minimal support, and can provide immediate feedback.

To this end, we developed a group of assessment techniques for use on individual software development projects. These assessments help determine a project's maturity relative to a maturity model and show which areas need improvement. They also provide feedback on progress and help participants reflect on and incrementally improve their practices.

Maturity Assessment Methods

The project assessment techniques we present in this chapter are among several maturity-model-based techniques. Others are described in the literature. For example, Synquest (www.synspace.com) is a computer-based tool that lets practitioners evaluate practices against both ISO 9001 and SPICE (Steinmann 1996). The tool is a questionnaire containing 37 questions relating to different processes. Members of the development group respond to each question by rating their processes according to eight attributes: existence, documented, inspected, recordings, responsibility, training, usability, and stability. The results are displayed graphically in several ways.

Another example is Motorola's Progress Assessment (Daskalantonakis 1994), which is based on CMM level 2 and was originally used to drive the company's cellular infrastructure group to level 2. Like Synquest, Motorola's method includes a group session in which representatives from the entire development organization agree on ratings for all CMM key practices. However, in this case, the assessment is also facilitated and supported by an assessment champion. The assessment instrument is a table in which all the CMM key practices can be evaluated from 0 to 10. The assessment is conducted quarterly to help participants track their progress.

Progress assessment is also the basis for many other methods, including the CMM Light Assessment used at Ericsson Denmark (see Chapter 3). Although such methods differ from our own, they all focus on individual projects and thus many of our conclusions here may have relevance for alternative techniques.

Here, we illustrate how project assessments can support an SPI effort by describing how two organizations developed and used their own methods for assessing individual SPI projects. In the first case, the main reason that Ericsson Denmark introduced project assessments was to quickly move projects to CMM level 2. In the second case, Danske Data used project assessments as part of a long-term improvement effort. The goal of this effort was to establish a grassroots movement aimed at getting project managers to take responsibility for their own learning and professionalization.

Based on these cases, we discuss three recommendations for using project assessments to facilitate and support improvement efforts on the project and organization level. Our recommendations can also be used by SPI practitioners to guide the implementation of similar approaches.

10.1 CASE 1: ERICSSON DENMARK

Ericsson Denmark has been developing software for almost two decades and has participated in Ericsson's corporate SPI program since 1993. Ericsson Denmark's first

CMM assessment was conducted in 1995 and rated the company at level 1. Before the assessment, there was no focus on improving the CMM level; the assessment was intended to kick off a new focus on CMM level 2 KPAs.

Although it was not formally stated, the corporate SPI program put a lot of pressure on Ericsson Denmark to reach CMM level 2 by the next CMM assessment, which was scheduled for 1997. However, when the time arrived for the second assessment, the CMM activities had shown little progress. Ericsson Denmark thus postponed the CMM assessment until 1998, and we went to work implementing CMM level 2 KPAs in projects. However, to improve the state of practice at Ericsson Denmark, we needed a new approach.

The Challenge

Although the contents of CMM level 2 are not beyond the typical level of Ericsson's policies, processes, and procedures, CMM does include significant new terminology. Earlier attempts at implementing CMM level 2 at Ericsson Denmark had been unsuccessful because project managers viewed CMM as too theoretical, and they didn't feel they had time for improvement—a typical attitude in low-maturity organizations. The problem was that the project managers couldn't get a feel for CMM until they had actually tried to *use* it, and they didn't use it because they didn't have a feel for it. It was a vicious circle, making it difficult for the company to succeed with a CMM project.

Another problem was with our initial improvement approach. We put a lot of effort into working groups aimed at defining KPA procedures for the projects. But the results of the working groups were sometimes so generic that project practitioners had to put a great deal of extra effort into tailoring a practical routine for actual use. Because practitioners were not given sufficient support for such efforts, they could easily claim that they were unable to live up to CMM level 2 as required.

The third problem was that, despite their commitment to SPI, management had very little expertise and insight into the CMM implementation's progress and therefore couldn't take the appropriate actions. For management commitment to be effective, management needed measurements to stay informed.

Experiences from other Ericsson companies indicated that regular use of CMM UltraLight Assessments (ULAs) could address Ericsson Denmark's problems and thus speed up the implementation process. ULAs are a simple self-assessment tool that lets projects rate their implementation of and compliance with each CMM level 2 KPA (see Figure 10.1). Faced with pressure to quickly reach CMM level 2, senior management demanded that every project perform monthly ULAs and report the results to the steering committee.

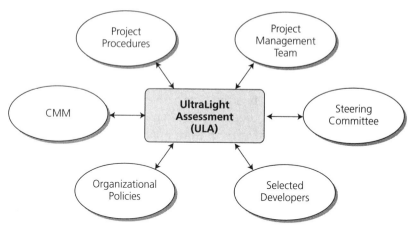

Figure 10.1 *The UltraLight Assessment process*

Results

Our experience with ULAs, both as a means of creating an awareness of CMM and a tool for implementing level 2 practices, has been very positive. Compared with previous approaches, it felt like a turbocharged implementation of CMM.

CMM UltraLight Assessments

Unlike other assessments at Ericsson Denmark, which typically are performed by CMM experts, the ULAs are performed by practitioners—usually the project management team. In our early ULAs, experts helped project teams with CMM terminology, but gradually the teams performed the assessments without extra help.

The ULA consists of a document that lists and describes all CMM level 2 key practices in separate boxes. The project team writes its own *compliance statements* below the CMM text in a color that matches its degree of compliance:

- Green: The key practice is in place and working or planned (includes reference).
- Blue: Minor things are missing, or status is uncertain.
- Red: The key practice is not in place.

Project members should make their compliance statements as concrete and precise as possible, stating the names of the people responsible for the KPA and the procedures needed to fulfill it.

Gradually, as the document is completed and more text is entered in green, the time it takes to perform the assessment decreases. Results are reported to management using a spreadsheet that summarizes the number of red, blue, and green statements.

Table 10.1 shows a sample compliance statement, and Figure 10.2 shows a sample spreadsheet.

One of the ULA's key benefits is that its results provide a quantitative and visual indication of the status of each project, each KPA, and—when aggregated—each department, as well as the company as a whole. Also, the simple color-coding scheme makes it easy to spot weak areas in the CMM implementation.

In our project, such visibility also made it easy for management to pinpoint problems, set goals such as "75% green" at a certain milestone, and easily track progress toward them. The simple reporting format helped management focus the effort and show active commitment to it without requiring deep insight into the details of CMM.

Our project managers also liked the pragmatic approach to CMM and (eventually) viewed the ULA document as a useful source of project information. Many projects printed large-scale versions of the ULA document and posted it outside the project manager's office. It thus served as a way to capture and communicate important project decisions, responsibilities, and standards to project staff, supplementing information from Web pages and minutes from project meetings.

Because the ULA document is structured according to the CMM model and was familiar to all projects, the public posting of results served as a best-practice mapping for the entire organization. For example, if a project manager had specific problems in requirements management, activity 3 (changes to the allocated requirements are reviewed and incorporated into the project), he or she could find inspiration for solving the problems by looking at how other project managers had implemented that key practice.

Project managers soon realized that it was important to "think CMM" from the beginning of a project if they were to achieve management's CMM implementation

Table 10.1 *Sample ULA Questions (CMM Key Practices in Italics)*

RM 1 For each project, responsibility is established for analyzing the system requirements and allocating them to HW, SW, and other system components.	*SPP 1 A documented and approved statement of work exists for the SW project.*	*SPT&O 1 An SW development plan for the SW project is documented and approved.*
The Technical Coordinator N.N. is responsible for analyzing requirements and writing the Implementation Proposal (green).	The Assignment Specification (FCPD 123 4321) has been written, but awaits approval (blue).	The Project Specification is on its way, but major parts have yet to be written due to lack of estimates (red).

	Red	Red%	Blue	Blue%	Green	Green%	
	Not implemented		Partly implemented/Don't know		Implemented		Check
RM	3	19%	8	50%	5	31%	100%
SPP	5	19%	10	38%	11	42%	100%
SPT&O	0	0%	2	67%	1	33%	100%
SSM	2	20%	1	10%	7	70%	100%
SQA	3	17%	5	28%	10	56%	100%
SCM	0	0%	5	45%	6	55%	100%
	13	15%	31	37%	40	48%	

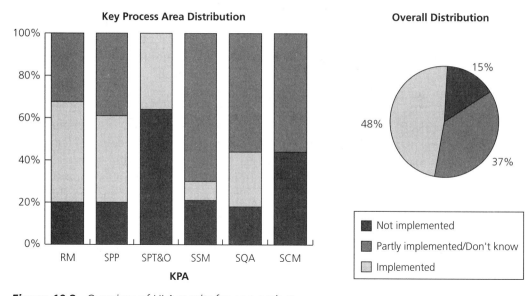

Figure 10.2   *Overview of ULA results for one project*

goals. For example, if a project manager hadn't recorded his or her planning data during project planning, the box for project planning, activity 15 (requesting the recording of project planning data) would stay red for the rest of that project. This created some frustration when the ULA technique was introduced because established projects could not get satisfactory levels of green in some key practices, no matter how hard they tried to satisfy CMM level 2.

Ultimately, the use of ULAs and strong management follow-up resulted in our achieving CMM level 2, which was verified by the formal CMM assessment in 1998.

Analysis

Today, the use of ULAs is a routine part of all Ericsson Denmark projects, although their use is less intensive than it was before the 1998 CMM assessment. Not only were ULAs a key component in our success in achieving CMM level 2, but also they are now recognized by project managers as a useful tool for implementing and maintaining project processes. Relying mostly on the participation of practitioners, the ULAs have created a common understanding of CMM across the organization rather than only among a few CMM specialists.

Because CMM level 2 represents the threshold of maturity (as defined in the CMM), it also represents a big mental barrier for the organization. However, ULAs have proven to be a good technique to break the "level 2 barrier" in that they involve both practitioners and managers in identifying, mapping, and developing practical, daily routines based on the CMM while also helping them solve real problems in projects and the organization. Before we used the UCLs, we introduced generic procedures to satisfy the CMM and then we tailored them to a project's specific problems to satisfy the business. Such an approach is a tempting but unfortunate choice in a level 1 organization, especially if the organization actually expects better business results from maturity and not just the status of CMM level 2.

However, ULAs are less beneficial when organizations are striving for level 3. CMM level 2 alone consists of 121 key practices, each represented by a box that project staff must fill out. If the ULA document were expanded to include level 3 key practices, the sheer number of boxes would be cumbersome. Furthermore, many of the level 3 key practices focus on organizational issues that must be addressed above the project level. Positive experiences with ULA techniques have nevertheless inspired some Ericsson Denmark project teams to continue using ULAs with the applicable level 3 key practices.

10.2 CASE 2: DANSKE DATA

In May 1997, Danske Data conducted a combined CMM–Bootstrap assessment. The assessment resulted in a list of seven improvement areas for the company, including *strengthen project management*. In their recommendation, the assessors argued that "project management at Danske Data lacks formal control" and that "management rests primarily on the experience of the individual project manager."

To address this improvement area, the SPI group established the Project Management Competence Center at Danske Data (see Chapter 5, The Grassroots Effort). The cornerstone of the PMC Center was the Danske Data Standard for Professional Project Management, which sets the standard for good, competent project management within the company.

The idea was new to Danske Data. Instead of developing a set of standards and mandating that it be strictly followed, we wanted to inspire managers with a visionary standard that they might strive to reach. Consequently, it was important for us that project managers be able to assess and compare themselves to the standard and in this way identify and prioritize areas in which they felt a need to improve. We also wanted the assessment tool to be available over the company's intranet and for all project managers to use it to assess themselves at the end of each project. Our overall goal was for the project managers to take responsibility for their own development. Our improvement effort was aimed at the grass roots.

The Challenge

Before presenting our idea to the organization, we wanted key people to commit to the concept. We invited representatives from both senior project management and project management from all parts of the organization to participate in a workshop to discuss and decide on basic principles. In this workshop, it was decided that project managers alone would be responsible for conducting project assessments, although other project participants could be involved in completing the questionnaire.

We now faced a dilemma. We wanted project managers to assess themselves regularly, but—in keeping with our grassroots vision—we also wanted such assessments to be voluntary. Thus, being unwilling to mandate project assessments, our challenge was in how to get project managers to conduct self-assessments as a routine part of completing a project.

Developing and Implementing Project Assessments

Developing the project-assessment questionnaire gave us a unique opportunity to create coherence between the vision of Danske Data's standard and that of the best practices embedded in the company's development model. To ensure this coherence, we submitted the questionnaire to members of the methodology department and the PMC Center.

As Chapter 5 describes, using CMM as inspiration in developing the standard enabled us to reuse and extend the CMM questionnaire that was used in the overall company assessment.

Developing a project-assessment tool gave the methodology department an opportunity to compare the level of project management at Danske Data with the new standard's expectations. We thus decided to store data from project assessments in a central database. Authorized staff from the methodology department can access the database and analyze data by differentiating on such parameters as time, product type, and the project manager's experience, educational background, and location in the company. Other parameters include the individual questions, goals, and KPAs. Each project manager can view only his or her own score and the average of all project managers.

To encourage diffusion and adoption of the tool, we held an implementation workshop (see Chapter 15). In the workshop, representatives of project management from throughout Danske Data reviewed the questionnaire and tested the assessment tool.

We also decided to use project managers as ambassadors in diffusing the project assessments. To do this, we used a stepwise approach. Before its launch, the project-assessment approach was included in Danske Data's project-manager education (described in Chapter 5). Project managers use the assessment to prepare themselves for the education program, which also includes a lesson on project assessments.

Results

During 1999, the project assessment was introduced to 48 project managers as part of the project-manager education program. Their reaction has been positive. On a scale of 1 to 6, with 6 as maximum score, they gave our project assessment method a 5. Among the comments we received as part of the education evaluation were that the assessment tool was "exciting" and made them, as one manager put it, "attentive towards deficiencies" in their management practice.

In October 1999, Danske Data held a formal Bootstrap assessment. The maturity assessment was supplemented with results from project assessments performed by project managers who had completed the education program. The results of the project assessments were consistent with those of the Bootstrap assessments. The methodology department regarded this as a validation of our project assessment, and that has increased confidence in our approach.

In 2000, we introduced the project assessments tool to all project managers in the organization.

Analysis

Through its questionnaire, the project assessment concretizes the Danske Data standard for professional project management. Assessing projects helps project managers to understand the standard and how to meet its expectations. This enhanced understanding, in turn, helps project managers develop informed opinions about the standard.

The project assessment is also a sales window for Danske Data's development model. Assessing projects helps project managers to identify and prioritize areas for improvement. The assessment tool also allows direct online access to development model guidelines and instructions that can help project managers to better meet the requirements of each of the standard's KPAs.

Finally, project assessments support the company's SPI initiative. The assessment tool gives the methodology department access to project assessment data that helps them monitor and analyze SPI development and prioritize and focus SPI initiatives. However, as we discussed earlier, deriving such benefits requires that project managers adopt our vision. Unless most project managers assess their projects, Danske Data will not experience these benefits.

The fact that project managers *appreciate* the project assessment concept does not automatically imply that they will assess their projects regularly. For example, only a few of the project managers who have completed the education program have voluntarily conducted a second assessment. In fact, it might prove impossible to get people to assess themselves voluntarily—no one enjoys being examined. It might be that top management will have to mandate project assessments. Or it might be that Danske Data is simply not mature enough for a voluntary program of this sort. At the end of 2000, we will be in a better position to conclude whether we have chosen the right strategy for implementing project assessments at Danske Data.

Project Assessment in Action

Danske Data's project assessment approach differs from other model-based assessments in that it is based on a model developed especially for the company. Projects are assessed based on a questionnaire that makes the standard's goals concrete in 10 KPAs. The questionnaire comprises 130 questions, each phrased as two scenarios describing the best and worst practice, respectively, on a bipolar scale. Figure 10.3 gives an overview of Danske Data's project assessments process.

The four steps are as follows:

1. Using a Lotus Notes–based tool at their workstations, project managers fill in the questionnaire based on their project experience.

2. The tool has many references and direct links to relevant online guides and instructions that help project managers meet the requirements in each of the 10 KPAs.

3. The tool processes questionnaires electronically and presents the results, which let project managers compare their individual scores with the current level of project management at Danske Data.

4. Data from the project assessment are stored in a central database. Authorized staff in the methodology department can access the database to analyze the data using several different views.

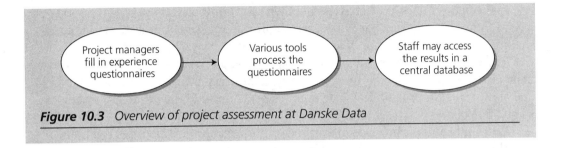

Figure 10.3 *Overview of project assessment at Danske Data*

10.3 SUPPORTING SPI WITH PROJECT ASSESSMENTS

One of the most important reasons to conduct project assessments is to support your organization's SPI effort. The cases of Ericsson Denmark and Danske Data exemplify the challenges of assessing projects. Although the two companies have different cultures, their experiences reveal valuable lessons about the benefits and pitfalls of project assessments.

In the following sections, we discuss three recommendations for using project assessments to support improvement efforts at the project and organization level. Figure 10.4 shows the three primary processes influencing the success of project assessments. The figure also shows how our three recommendations relate to these processes. By using our recommendations to establish your own project assessment initiative, you might avoid some of the difficulties and problems we encountered.

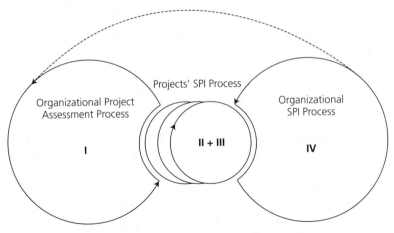

Figure 10.4 *Project assessments support the improvement efforts of projects and the organization*

As the figure shows, project assessment typically is initiated at the organizational level. From the organizational SPI process, a project assessment process is initiated that includes responsibility for defining the vision and approach, planning the initiative, and rolling it out to projects. When the projects start using assessments in their daily practice, the results are used to foster the projects' own improvement efforts and also to support organizationwide improvements through the extraction and dissemination of best practices.

As projects become involved in the process, the organization monitors and evaluates their ongoing efforts continuously or periodically to determine improvements that should be made to the assessment approach. At the same time, any lessons learned from applying project assessments can be collected and aggregated by the organization's SPI process.

Recommendation 1: Establish a Separate Process for Project Assessments

As Figure 10.4 shows, it is important to establish a separate process to explicitly handle all issues related to project assessments. Such a process should include at least six activities.

Establish a Clear Vision or Mission for Project Assessments

As with any initiative that changes the established order, it is important to be clear about the purpose of project assessments. Your vision should clearly and briefly establish the benefits expected for both the projects and the organization. In general, projects can expect to benefit from the best practices that are either embedded in the underlying maturity model or used by other projects in the organization. You should also direct projects toward opportunities for improving their performance and comparing it to other projects. Finally, project managers can use the assessment as an informal evaluation of their project operation. Because implementing project assessments is typically decided at the organizational level whereas its success is inherently linked to widespread adoption by projects, it is crucial to ensure that projects will see concrete benefits. The organization will benefit from project assessments in that best practices in some projects are easily identified and thus can be recommended to other projects. Also, project assessments can give management increased project oversight and give the SPI group greater exposure throughout the organization. Whatever the benefits of your approach, you must be clear about what is expected and how the approach ensures that those expectations will be met.

Use an Accepted Norm, Standard, or Maturity Model as the Basis for Project Assessments

For the project assessment to be on firm ground, its foundation should be well documented. For example, you might choose a maturity model such as CMM as in the Ericsson Denmark case, or a customized model as in the Danske Data case. Other options include ISO 9000, for example, or an organization-specific description of project best practices.

Ensure Support

You should support your approach with both a method and knowledgeable people. To ease its use in projects, your approach should be accompanied by a well-defined method, including all necessary descriptions, manuals, and tools, such as questionnaires, spreadsheets, and so on. You might also establish a hotline where experts can answer practitioner questions about how to apply the approach. The hotline staff can come from people in your organization's SPI group or people from other projects who have experience applying the approach.

Implement Project Assessments in the Projects' Daily Work

To ensure that assessments are actually performed, it is important that they not pose undue requirements on a project team's time. Thus, project assessments must be integrated into project operations, and project managers should have options in terms of how assessments are run.

Evaluate Usage in Projects

To detect early signs of problems with your approach, you should regularly evaluate how projects are applying it. This evaluation could range from a simple count of how many projects are performing assessments and how often, to a review by management or the SPI group to determine how projects are using the assessments, which benefits they're seeing, why some might not be using assessments, and so on.

Improve Your Approach

Based on the evaluation results, it may be necessary to refine your approach. Even if the process has been working well for some time, your organization might mature or develop in other ways that make it necessary to change the project assessment approach. One way to make improvements is to use the five activities shown here as a checklist, see how each is working, and identify problems.

Recommendation 2: Support Dedicated, Project-Specific Improvements

SPI should be evolutionary, focusing on implementing incremental improvements rather than on taking quantum leaps from one state to another and avoiding the often painful learning process and behavior modifications associated with sustainable change. Project assessments provide several opportunities to support an evolutionary and incremental improvement strategy in which improvements are situated in and dedicated to actual software development projects. It also poses a few risks.

Opportunities

First, project assessments support dedicated and tailored improvement initiatives. SPI is a complex and challenging change initiative, and what succeeds in one project might fail in another. Successful SPI can therefore require different change strategies for different projects. By providing opportunities to draw on previous projects' experiences while still recognizing each project's uniqueness, project assessments support projects in establishing their own tailored strategies for improving their processes. At Danske Data, project managers used project assessments as inspiration for improvement strategies in their next project. Each project at Ericsson Denmark established local and dedicated improvement strategies to implement missing practices.

Second, project assessments foster a desire and commitment to improve the practices that need it most. Project assessments encourage software developers to reflect on their own practices and identify opportunities for improvement. Developers are involved in deciding what to improve based on a shared understanding of their current practices, and they themselves decide how to improve their practices, possibly inspired by other good practices and support from the SPI group. This should make project members more committed to change practices. At Ericsson Denmark, for example, the use of project assessments made project managers more committed to CMM and SPI. They realized that CMM was not rocket science but rather reflected common sense that they could use to improve their behavior. At Danske Data, it has yet to be seen whether project assessments will succeed in motivating and sustaining commitment from project managers.

Third, project assessments make improvements part of daily work instead of adding to it. One possible approach to SPI is to create ad hoc improvement teams—often called technical working groups—composed of competent practitioners who develop process specifications for key practices. Ericsson Denmark adopted this approach before project assessments were introduced, but it was difficult to allocate the necessary time and resources to the working groups, and thus improvement tasks were simply added to practitioners' workload. Project assessment changed this approach and focused on integrating improvement into their daily work.

Risks

One possible risk with project assessments is that project managers can become too committed to the recommendations in the underlying model and enforce rule-oriented behavior, failing to tailor the approach to the project's needs and context. At Ericsson Denmark, for example, some projects "chased green percentages" (in part because of management pressure), focusing on what was written on the self-assessment chart rather than on CMM's real intention: continuous improvement.

There is also a risk that some projects won't engage in improvement efforts and thus will slow the organization's overall improvement rate. Some practitioners view process improvement as hindering "real work." The fact that Danske Data's project assessment is voluntary has made implementation difficult and somewhat of a balancing act. We've had to try to convince project managers that assessment is an advantage to them and the entire organization, but without giving them the impression that it was required. Success depends on project managers' acknowledging the value of assessments but also requires that the maturity model actually represent good practice or that it can at least be customized to suit the project. Depending on your organization's culture, you can compensate for these problems by using peer pressure or competition.

Recommendation 3: Support Organizational Improvements

One of the problems in managing an SPI effort is obtaining detailed and accurate information about how widespread the improvement initiative's implementation actually is. Without such information, it becomes difficult to make informed evaluations and decisions about which improvement strategies to choose. Project assessments provide several opportunities for supporting the organizational improvement initiative, along with a few risks.

Opportunities

First, if projects widely adopt assessments, an organization can access information about the relative maturity of projects and thus about which projects have adopted new practices. This type of information is interesting to both the SPI group and management. The SPI group will be able to fine-tune its implementation effort to target only those projects that have not embraced the improvements, whereas management will be able to detect the value of its SPI investments relative to project progress.

Second, the SPI group can use project assessments as input to detect new improvement areas, thus supplementing the formal maturity assessments. At Danske Data, for example, the second Bootstrap assessment in October 1999 was supplemented with additional information, including project assessment findings. The two assessment techniques showed similar results, which gave the organization added confidence that the methods had detected real problems.

Third, organizations can use project assessments as preparation for a formal maturity assessment, serving two specific needs. Project assessments can guide highly focused local improvement efforts to ensure that each project meets the requirements of the company's target maturity model. Ericsson Denmark used this approach to prepare for the formal CMM assessment. Project assessments can also provide management and the SPI group with hints about the organization's current maturity and thus help them to better schedule a formal assessment.

Fourth, management can use project assessments as an information tool to track the progress of projects and individuals. If a project assessment is performed several times during a project, the results will show the project's progress, which can be compared to other projects. Ericsson Denmark did this to some extent when it used project assessment results in the regular project status meetings. Project assessments can also facilitate discussions about personal and career development, such as at Danske Data, where they were used in discussions between project managers and senior managers. Finally, project assessments can be used before the project starts, helping participants agree on the expectations and ambitions.

Fifth, project assessments enable internal benchmarking to identify, share, and disseminate good practices throughout the organization. As more projects use assessments, the common knowledge base of existing practices expands. To identify and transfer good practices, we recommend two approaches. First, when the SPI group participates in project assessments, learning opportunities can emerge. Group members will be able to identify which projects are handling some process particularly well, for example, and study that process in more detail, possibly disseminating it as a best practice throughout the organization. The second approach is the "Wall of Fame." Learning opportunities can emerge when projects make their assessment results available to everyone. At Ericsson Denmark, for example, project managers printed large-scale versions of their assessment results and posted them outside their offices. By making results available, this method lets everyone see the status of projects in process-maturity terms, which acts as a supplement to regular project information. Such public results might also facilitate the transfer of knowledge and experience among projects.

Finally, at Ericsson Denmark, project assessments enforced a common terminology in the organization, making it easier to transfer people and experiences between projects. Danske Data had a similar experience, in which the common frame of reference made it possible for project managers to exchange experiences and discuss the standard across organizational units. The project-manager education program proved to be an excellent forum for this purpose.

Risks

A major risk of project-based SPI is that it can encourage discrete, uncoordinated improvements, resulting in loss of control of the overall SPI initiative. Because the SPI group is responsible for the organizationwide SPI, project assessments might make it difficult to create strategic and tactical SPI plans and develop an organizationwide improvement strategy and schedule.

Also, care must be taken when the results are used for purposes outside the projects themselves. You must ensure that information submitted by project participants as part of a project assessment is not used against them; otherwise, the data will not be trustworthy. A project manager can easily get excellent scores on a questionnaire; it is obvious what the answers *should* be. Also, if project assessment results are primarily used outside the project group, project participants will experience only an added administrative overhead without benefits. This will surely seal the fate of a project assessment program. At Danske Data, the issue of protecting against wrongful use of the data was dealt with explicitly: Only anonymous project assessment results are entered into the company database, which is, in turn, searchable only by SPI group members.

10.4 CONCLUSION

As we have illustrated here, a project-specific assessment approach can situate improvement initiatives in the projects' daily practice and can help projects conduct local improvement efforts. Such an approach has the potential to completely change how an organization conducts SPI.

Our experiences in two companies helped us to identify our recommendations for organizations embarking on their own assessment programs. Those recommendations are to establish a separate process for project assessments; support dedicated, project-specific improvements; and support organizational improvements.

We plan to follow both companies over the next few years to see whether their assessment approaches change and new usage patterns emerge as the companies and their projects face new challenges. Both companies recently completed formal assessments and were rated at level 2. They will thus work on consolidating their level 2 ratings and begin work toward level 3. It will be interesting to follow these ongoing efforts and see whether the project-assessment approaches can support their movement toward higher maturity, where the focus shifts from project-specific improvements to organizationwide improvements.

10.5 REFERENCES

Steinmann, C., and H. Stienen. 1996. "SynQuest—Tool Support for Software Self-Assessment." *Software Process—Improvement and Practice*. 2:1:5–12.

Daskalantonakis, M.K. 1994. "Achieving Higher SEI Levels." *IEEE Software*. 11:4:17–24.

Chapter 11

A Framework for Selecting an Assessment Strategy

Peter Axel Nielsen and Jan Pries-Heje

Assessing your organization's software process before launching an improvement effort is crucial. Without an assessment of some kind, your improvement plan would be at best groundless and ad hoc and at worst counterproductive. Consequently, the SPI field has always focused strongly on assessment models and methods. Some of these models, such as the Software Engineering Institute's CMM, have gained widespread attention. Others, such as the Bootstrap Institute's Bootstrap assessment, include both a model and a method. The need for assessments has also increased the interest in software process measurements, producing something of a renaissance for software metrics research.

Given the many types of assessment, there is a predictable clamor over superiority. Some claim that CMM is better; others champion Bootstrap or other, lesser-known models. In most cases, however, any such sweeping claim is misguided. No one strategy will be best in all situations. Methods and models suit different purposes and have different strengths and weaknesses. Also, organizations typically include more than one assessment method in their overall assessment strategy.

The first step in choosing an assessment strategy is to decide the purpose of your assessment. This is no easy task. Inevitably, you must consider your organization's history, culture, environment, and desire for change as well as its vision for the future. When you reach an understanding of the assessment's purpose, you are halfway to finding your assessment strategy. Your next task is to select your strategy from among the many options, knowing full well that many are largely incompatible.

There are several surveys of SPI assessment strategies. For example, Messnarz (1999) reports on several SPI projects in different organizations that used different software process models in different combinations. Tully and his colleagues (1999) compare and catalog some of the well-known assessment models, examining Bootstrap, CMM, and SPICE in great detail. Their catalog is based on a formalization of six elements: a set of features, a feature scale, a set of conditions, a condition scale, an assessment result, and supplementary information. CMM's catalog entry, for example, lists the KPAs and the practices within each of them. Although such a catalog is informative, it does not provide the information you need to select an assessment strategy.

We have developed a framework to help organizations make sense of different assessment strategies, models, and methods and link them to their particular assessment goals. Our framework distinguishes between three significant dimensions: rigor versus relevance, model-driven versus problem-driven, and intervention versus day-to-day management. These dimensions form eight possible categories that can help you examine your organization's needs and then select an appropriate assessment strategy in an informed and systematic way.

We developed this framework based on three years' experience working with four companies actively engaged in SPI improvements. Each company carried out several kinds of assessments during this period, including CMM, Bootstrap, self-assessments, interview-based problem diagnosis, and error-report analyses. Based on these assessment experiences and a study of their outcomes, we developed our framework. We describe it here in detail, along with the steps involved in choosing an overall assessment strategy.

11.1 THE FRAMEWORK

We identified three dimensions that are important for distinguishing between assessment strategies.

◆ Rigor versus relevance: At one extreme, an assessment strategy may have a strict approach to collecting data and using it to draw conclusions. We call this a rigor-based strategy. Typically, a rigorous method follows rules to achieve systematic and defensible results that are even considered objective in some cases. The opposite of a rigor-based strategy is a relevance-based strategy. Here the strategy focuses on eliciting results relevant to one or more of the stakeholders. Or said in another way, a relevance-based strategy may not lead to an assessment that is full or complete or rigorous, but it will lead to results and conclusions that concern the involved organizational actors.

◆ Model-based versus problem-based: A model-based method puts its faith in maturity models such as CMM, Bootstrap, and SPICE. More generally, the model-based strategy focuses on models of best practices and, consequently, models of general software-process problems. A problem-based assessment strategy focuses on what software practitioners and their managers perceive as problems in the software process.

◆ Intervention versus day-to-day management: At one extreme, the intervention strategy relies on some kind of assistance from outside actors, such as SPI or measurement consultants, to assess the organization. The outside assistance is often organized as a specific project with a start date and an estimated completion date. At the other extreme, the day-to-day management approach independently implements assessments into the routine work of organizational actors.

As Table 11.1 shows, these three dimensions form eight possible categories of assessment strategies.

Assisted Model-Based Assessment

◆ Category: Rigorous, model-based intervention

One example in this category is use of the SPICE model. Work on SPICE (ISO 15504) started in 1993, and it was proposed as an international standard in the late 1990s. SPICE covers more than 40 software processes, encompassing those in CMM version 1.1 and Bootstrap version 2.3. A full SPICE assessment demands rigorous data collection and processing; to complete it, your organization must devote the effort of many people over two or more weeks' time. A SPICE assessment compares your software practice directly to 40 model processes and typically is carried out by external SPICE-trained assessors.

Bootstrap version 2.3 is another example of a maturity model that requires outside intervention and rigorous data collection and processing. Seven partners from five European countries developed the Bootstrap assessment model from 1990 to

Table 11.1   *Three Dimensions, Eight Categories*

		Model-Based	Problem-Based
Rigor	**Intervention**	Assisted model-based assessment	Assisted metrics program and benchmarking
	Day-to-Day Management	Independent model-based assessment	Independent project-based metrics program
Relevance	**Intervention**	Assisted model-based assessment (small sample)	Assisted problem diagnosis
	Day-to-Day Management	Independent model-based self-assessment	Independent project-based self-assessment

1994. The model consists of 21 software processes divided into three groups: organization, methodology, and technology.

CSC Denmark (formerly Datacentralen) has used the assisted model-based assessment strategy. In 1997 the company decided to have all its projects assessed and did so, using outside consultants as well as people from inside the software house who had attended an official assessor training. Even though the full assessment of all projects was expensive, it was believed to have initiated such valuable software process improvements that the assessment of every project within the company was repeated in 1999, again with outside consultants as lead assessors.

Assisted Metrics Program and Benchmarking

♦ Category: Rigorous, problem-based intervention

One example in this category is the Compass development program for measuring productivity and quality. Compass is based on a large, general metrics program that is common to all the companies using it. The participating companies collect a large amount of data and process it using algorithms. They then send the data to the Compass organization. Compass then sends each company results that indicate several dimensions, including productivity, time to market, quality, and precision of estimates. The results also indicate where the company is relative to other, similar companies. Compass does not disclose how it calculates these indicators, and only Compass can analyze the data. It is thus an intervention-based assessment. The rigor of this approach comes from the scrutiny in data collection and processing and the fact that data from all companies are analyzed using the same procedure. Compass Development is based on a metrics program and does not use any kind of model of software process maturity.

Another example in this category is the Goal Question Metric (GQM) method. In this method, you define your goals and then formulate a set of questions that you might ask to help you to assess whether you are achieving your goals. You then decide how to measure the answers to these questions. This method works well with consultants, but you can also use it yourself in day-to-day management.

Independent Assessments of Individual Projects

♦ Category: Rigorous, model-based, day-to-day management

An example in this category is Danske Data's strategy during its two assessments (see Chapter 5). The first assessment integrated a Bootstrap assessment with a questionnaire-based CMM level 2 assessment (called QBA). The assessors performed the Bootstrap assessment by first interviewing project groups and then filling out questionnaires. The QBA also used questionnaires, but they were filled out by the project participants themselves. The two assessments supplemented each other (Iversen et al. 1998). A matrix was used to combine the results from the assessments.

Danske Data's second assessment used an ordinary Bootstrap assessment along with data from self-assessments, problem lists from quality meetings, and problem lists from a project-manager education project. Again, the data sets supplement each other. When four independent sources point at the same problematic software processes, the result is more powerful and the resulting strategy more rigorous. The Bootstrap and CMM maturity models supported this strategy. During data analysis, the models played an important role, providing the framework for comparing data from the different sources. This strategy was more day-to-day management than intervention because it anchored the assessment-process knowledge within the organization.

Another example of this strategy was one used at Ericsson Denmark. As Chapter 3 describes, Ericsson Denmark assessed its software practices using the CMM maturity model. The assessments were performed by well-trained, internal practitioners who had been certified as CMM assessors.

Independent Project-Based Metrics Program

  ◆ Category: Rigorous, problem-based, day-to-day management

Brüel & Kjær's strategy is one example in this category (see Chapters 6 and 8). Brüel & Kjær's first strategy was based on knowledge and experience in the form of existing defect reports. The SPI actors selected approximately 20% of 1,000 defect reports on one of the company's marketed products and rigorously analyzed the reports using a publicly available taxonomy. Through this analysis, they identified two problem areas specific to Brüel & Kjær's software development: testing and requirements specification. They then launched and successfully completed two related SPI efforts. Chapter 8 explains the strategy in detail; the authors conclude that their use of defect analysis is a valid and effective alternative to formal SPI assessments.

Assisted Model-Based Assessment (Small Sample)

  ◆ Category: Relevance-driven, model-based intervention

CMM or Bootstrap assessments that use representative project samples are typical examples in this category. Although the rigor of such an assessment can be questioned, its relevance is typically high. For example, a weeklong Bootstrap assessment ends with a closing session in which assessors present preliminary results and software managers and developers have the opportunity to confirm or object to them.

Originally, CMM presented two ways to carry out an assessment: *software process assessment* and *software capability evaluation.* In the first case, an organization could carry out an assessment themselves (what we have called independent or day-to-day management) or do it with assistance. In the latter case, only outside assessors can give the assessed organization a proof or certificate of the assessment results.

At Systematic, assessors carried out two traditional Bootstrap 2.3 assessments and one CMM 1.1 assessment in the period from 1997 to 1999 (see Chapter 4). In all three assessments, the company used external assessors to examine four representative projects. The project-selection criteria were size (small and large), application area (military and business), actual development phase (from analysis to testing), and customer relationship (fixed price versus process contract). The company considered the strengths and weaknesses revealed by the assessments to be so relevant that it used the results as a basis for a three-year SPI program.

Assisted Problem Diagnosis

- ◆ Category: Relevance-driven, problem-based intervention

Brüel & Kjær's problem diagnosis is an example of this category (see Chapter 9). Brüel & Kjær's strategy applied little rigor but much relevance in collecting related data for qualitative analysis. SPI actors interviewed only project managers, with the goal of identifying the problems they perceived in their software practice, irrespective of process models. Although process models played a role in problem diagnosis and analysis and served as a context for the interviewers, such models were deliberately ignored during the interviews themselves. The effort was an intervention in that the interviews proved more successful when the interviewers were drawn from outside the organization. Although interviewers arguably can be drawn from internal SPI practitioners, the quality of the interviews improves if curiosity and empathy, rather than a priori insight and organizational bias, prevail.

Independent Model-Based Self-Assessments

- ◆ Category: Relevance-driven, model-based, day-to-day management

We can readily illustrate this category by making a simple change to the Systematic example. Systematic displayed a strong belief in maturity models and focused on relevance by selecting representative process samples. If the company had opted for doing the assessment itself without external assistance, its approach would provide a clear example of this category.

Ericsson Denmark's effort is a more exact example of this approach (see Chapter 3). Some years ago, Ericsson's corporate offices decided to build an improvement program based on CMM. Corporate managers selected internal assessors from every Ericsson development organization. These assessors were taught CMM principles and how to perform assessments. From 1997 to 1999, Ericsson Denmark carried out one major assessment and numerous UltraLight Assessments (see Chapter 10). The organization clearly had the knowledge to carry out its own assessments and created several mechanisms to avoid the bias that can result from using insiders instead of outsiders. However, it is the UltraLight Assessments in particular that contribute to day-to-day management.

Independent Project-Based Self-Assessments

◆ Category: Relevance-driven, problem-based, day-to-day management

Danske Data's self-assessments for project managers are an example in this category. The self-assessment questions are directly linked to Danske Data's own standard of project management (see Chapters 5 and 10). In creating the standard, SPI actors emphasized the relevant criteria needed for good project management. The assessment questions reflect this relevance and are also problem-oriented. Although the standard's developers borrowed many ideas from a maturity model, self-assessment analysis and results are not directly related to the model. This strategy meets the day-to-day management criterion in that project managers themselves collect and analyze data and present the results (hence "self-assessment").

11.2 CRITERIA FOR SELECTING AN ASSESSMENT STRATEGY

The three dimensions of our framework form a decision space. The following steps can guide you in planning your assessment, making an informed and systematic choice about your primary strategy, and managing the details of the assessment.

Step 1: Select a Primary Strategy

First, you should select a primary strategy. Each of the three dimensions has specific questions; when you've answered the questions in each dimension, you should have a good idea about which of the eight categories offers the best primary strategy for your particular situation.

Rigor Versus Relevance

The discussion of rigor versus relevance is as old as social research. The "pure" scientists argue that true knowledge comes from a rigorous research approach. Practice-oriented researchers argue that rigor means nothing if it fails to produce relevant results. Although an assessment is not research, it shares with research the desire to produce sound knowledge that actors can rely on to better plan ahead.

In comparing a Bootstrap assessment with a CMM assessment, we found some interesting differences (Iversen et al. 1998) that show why the debate between rigor and relevance is not easily settled. The Bootstrap approach is based on qualitative group interviews that feature open-ended questions. Because Bootstrap assessors focus on a relatively small number of interviews, interviewees must be carefully selected to represent the whole organization. Assessors then interpret the interviews and turn the qualitative data into quantitative data by filling out the Bootstrap questionnaire. They can later supplement their analysis of the quantitative profiles with the original qualitative data. The profiles provide general, overall impressions of maturity, and the qualitative data offers the details needed to make the results comprehensible. Using only a few interviews reduces the model's rigor but offers potentially high relevance. Also, rigor is later increased by systematic data analysis.

In another assessment, CMM served as the underlying model for an approach based on a questionnaire-based assessment (QBA) that was filled out by many respondents. Assessors analyzed the resulting quantitative data in a traditional way. Rigor is high in this method, but it is also risky in that the QBA questionnaire might miss certain problems altogether because its questions are drawn only from CMM level 2.

A rigorous assessment approach is needed if assessors and others are to trust the assessment results. On the other hand, a relevance-based assessment approach is crucial in creating confidence in the results and thus letting assessors and others trust the ensuing improvement plans.

The following three questions are important in determining your direction in this dimension.

- Do you believe that indisputable data is the source of knowledge?
- Do you think it is better to get a general picture of existing software processes as they really are (as opposed to a more detailed picture of problems as software practitioners perceive them)?
- Do you think that objectivity is crucial and worth pursuing vigorously?

If you answered yes to two or more of these questions, your primary strategy for data collection and interpretation should be based more on rigor than relevance.

Model-Based Versus Problem-Based

The CMM framework characterizes a path for SPI, describing key practices and KPAs at each of its five levels. This description includes several goals at each level, and a software organization must meet each of these goals to advance to the next level. Recent figures from the SEI suggest that around 66% of all software development organizations are at CMM level 1, and another 25% are at level 2. Empirical evidence supports claims that CMM reasonably describes how software organizations can improve (Humphrey 1987), but with so few real-world examples beyond level 2, the data is indicative rather than descriptive. Put another way, to use CMM or similar models as a basis for your assessment is an expression of faith in the maturity model paradigm rather than a strictly rational act.

Given this, an obvious question is, What are the models' underlying assumptions? There are at least three interesting answers to this question. The most obvious answer is that process maturity models focus solely on one factor in a company—processes—and neglect other aspects. This answer rests on the assumption that good processes alone will lead to the goal of better software development.

A second possible answer is that the models measure maturity by counting how many best practices exist in an organization. However, this way of counting assumes that what is best for one kind of company is also good for another kind. That is, it assumes that you can generalize best practices across the software industry.

A third assumption of maturity models is found in their two underlying philosophies. The first is Total Quality Management, which is a "management philosophy embracing all activities through which the needs and expectations are satisfied in the most efficient and cost effective way by maximizing the potential of all employees in a continuing drive for improvement" (British Standard 1991). The second philosophy is step-by-step, one-small-step-at-a-time learning, such as that practiced in the Japanese Kaizen strategy (Colenso 2000).

Problem-based strategies, on the other hand, take problems found in practice as their starting point. The belief is that every problem is special in itself and must be addressed in a unique way. Thus, no model or best practice from other organizations—even those contending with the same type of problem—will be useful for solving the problem at hand.

The following three questions are important in determining your own assumptions and how they align with your choices in this dimension.

- Do you believe that better software products are primarily (or solely) the result of good software processes?
- Do you believe that best practices from one kind of software development company—typically a large, North American company—will be useful for you?
- Do you believe that the best way of improving your software organization is to focus on efficiency and cost-effectiveness and to change one small thing at a time (as opposed to, say, more revolutionary changes)?

If you answered yes to two or more of these questions, you should select a primary strategy in the model-based category.

Intervention Versus Day-to-Day Management

Intervention involves coming into an organization from outside, grasping the essence of what drives the organization and its actors, and identifying the actors' practices and defense mechanisms. Intervention has several advantages. Interventionists are open to discovering how the organization works without the biases that come from living within it. Also, interventionists are often specially trained to consult, assess, and apply maturity models and can sometimes generalize based on their experiences with other organizations.

A proper Bootstrap assessment must be conducted by outside assessors who are trained in the Bootstrap model and accredited by the Bootstrap Institute. An SEI-certified CMM assessment must be conducted by SEI-accredited assessors. Thus, if your organization wants or needs the official certification of either model, you must choose a strategy from the intervention category.

Another possibility is to use assessments to directly influence the day-to-day management of your software organization. Our experience with assessments has shown that organizations find their own ways of assessing software processes and often gradually turn away from intervention-style assessments in favor of internal, management-style assessments. These internal assessments depend on managers being involved (rather than detached), part of the organization's history (rather than objective), and committed to the consequences of decisions (rather than the defensibility of their conclusions).

The following three questions are important in determining your choice in this dimension.

♦ Do you think that problems with your software process are more likely to be identified by external consultants who have little or no history with the organization?

♦ Does your organization want or need externally recognized certification?

♦ Does your organization lack internal SPI knowledge and the resources needed to educate and train internal actors?

If you answered yes to two or more questions, you should select a primary strategy based on intervention rather than day-to-day management.

Step 2: Consider a Combined Strategy

A single primary strategy is rarely sufficient in the real world. It is often better to use several approaches or to supplement your primary strategy with a secondary strategy.

Danske Data's first assessment was conducted with a combined Bootstrap–QBA approach (see Chapter 5 and Iversen et al. 1998). This combined approach was more reliable, increased confidence among participants, and allowed them to plan their efforts in more detail.

Danske Data now has an almost eclectic assessment strategy. The organization undergoes a Bootstrap assessment about every two years; it bases its improvement plans on the Bootstrap results as well as on the accumulated results from self-assessments, systematically collected information from quality meetings, evaluations of employee job satisfaction, and the company's metrics program. Often, the information gathered from these sources coincides, thus increasing confidence in the improvement plans.

Step 3: Design the Assessment

After you've selected your primary strategy or strategies, you are ready to design your assessment. In doing this, you should be able to answer questions regarding five key issues. If you can answer the questions related to each issue, you have a complete design. Keep in mind that many complete designs already exist. One example is the method behind a Bootstrap assessment. Other examples include the examples offered earlier in each of the eight categories. Existing designs are specific and thus have a specific combination of answers to the following questions. However, there are many other design possibilities.

- ◆ Staffing: Who will perform the assessment? What is their knowledge of the assessment process?
- ◆ Assessment process: Which assessment process will be used? In what ways will this process be guided by an assessment method?
- ◆ Data collection: How will data be collected and stored?
- ◆ Data analysis: Who will analyze the data? How will they analyze it?
- ◆ Presentation of results: How will the assessment results be presented to relevant actors in the organization?

Figure 11.1 shows how DELTA performs its Bootstrap 2.3 assessment. Figure 11.2 shows risk assessment techniques. To use this list, first ask yourself, What do we need to know? Your answers constitute your core questions. Next, ask yourself, Who has the knowledge we need? You can use your answer to this question to select the appropriate data-collection technique from Figure 11.2. Third, select a data medium for the selected strategies. For example, if you choose a rigor-based strategy, your data must be as objective and repeatable as possible. Finally, ask yourself, Who needs the

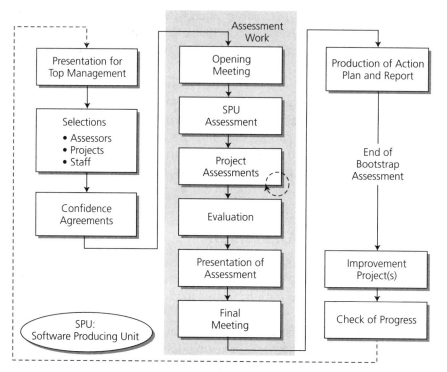

Figure 11.1 *A sample assessment. The middle section shows assessment week; to the left are activities carried out before assessment, and to the right, activities that follow assessment week*

information that the assessment provides? Your answer can help you select the appropriate techniques for presenting results.

After you've completed the assessment, you can evaluate your design by comparing the assessment outcome with your design ideas.

11.3 CONCLUSION AND DISCUSSION

Based on our experiences over a three-year period with several types of assessments, we have identified three dimensions—rigor versus relevance, model-based versus problem-based, and intervention versus day-to-day management—that yield eight categories that you can use to select your assessment strategy. Thus far, we've found that our framework and our dimensions are both useful. Whether the three questions for each dimension are useful is the subject of further research. In the future, we

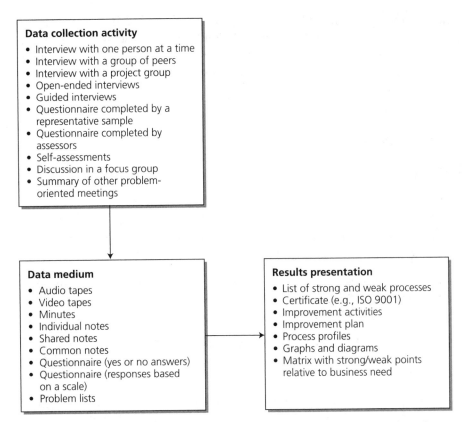

Data collection activity
- Interview with one person at a time
- Interview with a group of peers
- Interview with a project group
- Open-ended interviews
- Guided interviews
- Questionnaire completed by a representative sample
- Questionnaire completed by assessors
- Self-assessments
- Discussion in a focus group
- Summary of other problem-oriented meetings

Data medium
- Audio tapes
- Video tapes
- Minutes
- Individual notes
- Shared notes
- Common notes
- Questionnaire (yes or no answers)
- Questionnaire (responses based on a scale)
- Problem lists

Results presentation
- List of strong and weak processes
- Certificate (e.g., ISO 9001)
- Improvement activities
- Improvement plan
- Process profiles
- Graphs and diagrams
- Matrix with strong/weak points relative to business need

Figure 11.2 *Assessment techniques for data collection, data medium, and results presentation. For each of the eight strategies, you should choose a specific combination of techniques*

might also link the strategic categories more firmly with various contingent assessment designs.

One dimension that we have not taken into account is the cost of an assessment. For example, it is probably more expensive to follow a rigorous strategy than a relevance strategy. Following a problem-based strategy is also typically more time-consuming (and thus more expensive) than using a standard model-based strategy. Finally, although hiring outside consultants to intervene may seem expensive at first glance, it can be cheaper than a day-to-day management strategy when you add up all the required internal work hours.

The reason that we have yet to explore the cost dimension is that it was not well represented in the empirical data that we used to build our framework. There are several reasons for this, including that the companies in the SPI project were funded in part by outside sources and they did not count hours logged by external researchers. However, you can add a cost benefit analysis of different approaches after you have used our framework to explore your options and select appropriate candidate strategies for your organization.

11.4 REFERENCES

British Standard 4778: Part 2. 1991.

Colenso, M. 2000. *Kaizen Strategies for Successful Organizational Change: Enabling Evolution and Revolution within the Organization*. New York: Prentice Hall.

Humphrey, W.S. 1987 "Characterising the Software Process: A Maturity Framework." Technical Report CMU/SEI-87-TR-11. Pittsburgh: Software Engineering Institute.

Iversen, J.H., J. Johansen, P.A. Nielsen, and J. Pries-Heje. 1998. "Combining Quantitative and Qualitative Assessment Methods in Software Process Improvement." *Proceedings of European Conference on Information Systems*. IAE, Aix-En-Provence.

Messnarz, R. 1999. "A Roadmap to the Book." R. Messnarz, ed. *Better Software Practice For Business Benefit: Principles and Experience*. Los Alamitos, CA: IEEE Computer Society.

Tully, C., P. Kuvaja, and R. Messnarz. 1999. "Software Process Analysis and Improvement: A Catalogue and Comparison of Models." R. Messnarz, ed. *Better Software Practice For Business Benefit: Principles and Experience*. Los Alamitos, CA: IEEE Computer Society.

PART IV

Organizing for Learning

Chapter 12

Knowing and Implementing SPI

Karlheinz Kautz and Peter Axel Nielsen

Traditionally, the software industry has held a simplistic view of implementing change. Software engineers typically have viewed the diffusion of ideas and innovations as the mere diffusion of technology. Thus, for example, to solve problems with requirements and documentation, you would use CASE tools. However, all SPI maturity models recommend that organizations implement fundamental software processes before using such advanced tools. To get these processes in place, organizations must learn about SPI. However, until recently, there has been little theoretical or practical understanding of how SPI knowledge can be transferred to organizations.

Currently, research on knowledge and technology transfer plays an important role in both IS and SPI (Levine 1994; Kautz and Pries-Heje 1996; McMaster et al. 1997; Larsen and Levine 1998). Using such research as a foundation, we have developed a practical framework that can help change agents understand SPI implementation as knowledge transfer. Our framework integrates theories of innovation and adoption. Using it, we examine organizational change from three viewpoints: an individualist perspective, a structuralist perspective, and an interactive-process perspective. The latter combines the first two and emphasizes the content, context, and process of SPI implementation.

We developed this framework based on our separate work on two SPI efforts. In these efforts, each of us was a member of action research teams tasked with transferring SPI knowledge in two Danish software companies: Network Products and Danske Data. Based on our individual experiences, we collaborated to create a single coherent framework that not only made sense of both projects but also gave us deeper insight into the process of knowledge transfer as a function of SPI.

We first describe our framework and then use it to examine our respective SPI experiences. Using this framework gave us a rich understanding of the interplay of the different elements influencing the SPI initiation process in each case.

12.1 FRAMEWORK FOR SPI IMPLEMENTATION AND KNOWLEDGE TRANSFER

Our approach to developing the framework was relatively unstructured and was consistent with leading European ideas on open-ended action research (Avison et al. 1997; Checkland 1991, Hult and Lennung 1980; Rapoport 1970). We began by drawing on several concepts from existing research on the adoption, implementation, and transfer of innovations.

As a starting point, we used Cooper and Zmud's (1990) six-stage model for implementing information technology. The model's stages are initiation, adoption, adaptation, acceptance, routinization, and infusion. In the SPI context, we view "adoption" as the phase in which management decides to invest resources into SPI implementation, and "acceptance" as the phase in which innovations are put into practical use.

We also draw on work by Lien (1995), who conceives technology transfer as supply-driven and diffusion as demand-driven; Heidtman (1994), who conceives technology transition as the institutionalization of new tools, techniques, and approaches; Damsgaard and his colleagues (1994), who describe an organization's uptake of IT as penetration; and Veryard (1995), who—favoring the concept of adaptation—criticizes transfer and penetration theories as focusing mainly on a one-way influence. Veryard also observes that technologies change when they are implemented into an organization.

With this as our background, we established our formal framework, which combines Slappendel's (1996) theory on innovation diffusion and adoption in organizations with Walsham's (1993) theory on IT development and adoption. We applied this framework to our experiences in the two cases that we describe here. Applying this framework helped us better understand the interplay of elements that influence and drive the implementation and knowledge transfer processes.

Following Slappendel, we view organizational innovations from three perspectives: individualist, structuralist, and interactive process (see Table 12.1).

- The *individualist* perspective focuses on characteristics of relevant individuals.
- The *structuralist* perspective focuses on the organization's structural elements, such as its task environment, its size, its organizational complexity, and its level of job formalization, power centralization, and professionalism (viewed through its use of plans and methodologies).
- The *interactive-process* perspective views innovation implementation as a complex interaction of individual and structuralist elements.

From the individualistic and structuralist perspectives, innovation is a simple, linear phenomenon. The interactive-process perspective views innovation as nonlin-

Table 12.1   *Perspectives on the Implementation of Innovations (Adapted from Slappendel)*

	Individualist	**Structuralist**	**Interactive Process**
Basic assumptions	Individual actions create change and innovation	Structural characteristics determine change and innovation	The interaction between individuals and structural influences produces change and innovation
Theory of change and innovation	Objects and practices are static and objectively defined	Objects and practices are static and objectively defined	Focus on content of change; change and innovation can be reinvented and reconfigured to suit context
Theory of the process of change and innovation	Change is a simple, linear process; focus is on the adoption stage	Change is a simple, linear process; focus is on the adoption stage	Change is a complex, social process; interrelated events and stages are explored from different perspectives
Core concepts	• Champions • Leaders • Entrepreneurs • Change agents	• Environment • Size • Complexity • Normalization • Centralization • Professionalism	• Context • Innovative capability • Proliferation • Shocks

ear. It is the most comprehensive and complex of the views, as Figure 12.1 shows. We therefore supplement the interactive-process perspective with Walsham's general ideas on IT and organizational change (1993). Walsham's ideas center on a continuous interplay between three elements:

◆ The modification's content and the people affected by it: Innovations are not simply adopted; they are often adjusted, reconfigured, or reinvented.

◆ The context of the change: This context operates in terms of both external circumstances (the political and market-related context) and internal circumstances (interdepartmental conditions). Innovations depend on the organization's general ability to change and to generate and use new ideas. Also, the decision to innovate is often motivated by a shocking event or realization.

◆ The social process of change: Rather than simply record a linear flow of events, we must also explore the cultural and political aspects of the change process.

To illustrate how you can use our framework, we now examine two cases of organizational change.

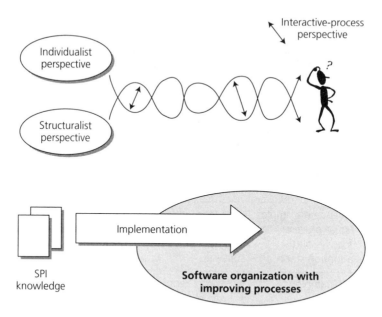

Figure 12.1 *With the interaction-process perspective, the SPI practitioner uses both the individualist and the structuralist perspectives to make sense of SPI knowledge implementation*

12.2 CASE 1: SPI IN NETWORK PRODUCTS

Network Products' (NP) business plan is to create an innovative warehousing systems application that performs fast, structured searches on as many as 20,000 inventory items on a slow network and displays results on a 14-inch screen. NP's goal is to be the first company to get such a product to the market.

NP was one year old when we began the improvement effort in 1998. At that time, the company had 25 employees: 15 in software development and 10 in business administration, marketing, and sales. NP had two software development divisions of roughly equal size. The production division delivered standard intranet and Internet solutions and generated much of NP's income. The R&D division was focused on developing the warehousing application and was financed by the production division, with some public R&D funding. Our SPI effort was directed at software development in R&D, where developers were working on the first version of the product.

From the start, NP managers had shown an interest in quality and quality management matters, and they wanted all basic software processes established and under control as soon as possible. This was particularly important in that they were expecting a considerable staff increase. They contacted three outside action researchers and set the SPI effort in motion.

Individualistic Perspective

The most influential people involved in NP's SPI implementation were a managing director, our action research team, and a project manager. One of NP's managing directors is an active entrepreneur and was the single most important driving force behind the effort. Seeing the need for SPI knowledge at NP, he took the initiative and brought in the action research team. He also provided the necessary resources and actively participated in our meetings with the development staff. If anything, he was at times too enthusiastic and his expectations too high.

The role of the action research team was to serve as the SPI specialists, perform an assessment, and prepare and present oral and written results. As *change agents*, we also facilitated the implementation process and supported developers during the planning and implementation of the improvement proposals.

One of NP's project managers also played a significant role. As a respected employee, he served as mediator between our team and management and *championed* the initiative through his active involvement in all activities.

Structuralist Perspective

Structurally, NP is simple. The two founders are NP's managing directors and are involved in all major decisions. In their view of NP's *environment*, unless the company adopted SPI, it risked being beaten by competitors.

Because of the complexity of its development task, work in NP's R&D division is project-oriented. Two project managers coordinate several subprojects, in which groups of four or five developers perform all development tasks. These project groups often emerge on an ad hoc basis. They typically exist only for a short period and are dissolved when they complete their task.

NP formally contracted with the action researchers. Our contracts contained a preliminary project plan and defined the project's resources and expected deliverables. Beyond that, little was formalized.

The SPI group consisted of two of the three action researchers and the influential project manager. The group's task was to supervise, support, and perform improvement activities. We also established two temporary technical working groups to develop and implement specific improvement plans. This more centralized approach was aimed at bringing more formalization and professionalism to the developers' work.

Interactive-Process Perspective

Contents

NP's SPI implementation consisted of importing SPI knowledge (via our action re-search team) and organizing the initial improvement activities. These activities con-sisted of analyzing the company, assessing its software process, producing an assessment report and action plan, and implementing the first process improvement. The activities' effect was to significantly change developers' work practices and slightly change the overall organization. The action researchers managed the over-head of change, which consisted of the administrative procedures that supported the change process, such as writing proposals, organizing meetings, and taking minutes.

Context

NP's external circumstances include a growing market for its target product and in-creasing competition. NP's goal is to establish itself as a company known for compe-tence and committed to quality, with products that are professionally crafted and meet high standards.

Another external factor is NP's economic foundation, which is based in large part on the EU's support for new business development. In NP's business plan, which serves as its contract with the EU, the company committed itself to creating a quality assurance group or division. Some of NP's EU funding was earmarked to meet that objective.

NP's internal atmosphere is entrepreneurial and frank, and that supports com-munication and makes it easier to adjust to change. The company is project-oriented, and a creative and dynamic—and at times, hectic—atmosphere prevails. To nourish this energetic culture, NP mainly hires recent graduates from information systems and computer science programs who are typically young, have no "bad habits," and are open to innovations. Thus, the collective efforts typically are quite innovative, particularly when it comes to the adoption of new software.

NP's managers make all the strategic decisions on business and products. They expect all employees to take responsibility for their own work and to work for the common interest. The managers' style is "management-by-walking-around." Project managers oversee technical tasks and achievements, and software developers are largely autonomous. This autonomy extends to solving technical problems as well as purchasing tools and other materials. Developers appear both committed and moti-vated, and they often work overtime.

Process

We implemented the initial SPI activities according to the IDEAL model, which con-sists of five phases: initiating, diagnosing, establishing, acting, and leveraging. Following initiation, we ran through the final four phases as part of the first cycle in a structured approach to continuous improvement. Adjusting the abstract model to NP's concrete situation was itself part of the project. We now describe the four phases and their activities.

In the *initiation* phase, we clarified the expectations of the various groups and established the immediate goals. We also signed contracts and established the SPI group. Although the most active participants in this phase were the top managers, the action researchers, and the influential project manager, we held a meeting to inform all developers about the project and reached consensus on the value of improving software processes.

In the *diagnosis* phase, our action research team assessed the organization. We did this primarily through staff interviews and a project-manager survey, but we supplemented this by reviewing requirements specification and design documents and observing the culture in NP. In this stage, we invited everyone to contribute concrete experiences. Based on this work, our team identified acute problems and long-term improvement needs and then presented these at a staff meeting.

In the *establishing* phase, we further elaborated on the improvement proposals and placed them in a lifecycle model that showed where they best fit into NP's software development process. This made it easy to prioritize required actions and also showed both management and developers that rapid progress was possible. The SPI group performed most of these activities. However, two working groups of developers helped with work on the two acute problems: unstructured meetings and the lack of code documentation guidelines.

The *acting* phase was brief: Within a week, both problems were solved and the solutions implemented.

The *leveraging* phase—in the sense of leveraging knowledge—took place throughout the effort. Our general approach was to implement improvements through proliferation rather than follow a complete and visionary strategy. After the original project period, we evaluated the entire process. The improvement to better structure meetings (complete with rules) had been implemented. However, after some use, the code documentation guidelines were abandoned. According to the project manager, the reason was time pressure and lack of quality control over the documentation. In general, management liked things as informal as possible, whereas the developers would have liked a little more formalism.

Despite their differing attitudes on structure, NP's managers and developers considered the SPI project a success. More than a year after the initial improvement project, NP still employs two action researchers full time as process improvement specialists. We have used the lessons learned and a refined action plan to continue the improvement effort and implement new processes and procedures for project planning, quality assurance, and configuration management.

Discussion

NP has efficiently and effectively improved some of its software processes. The individualist perspective would attribute this success to the company's powerful improvement champion. One of NP's managing directors was passionate about the need for SPI; he encouraged, argued with, and eventually convinced the SPI group and the software developers to get improvements implemented. Although this individualistic view is useful, it provides only a partial explanation of NP's improvement experience.

From a structuralist perspective, NP is small and young, and everyone literally works in the same room. The SPI group was visible and central: Two of its members were devoted solely to driving the implementation process forward, and another managed NP's most significant project. Like the individualist view, the structuralist perspective is useful but insufficient on its own.

Combining the individualistic and structuralist perspectives lets us explore how their respective elements interact and thus lets us better interpret NP's improvement experience. The interactive-process perspective focuses on how individuals interact with the structures around them. At NP, the combination of the SPI champion's actions and the fact that the SPI group was centrally positioned provided momentum for implementation.

The interactive-process perspective also lets us interpret the case in more detail. NP's context was dominated by the company's strong desire to be among the best organizations in its market. Management realized early on that SPI might increase the likelihood of achieving this goal. Because project managers and systems developers were under permanent pressure to reach immediate deadlines, NP's top management alone had the time and energy to think of the future. However, management communicated their goals to everyone in the organization. Unlike many companies, NP was not "shocked" into implementing SPI. The company's whole philosophy was based on a huge risk: Its very existence was based on the goal of developing a single major product, with the hope that it would lead the market. This focus and its inherent risk certainly fed the aspiration to improve.

Furthermore, NP's environment made it easy to proliferate innovation. Management constantly encouraged new ideas and practices, and the software developers—most of them just graduated from university—had considerable innovative capabilities. The prevailing attitude among developers was that many things are still worth learning. Such curiosity led to an openness toward any innovation that might enhance their work routines and products. That provided a solid ground for SPI improvements.

12.3 CASE 2: SPI IN DANSKE DATA

As Chapter 5 describes, Danske Data maintains and develops a huge portfolio of banking and administrative systems for Denmark's largest bank. The company has more than 700 systems developers in four geographical locations, each of which has its own management hierarchy. Although the development activities are distributed, the company has a common support staff, which includes a methodology department, database administration, and an SPI group.

Individualist Perspective

From an individualist perspective, Danske Data's SPI effort included a few significant people who played different roles and had different attitudes toward improvement. In the initial SPI implementation, those individuals were the managing director, the SPI project manager, and the action research team, whose manager was particularly influential.

The managing director was convinced that SPI would benefit Danske Data, and he championed the initiative. However, he also had many initiatives of various types competing for his attention. He appointed the SPI project manager to lead the initiative and gather the relevant organizational change agents. Waiting for these agents to become operative took a lot of time, but after the initiative rose above the grassroots level they became vital, if not indispensable, to the SPI effort.

The action research team fed the improvement effort with SPI knowledge—general theories as well as models and assessments of Danske Data's particular processes. Although the individualistic perspective does not view knowledge transfer as crucial to implementation, it must take place. After the implementation process had been under way for some time, the research manager held meetings with the managing director to increase his awareness of the SPI project. In this respect, the research manager acted as an entrepreneur, using several different channels to ensure a continued focus on process improvement.

Structuralist Perspective

Danske Data is an old and large organization. Its environment is stable, even though its products are innovative: It provides the latest IT solutions to the bank, which is its main customer. The company's software development is complex for two reasons: banking itself is complex, and most new applications for the industry depend on an existing portfolio of applications. Many of Danske Data's work practices are formalized, but the company basically relies on its highly professional culture, which takes pride in application quality rather than time to market.

None of this explains why Danske Data's SPI implementation occurred. However, it does help explain many of the SPI project's obstacles. It is actually easier to see the company's structures than it is to identify the individuals who made the improvements happen, both because of and despite the structures. Danske Data is bureaucratic and divisionalized. The divisions are quite different and have different professional cultures that originated in the IT departments of three different banks and an insurance company. Suspicion and superstition among divisions has long been common. Finally, the divisions' software processes varied considerably. The SPI group members struggled with these differences and also the fact that they were located within one of the divisions.

Interactive-Process Perspective

Contents

Danske Data's SPI group took an SPI effort that had been marginalized by most developers and middle managers and turned it around, successfully implementing improvements and, in the process, achieving increased visibility. Initially, our action research team offered general SPI knowledge and conducted the assessments. Gradually, our role changed to encompass the task of adapting SPI knowledge to suit Danske Data's conditions.

Context

On the one hand, Danske Data's environment was quite stable in terms of the tasks banks desired. On the other hand, Danske Data was shocked by several events that transpired during the implementation. Some of the shocks and the turbulence that followed were widely evident. For example, the influential SPI project manager was promoted to another job, then came back, and then finally left Danske Data for another company. Other shocks were more subtle, such as when senior management prevented the SPI group from publicizing its metrics reports (see Chapter 17).

Process

Chapter 5 describes the improvement process and results in detail. Here we focus on the implementation process. Despite the structural difficulties, the SPI implementation at Danske Data was a firm and consistent effort that included several phases.

- Establishing the need for SPI: Although Danske Data's need for better quality, productivity, and time to market had long been realized, the need for SPI was clear to only a few people. It took a careful and systematic persuasion of senior management to actually start the initiative.
- Assessing the maturity of software processes: Our action research team assessed the company's maturity level and pointed directly to processes that needed improvement. We then presented our results to senior management and the projects we assessed.

◆ Planning improvement activities: Following the assessment, we planned a few detailed improvement activities. However, it was difficult to find people to lead the activities. Danske Data does not have an experimental culture, and hence success and failure depend largely on preparation and planning.

◆ Conducting the improvement activities; Chapter 5 describes these activities and the accompanying challenges.

During these phases, the SPI group also engaged in several activities:

◆ Organizing the SPI work: Within the SPI group, members were constantly debating how to organize the work. The primary debate was over whether they should strive to be a centralized organization, with the risk being that no one would listen to them, or a distributed organization, with the risk of fragmenting their results.

◆ Monitoring progress: At its periodic meetings, the SPI group monitored the progress of the improvement activities and intervened when necessary.

Throughout this process, our action research team worked closely with the SPI project manager and his group. Group members from inside Danske Data offered detailed knowledge of the context and culture, and we provided state-of-the-art SPI knowledge. We thus brought together the two knowledge domains.

Discussion

Danske Data's SPI group frequently struggled with losing the attention of senior management, software developers, and middle managers. The individualist perspective offers a simple explanation here: The champion also had to champion other initiatives. That perspective might also claim that the change agents were ineffective and failed to produce results that software developers considered relevant. Although this explanation has some validity, it is also true that it took a long time to organize the change agents, and they could not be effective until they were properly organized.

From a structuralist perspective, Danske Data is old, large, and divisionalized. Although the SPI group was responsible for implementing SPI, several members had many other competing obligations. The SPI group fought a constant battle to get sufficient resources and commitment for the effort. Also, the SPI group lacked a central position at Danske Data. This sparked vigorous and ongoing debate within the group about its own organization. In particular, there was concern over the group's relationship to the old methodology department. A few members had long been dissatisfied with that department and did not think it should be entrusted with new SPI ideas; a few others had worked in the methodology department and were confident that the two groups could work closely and successfully together. These debates and others like it—such as that over the possibility of empowering several project managers as change agents—cannot be understood without returning to the individualist perspective.

At Danske Data, the relationship between structural influences and individual roles and actions is complex. In the interactive-process perspective, the company's SPI implementation cannot be understood without paying particular attention to the context and the shocks discussed earlier. Also, although there were certainly people with innovative capability, innovative ideas have a hard time taking root in this context. Traditional defense mechanisms, such as "Don't tell us, we know better," were common. Danske Data is an organization in which only the most well-prepared ideas survive. At the same time, implementing SPI through proliferation would have been difficult in this context because new ideas stand a much better chance of catching on if they are consistent with all previously established procedures.

12.4 IMPLEMENTATION AND KNOWLEDGE TRANSFER

At both NP and Danske Data, external actors, action researchers, and sometimes consultants brought SPI into the organizations from outside. Thus, the SPI implementations were in part a process of technology transfer. Furthermore, SPI consists largely of a body of knowledge that—to be implemented—must be transferred to the organization and adopted by it or, better yet, adapted to its particular needs.

At NP, assimilating and accommodating SPI knowledge was a considerable effort: Two of 25 staff members did nothing else. The transfer was initiated when the action research team brought the SPI knowledge to the company. Through our cooperation with a project manager in the SPI group, we were quickly adopted and respected at NP. The transfer was facilitated by two facts: The project managers and systems developers were eager to incorporate new ideas, and they relied on the experience of others when they had insufficient knowledge and competence.

At Danske Data, the SPI group was responsible for assimilating and accommodating SPI knowledge. Our action research team worked closely with the SPI group, but we had only modest contact with other people at Danske Data. In that respect, SPI knowledge transfer was a two-step process: We transferred it to the SPI group, and they transferred it to the wider organization. This was problematic in that we had credibility as external actors and were perceived as experts, whereas the SPI group members were perceived largely as formalists.

12.5 CONCLUSION

As our experiences show, neither the individualistic nor the structuralist approach is sufficient on its own. The implementation process occurs through a complex interaction between individual action and structural influences and thus must be understood through an interactive-process perspective. Using such a framework to examine our experiences helped us gain a deeper understanding of this complex process and provided at least a partial roadmap for better implementing SPI. Thus, beyond supporting our understanding of these two cases, we are confident that the framework will be useful for planning and reflecting on SPI implementations in other organizations. When using the framework for planning SPI or reflecting on past SPI implementation, it is important to ask yourself the following questions:

- Looking at future (or past) SPI activities through the framework's lenses, what obstacles can you identify?
- Based on the framework, which countermeasures might you take (or have you taken)?

The framework will be particularly useful when you view it as providing general knowledge about change rather than direct advice on what to do in a specific situation. It is your task to adapt the information it provides to your particular needs. The framework's strengths are in how it points out complexities in relationships that are often viewed as much more simplistic.

12.6 REFERENCES

Avison, D., F. Lau, M.D. Myers, and P.A. Nielsen. 1999. "Action Research." *Communications of the ACM*. 42:1:94–97.

Checkland, P. 1991. "From Framework Through Experience to Learning: The Essential Nature of Action Research." In H.E. Nissen et al., eds. *Information Systems Research: Contemporary Approaches & Emergent Traditions*. Amsterdam: North-Holland.

Cooper, R.B. & R.W. Zmud. 1990. "Information Technology Implementation Research: A Technological Diffusion Approach." *Management Science*. 36:2:123–139.

Damsgaard, J. et al. 1994. "How Information Technologies Penetrate Organizations: An Analysis of Four Alternative Models." In L. Levine, ed. *Diffusion, Transfer and Implementation of Information Technology: Proceedings on the IFIP TC8 Working Conference*. Amsterdam: North Holland.

Heidtman, S.E. 1994. "Exploration of an Incremental Approach to Technology Transfer and the Issues Affecting its Implementation." in L. Levine, ed. *Diffusion, Transfer and Implementation of Information Technology: Proceedings on the IFIP TC8 Working Conference*. Amsterdam: North Holland. (Referring to Fowler, P., and L. Levine. 1992. "Toward a Problem Solving Approach to Software Technology Transition." Van Leeuven, J., ed. *Proceedings of the 12th IFIP World Computer Congress Vol. 1.* Amsterdam: North Holland.)

Hult, M., and S.-Å. Lennung. 1980. "Towards a Definition of Action Research: A Note and Bibliography." *Journal of Management Studies.* 17:2:242–250.

Kautz, K., and J. Pries-Heje, eds. 1996. "Diffusion and Adoption of Information Technology." *Proceeding of the 1st IFIP 8.6 Working Conference.* London: Chapman & Hall.

Larsen, T., and L. Levine, eds. 1998. "Information Systems: Current Issues and Future Changes." *Proceedings of the IFIP WG 8.2 & 8.6 Joint Working Conference.* Laxenburg, Austria: IFIP.

Levine, L. ed. 1994. "Diffusion: Transfer and Implementation of Information Technology." *Proceedings of the IFIP TC8 Working Conference on Diffusion, Transfer and Implementation of Information Technology*, Amsterdam: North Holland.

Lien, L. 1995. "Toward a Management Model for the Transfer of Technology." In Kautz, K. et al., eds. *Diffusion and Adoption of Information Technology: Conference Notebook from the 1st IFIP 8.6 Working Conference.* Report No. 900. Oslo, Norway: Norwegian Computing Center.

McMaster, T. et al., eds. 1997. "Facilitating Technology Transfer through Partnership—Learning from Practice and Research." *Proceedings on the 2nd IFIP 8.6 Working Conference*, London: Chapman & Hall.

Rapoport, R.N. 1970. "Three Dilemmas in Action Research." *Human Relations.* 23:6:499–513.

Slappendel, C. 1996. "Perspectives on Innovation in Organizations." *Organization Studies.* 17:1:107–129.

Veryard, R. 1995. "IT Implementation or Delivery? Thoughts on Assimilation, Accommodation and Maturity." In Kautz, K. et al., eds. *Diffusion and Adoption of Information Technology: Conference Notebook from the first IFIP 8.6 Working Conference.* Report No. 900. Oslo, Norway: Norwegian Computing Center.

Walsham, G. 1993. *Interpreting Information Systems in Organizations*. Wiley Series on Information Systems. Chichester, UK. See also Kautz, K. 1996. "Information Technology Transfer and Implementation: The Introduction of an Electronic Mail System in a Public Sector Organization." In Kautz, K., and J. Pries-Heje, eds. *Diffusion and Adoption of Information Technology*. London: Chapman & Hall.

Chapter 13

Improving Customer Relations

Lars Mathiassen, Gro Bjerknes,
and Carsten Kristensen

When an organization pursues a systematic strategy to mature its software operation, there are serious implications for customers and clients. It is impossible, for example, to improve requirements management practices without changing software contracts and the way software teams interact with customers and future users. Systematic therefore decided to involve customers in its SPI program, initiating joint activities aimed at improving the customer–supplier relationship. In doing so, Systematic hoped to better understand and improve its own SPI efforts and to develop services that would also help its customers mature.

We began our efforts by organizing a one-day workshop with key customer representatives. To prepare for the workshop, we researched maturity models that address customer relations and studied state-of-the-art knowledge on the customer–supplier relationship in software development. Guided by this work and our workshop findings, we formulated concrete initiatives to improve Systematic's relationship with its customers. We first present an overview of our research on customer relations, then describe our efforts to improve them at Systematic.

13.1 UNDERSTANDING CUSTOMER RELATIONS

Most SPI initiatives take place within a software organization and focus on improving development processes from the supplier's perspective. That is, the development process begins when a project is formed—based on some type of contract with a customer—and continues until the system is delivered to the customer. This focus on internal processes has helped many organizations improve their software process by building project-management disciplines and supportive organizational environments.

There are, however, clear limits as to how much a software organization can change its processes without seriously affecting customer relations. As software organizations mature, they must therefore broaden their perspective on SPI to include customers and their viewpoints. From the customer's perspective, projects do not start with explicit contractual arrangements but rather result from unstructured, problematic situations. Different actors in the customer organization typically perceive such problems and their solutions in different ways. Also, projects do not terminate with system delivery but continue as the system is integrated into the organization's practices. Given this broad perspective, customer-centered improvement questions emerge. What are the key elements in understanding how customer and supplier organizations collaborate in systems development? What opportunities and challenges emerge for customers as their supplier organizations mature? How can customers help develop mature customer-supplier relationships?

At Systematic, we were interested in how to better collaborate with customers through a development project; we did not look at situations in which customers simply buy commercial off-the-shelf products. In collaborations, customers need new or modified systems to pursue business goals and achieve some desired changes. Typically, the customer is an organization consisting of many heterogeneous groups. Large organizations sometimes have a purchasing department that solicits systems for future owners and users in other parts of the organization. Smaller organizations typically establish a project to procure a new system, and the system owner participates from the beginning. Sometimes, the customer organization lacks the system-acquisition expertise and will purchases such expertise, usually by hiring consultants.

Suppliers, on the other hand, might produce off-the-shelf products, sell systems that require adaptation, or develop new systems based on specific contracts. In the latter case, the supplier might be the customer's in-house IT department or an independent software house, which might itself have many customers or might function as an outsourced IT department for one client.

Figure 13.1 shows the different roles and interests in customer–supplier projects. In many situations, the relationships are even more complicated. For example, if the buyer is a purchasing department, the supplier might not interact with future users at all. Such complexity in relations can make it difficult to establish good collaborations.

As Figure 13.2 shows, the customer–supplier relationship plays out on several parallel levels. Interactions at the constituting level take place over time and across different projects. Such interactions typically occur between the customer organization's middle management and the supplier organization's sales and marketing team and are aimed at maintaining the relationship and initiating new projects. Top management from both organizations might also interact at this level. At the contractual level, specific contractual negotiations take place and now include the project leader

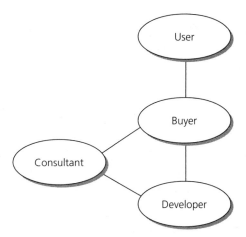

Figure 13.1 *Roles in the customer–supplier relationship*

from the supplier organization and the project owner from the customer organization. The customer might also bring in a consultant at this stage. Contract tracking and maintenance are handled by a steering committee with the help of project leaders or managers from both sides. This phase continues after system delivery until the warranty period is over. At the development level, project teams from both sides work together to develop the system.

The important milestones of each project occur at the contractual level: The contract is signed, the system is accepted, and the guarantee period is over. Looking at

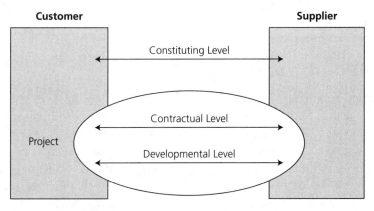

Figure 13.2 *Customer–supplier relationship levels*

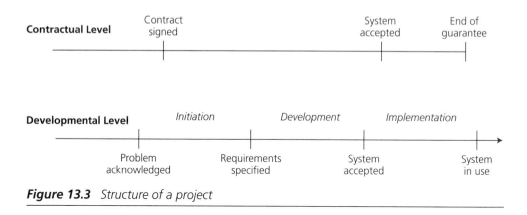

Figure 13.3 *Structure of a project*

the development level, however, we find other important milestones: The problem is acknowledged, the requirements are specified, the system is accepted, and the system is in use. Thus, a project typically lasts longer for the customer than for the supplier. It starts when the customer identifies a problem to solve, and it ends when the solution is implemented as an integral part of the customer's operation. Figure 13.3 shows this basic project structure. We use the term "IT project" rather than the more narrow "software project" to stress this broader perspective.

We now introduce pairs of contrasting concepts that illuminate the nature of the relationship between customer and supplier at each of the three levels in Figure 13.2: collaboration and competition at the constituting level, trust and control at the contractual level, and care and engineering at the development level. A well-functioning customer–supplier relationship requires that the involved actors constantly seek to balance these elements at each level.

13.2 COLLABORATION AND COMPETITION

The customer–supplier relationship includes three quite different contractual arrangements: teams, bureaucracies, and market relationships (Williamson 1975; Ouchi 1979; Ciborra 1993). At one extreme, teams collaborate closely and must have a high level of goal congruence. However, the performance measure typically is implicit and based on mutual trust and shared interests. At the other extreme, market relationships are based on explicit performance measures; that is, they are based on the price. In this case, there is no assumption about goal congruence because the basic form of market relation is competition. Bureaucracy is an intermediary form and has neither high goal congruence nor explicit performance measures. In this case, actors work for an organization's goals based on their employment contract.

At the constituting level, we can view the customer–supplier relationship in IT development as a dynamic network of exchanges governed by these three contractual arrangements. The customer buys services from the supplier, and the basic relation is the market. But a mix of all sorts of market–bureaucratic relationships can exist, depending on the dependencies between the customer and supplier organizations. Specific development efforts are organized as projects, in which the team is the ideal collaborative form. However, such teams are always embedded in bureaucratic arrangements within the respective organizations. The constituting level can thus be understood as a dynamic relationship that balances the intention and need to collaborate with inherent competing interests. Mastenbroek (1993) views this kind of relationship as a network of interdependent groups that are governed by collaboration *and* competition. The involved actors and organizational units are dependent on each other and also have their own interests; to succeed, they must form what Mastenbroek calls "coalitions of divergent interests."

Competition and divergence are, so to speak, embedded in the economic and structural foundation of the relationship, whereas collaboration is a more ephemeral and vulnerable dimension embedded in the relationship's culture. McConnell (1998) suggests that to build and maintain a well-functioning collaboration, both parties must respect the other's "Bill of Rights." Customers must, for example, formulate the goals and expect them to be followed, and they have the right both to make reasonable requirements changes and to know how much they will cost. Developers must, correspondingly, know the goals and the underlying priorities, and they must be able to finish each activity in a technically acceptable fashion. The challenge, in more general terms, is to build and maintain a collaborative environment and culture between the customer and the supplier in which the underlying competitive nature of the relationship is explicitly addressed and dealt with.

13.3 TRUST AND CONTROL

At the contractual level, we find both a psychological contract and a formal, written one (Sabherwal 1999). The psychological contract builds on trust and consists of a set of unwritten and largely unspoken but ideally congruent expectations. The written contract offers mechanisms for structural control and is the outcome of an explicit negotiation process. Sabherwal argues that in IT projects, trust—which he defines as confidence that the other's behavior will meet expectations and will be based on good will—improves performance, whereas distrust hurts performance. Trust is embedded in collaborative teams, whereas structural control is an expression of the bureaucratic and market dimensions of the relationship. Both structural control and trust are needed if the parties are to address unexpected problems, and project participants must constantly balance the two to effectively manage the uncertainties and risks they will face.

Structural control is important because it gives customers confidence in a project's outcome and give suppliers confidence that the users will not ignore the project or make endless demands for new requirements. However, too much control can lead to too much time spent reporting progress instead of developing software, whereas too little control can lead to inefficient or nonexistent communication and coordination, in turn resulting in distrust. On the other hand, too much trust indicates that one party is giving away its responsibility, and too little trust creates increasingly difficult communication.

Sabherwal distinguishes between four types of trust:

1. *Calculus-based trust* is rooted in project rewards and punishments. This type of trust is established in several ways. Examples include implementing structural control and penalty clauses, an approach that minimizes opportunistic behavior; using project management and reporting procedures; and helping customers recognize the supplier's desire to contract future projects.

2. *Knowledge-based trust* depends on the two parties knowing each other well. This knowledge might be based on experience from earlier projects and is increased by having the supplier demonstrate ability, either by running a test case (for standard software) or by building a small system first. Such trust might also be based on existing relationships between key people in both organizations or increased through *courtship,* in which the partners actively get to know each other before the project begins.

3. *Identification-based trust* occurs when parties identify with each others' goals. It is enhanced by establishing shared goals and mutual understanding through early team-building efforts or through collaboration in analysis and design.

4. Performance-based trust is based on project success. This type of trust is especially important when the customer and the supplier are geographically separated. Performance-based trust can be supported by a shared ritual when intermediate goals are reached or by demonstrating completed portions of the system.

Sabherwal argues that balancing trust with structural control leads to well-functioning customer–supplier relations: Structural control promotes decisions and monitors progress, whereas trust promotes creativity and mutual learning.

13.4 CARE AND ENGINEERING

The development level of the relationship is where things get done. At this level, the technical system is developed or adapted to the customer organization, a process that involves several software engineering activities. A strong focus on engineering is both natural and needed. But when this focus is combined with a neglect of the problems and challenges related to the organization's implementation of the new system, the situation becomes highly problematic from the customer's point of view. Ciborra (1996) suggests that when an organization introduces a new IT system, it should practice *hospitality*—that is, the organization should be open and friendly toward its new "guest." Hospitality is necessary because of the system's ambiguous nature. The system might turn out to be a good friend, supporting work in the customer organization in a flexible and efficient manner. Or it might turn out to be a monster, making everyday life difficult and troublesome for users. In the latter case, hospitality can easily turn into hostility. However, if the organization approaches a new system with the expectation of trouble or unexpected events, it will be in a much better position to address the problems and avoid failure.

For the organization to be hospitable, the new system must be cared for at three levels: perception, circumspection, and understanding. *Perception* is the care shown in anticipation of the new system. Project teams from both parties show care in this way by developing shared visions of the new system, building prototypes, adjusting their expectations, controlling changes, planning acceptance testing, and emphasizing user training at an early stage in development.

Circumspection is the care shown in making the system easy to use. This type of care includes preventing errors through user and operator training, correcting ad hoc errors, collecting change orders, and changing routines to provide a good fit between the system and the customer's work tasks. A help desk function is another example of this kind of care.

Understanding, the third level of care, is reached when the new system is integrated as a well-functioning part of the customer organization. In the circumspection level, the system is present-at-hand (Winograd and Flores 1995) and causes breakdowns in the customer organization. In the understanding phase, the system becomes ready-at-hand (Winograd and Flores 1995); that is, system becomes integrated into primary work tasks, and thus there is no longer a need to focus on the system.

The challenge in systems development is to build *and* implement a new or adapted IT system. Building a technical system requires that engineering disciplines be applied to perceived or stated requirements. If the development process is dominated by engineering concerns, however, there is a considerable risk that the effort's business impact will be weak in the customer organization. Care is needed to deal effectively with the social complexity involved in IT implementation.

13.5 RELATIONSHIP DYNAMICS

The three concept pairs are expressions of the contradictory nature of the customer–supplier relationship in IT development. Half of the pairs represent "soft" values: collaboration, trust, and care. These values are expressions of a romantic worldview focused on mutual learning, creativity, and change (Dahlbom and Mathiassen 1993). This romantic position is complemented with the "hard" values of competition, control, and engineering. These values are expressions of a mechanistic worldview that emphasizes prediction, method, and order (Dahlbom and Mathiassen 1993). Outsourced IT development tends to focus on competition, structural control, and engineering and to enforce these values in the face of uncertainty or when unexpected events emerge. What is needed instead is to create a balance in which both organizations deal explicitly with the contradictory relation between customers and suppliers, and between present and emerging organizational forms (Robey 1995).

The three levels of concept pairs are intrinsically related. If a customer and a supplier start at the constituting level in the spirit of collaboration and the acknowledgment of a common goal, trust often results. When unexpected events occur, as they invariably do, this typically leads to negotiations. In an atmosphere of trust, it is easier for each party to go for a win-win solution and to believe that its counterpart will do the same. Trust also leaves room for learning. For example, trusting parties are more likely to experiment when faced with uncertainty or to change decisions when emerging and unexpected insights call for it. Trust also encourages tight interaction from the lowest level upward. When projects are based on care, it reinforces trust at the contractual level, and this in turn enhances and further develops collaboration at the constituting level. The three levels are also connected by the "mechanistic" pairs. Competition, for example, results in each party enforcing structural controls on the other, such as that the supplier delivers software as promised or that the customer delivers involvement as promised.

Even in a well-functioning process that dynamically addresses and manages the relation between collaboration and competition, trust and control, and care and engineering, problems and unexpected events will still arise for two reasons: the task's complexity and uncertainty, and the social complexity inherent in such collaborations. A balanced approach is in no way a guarantee of success. However, it does reduce the risk of failure or unsatisfactory outcomes.

13.6 MATURITY MODELS

A few recent maturity models address the customer–supplier relationship in IT development. Here, we review two specific models—the Software Acquisition Capability

Maturity Model (SA-CMM) and SPIRE, in light of the concepts just discussed. Although the models are structurally different, their content overlaps.

Both models address competition management. For example, competition between suppliers is taken care of by offering customers clear evaluation criteria for selecting a supplier. Competition between the customer and the supplier is managed through a careful choice of contract type. The models are not specific on penalties and rewards, which are related to the type of contract chosen. Nevertheless, both models suppose some kind of fixed delivery date and fixed price. Both models also support structural control. They emphasize that plans and change control procedures are important and that the contract—including the requirements—should be tracked and monitored. Finally, both models support engineering by emphasizing the need to test and evaluate the quality of the delivered product. The models stress both acceptance testing and peer reviews of intermediate products. Thus, as Table 13.1 shows, both models score high on the mechanistic aspects of the customer–supplier relationship. The models differ, however, when it comes to the romantic criteria for a well-functioning relationship.

Customer-Focused Maturity Models

Like the Software Engineering CMM (SE-CMM) (Ferguson et al. 1996), SA-CMM organizes improvement around KPAs at five maturity levels. However, SA-CMM's focus is on acquiring a system rather than on engineering one. SA-CMM is most relevant for large organizations with separate purchasing departments and is oriented toward organizations that acquire systems frequently. It also helps match organizations with suppliers that use CMM (Kind and Ferguson 1997). This is especially relevant for companies that work with military organizations because they require all associated projects to perform at CMM level 3 and use sound project-management practices and organizational routines.

Like CMM, SA-CMM has KPAs at each level. Each KPA describes a goal, a commitment to perform, an ability to perform, activities performed, measurement and analysis, and a way to verify implementation. SA-CMM level 2 is most directly concerned with customer–supplier collaborations. This level has seven KPAs: software acquisition planning, solicitation, requirements development and management, project management, contract tracking and oversight, evaluation, and transition to support.

The SPIRE Handbook (European Community 1998) is a model for small software development companies (fewer than 50 developers). It describes how to conduct SPI. The handbook focuses on the customer–supplier relationship in Chapter 8, outlining several processes that suppliers can improve.

SPIRE describes the overall customer–supplier process in four stages: acquisition process, supply process, requirements-elicitation process, and operational process. The handbook further describes each process in terms of process basics and implementation guidance. Process basics include purpose, motivation, inputs, activities, outputs, industry best practice, and results expected. Implementation guidance includes information, things to do, things to avoid, things to think about, and further reading.

SA-CMM focuses on managing and controlling the software acquisition process. It recognizes the various affected groups and the need for communication among them. However, collaboration and trust are not seen as important aspects of the process. For example, the model does not emphasize collaboration as necessary for reaching the goal, and it offers no indication of how the customer and supplier might come to share goals and success criteria. Trust is included only through structural control; the psychological contract is not mentioned. In terms of care, SA-CMM shows perception care in that it involves affected groups in requirements development and management, and circumspection care in its "transition to support" process, which ensures that there is at least operational support for correcting errors, making changes, and taking responsibility for day-to-day operation. However, given that SA-CMM is a model for software acquisition, we would expect more emphasis on user training, the fit between procedures and the system, and the interface between the users and the supported system, including user documentation and support facilities such as a help desk. In summary, SA-CMM's target group in the customer organization seems to be system purchasers rather than users.

SPIRE is more concerned about collaboration, trust, and care. This is visible mainly in its sections on implementation guidance. SPIRE assumes that the cus-

Table 13.1 *Evaluation of Model Performance*

Worldview	Aspect of Relationship	SA-CMM	SPIRE
Mechanistic	Competition	★★★★★	★★★★★
	Structural control	★★★★★	★★★★★
	Engineering	★★★★★	★★★★★
Romantic	Collaboration	★	★★★★★
	Trust	★	★★★★
	Care	★★★	★★★★

* = poor, ** = deficient, *** = mediocre, **** = good, ***** = very good

tomer and a supplier have a shared goal: a successful system implementation. It also assumes that the customer and supplier organizations will perform joint activities. Nevertheless, SPIRE deals explicitly with situations in which disagreements often occur, such as deciding requirements, dividing responsibilities between the customer and supplier organizations, and deciding system acceptability. SPIRE is fairly direct about trust: "Suppliers must be able to deal effectively and appropriately with their customers in order to deliver their products and services predictably and profitably and in the first place give them confidence that this can be achieved" (European Community 1998, p.75).

SPIRE proposes various ways to promote trust. It secures calculus-based trust through structural control, as well as through recommendations such as, "Ensure that there is an agreed procedure for contact between you and your customer" (Ibid., p. 94), and "Understand customer expectations" (Ibid., p. 92), both of which support the psychological contract. SPIRE also proposes activities for increasing knowledge-based trust, such as learning about related projects; investigating staff turnover in relation to skills, qualifications, and experience; and examining the supplier organization's commitment to software improvement and quality assurance.

SPIRE is also focused on care. Perception care is promoted by emphasizing how the system meets needs and what its significance and value are to the business. The method also advises that real users validate requirements and that key users be involved in the initial needs analysis. SPIRE supports circumspection care by advocating appropriate user training, adequate user documentation, and a procedure for handling user requests, and by assisting and consulting with the product's new users. SPIRE thus gets a full score on collaboration and a nearly full score on trust and care. On trust, SPIRE falls short on courtship and performance-based trust, and on care, it does not address the need for a fit between organizational procedures and system use.

In summary, from a customer viewpoint, we consider SA-CMM to be a mediocre model for systems acquisition. It does not provide a useful balance between the mechanistic and romantic aspects of the customer–supplier relationship, nor does it offer guidance on implementing the new system in the customer's business processes. We consider SPIRE a good model for systems acquisition because it balances mechanistic and romantic criteria fairly well. It does not get a full score, however, because its explicit treatment of the relation between mechanistic and romantic criteria could be improved.

13.7 THE WORKSHOP

Systematic's management is committed to improving customer relationships, and the company views collaboration as a competitive advantage. Systematic therefore decided to organize a workshop to initiate collaboration with customers, to evaluate strengths and weaknesses in existing relationships, and to identify activities that would increase the maturity of collaborations. We designed the workshop as a mixture of prepared presentations and structured discussions. We asked several customers to present assessments of the collaboration, and we presented state-of-the-art knowledge on customer–supplier relations in IT projects. Given the theory we have outlined here, we then evaluated Systematic's customer–supplier relationships based on our workshop findings. We then discussed our initiatives aimed at improving collaboration.

The workshop itself was an obvious expression of Systematic's cooperative strategy. Beyond that, Systematic management demonstrated cooperation clearly in some projects by taking on unexpected costs in order to provide customers with satisfactory solutions. Customers emphasized Systematic's willingness to cooperate, and, overall, there seemed to be a useful balance between competition and collaboration at the constituting level.

Customers also mentioned trust as a key part of their relationship with Systematic. Identity-based trust—the will to identify with each others' goals—is strongly supported by Systematic management. However, this type of trust must be strengthened at the project level, as is clear in customer comments that mentioned "lack of sharing knowledge" and "one-sided dependency." The amount of knowledge-based trust varies with the customers. Some relationships are old, whereas others are fairly new. Nevertheless, lack of knowledge about the customer organization was mentioned several times and seems to be a common problem. In general, customers expressed trust in Systematic's knowledge. We heard comments such as "good professional knowledge," "good technical knowledge," and "good competence." In general, customers also seemed satisfied with Systematic's performance, and thus performance-based trust does exist. Nonetheless, statements such as "unpredictable delivery time" and "lack of domain knowledge" indicate room for improvement. The most pressing problems, however, relate to calculus-based trust. Even though our calculus-based trust is supported through contract-based penalties, both Systematic and its customers lack structural control. According to customers, Systematic's lack of structural control is manifest as "unclear expectations," "lack of control," and "unpredictable delivery time." Customers also said that they want more formalized contact and communication throughout the project and that they would like more structural control through such things as better project organization.

Because most Systematic projects do not have access to "real users"—customer participation is typically at the contract level—our involvement with the perception aspect of care is limited. From the customers' viewpoint, an important contribution to perception care is their ability to critically question the requirements and thus avoid expensive and unnecessary ones. Systematic supports circumspection only to a certain extent; our documentation could be better. At the seminar, customers admitted that they also offer too little at the care level with respect to both perception and circumspection. Customers mentioned problems with getting the right users to participate, motivating and training new users, and giving them proper support.

As our workshop shows, there are important imbalances between trust and control, and between care and engineering in Systematic–customer relationships. To some extent, Systematic management's general focus on collaboration balances out the lack of structural control and the possibilities for distrust it implies. This collaborative focus also helps minimize the impact of relatively weak attention to care on both sides and Systematic's strong focus on engineering and traditional SPI. Nonetheless, there are many good reasons to improve the relationship between Systematic and its customers.

Table 13.2 shows the proposals for improvement that were forwarded at the workshop. The participants divided the proposals into customer, supplier, and shared improvements. We then divided them further. Even though some proposals encourage stronger structural control—such as the suggestions under project management and requirements management—there is a striking focus on improved knowledge about and understanding of the other party. The suggestions on contextual issues, mutual understanding, and process support all point in this direction, as do the suggestions under organizational implementation and some of those under miscellaneous. The focus on mutual understanding and the communication needed to achieve it is a key aspect of the romantic worldview. This indicates that if Systematic wants to improve its customer relationships, it must expand the romantic aspects at the project level and must more systematically balance them with mechanisms for structural control.

Table 13.2 *Proposals for Improving Systematic's Customer Relations*

	Customer Improvement	Shared Improvements	Supplier Improvement
Contextual issues	• Establish flexible funding procedure • Inform supplier about IT strategy • Specify development strategy • Make goals visible	• Create two-phase contracts • Structure contracts to permit changes • Organize projects symmetrically • Know each others' strengths and weaknesses	• Communicate IT strategy • Make process visible

Table continued on next page.

Table 13.2 *Continued*

	Customer Improvement	**Shared Improvements**	**Supplier Improvement**
Mutual understanding	• Help supplier understand the customer's world • Allocate resources to project • Be available • Develop a strategy for involving end users	• Hold workshop before signing contract • Hold workshop after signing contract • Establish the project properly	• Acquire domain knowledge through visits and interviews • Offer workshops to increase customer competence
Process support	• Show real commitment throughout the project • Establish project culture	• Evaluate and discuss process	• Offer course on "being a customer" • Facilitate the process • Invite customers to take part in milestone evaluation
Project management		• Share risk management • Share estimation and scheduling • Share emergency plan • Be both open and in control	
Requirement management	• Be flexible with requirements	• Share requirements database and add procedure for update	• Be aware of requirements sliding
Organizational implementation	• Involve supplier in the implementation activities		• Increase focus on organizational implementation • Create documentation on maintenance
Miscellaneous	• Give testing priority • Reuse experiences	• Share tools • Enforce acceptance criteria for usability (four out of six users must be able to perform tasks)	• Build trust by communicating internally, maintaining customer contact at all levels, celebrating results with the customer, creating info-server for all projects, and making management engagement visible

13.8 EARLY INITIATIVES

Based on the workshop findings, Systematic launched specific improvement initiatives targeting the customer–supplier relationship. The first initiative is to design and implement six joint workshops that actively involve customers. Second, Systematic will support several customer initiatives to strengthen customer participation in projects. Among these initiatives are ones to develop project-management skills, establish a project culture, and create opportunities for Systematic developers to visit and interview "real users." Finally, Systematic will develop simple frameworks, based in part on available models, that can be used to critically assess specific customer-supplier relationships.

As part of its first initiative, Systematic is planning six workshops for improving customer relations.

- ◆ In the Project Establishment Workshop, participants will outline the project's vision, focus on goals and customer and supplier roles, and analyze risks.
- ◆ In the Establishing Requirements Workshop, relevant stakeholders will identify key requirements and select procedures for managing requirements changes.
- ◆ In the Project Diagnosis Workshop, participants will first review the project's schedules and budgets and then evaluate results and hold another risk-analysis session.
- ◆ The Rollout Workshop focuses on helping the organization use the new system. Participants define a rollout strategy, identify the various roles involved, analyze education and training needs, and plan the implementation process.
- ◆ The Test Planning Workshop emphasizes test strategy. Participants design acceptance criteria, develop test plans for the customer and supplier, and make test data provisions.
- ◆ In the Project Evaluation Workshop, participants analyze positive and negative experiences and develop proposals for improving future cooperation.
  We plan to hold all six workshops with each customer in the future.

A Sample Workshop

We held a Project Evaluation Workshop with a customer who had several years' experience with large Systematic projects. The workshop was carried out as a structured brainstorming session, focusing on why the most recent project went well and how it could have been better. We recorded comments and grouped them according to subheads to capture their essence. We then presented and discussed the subheads. According to our findings, the project went well for the following reasons:

- A "fantastic partnership" with mutual goals, respect, and trust led to a flexible approach that ensured project success.
- Meetings were well organized with clear agendas and constructive discussions.
- Management meetings and technical meetings were held separately.
- There was contact at all levels between the parties involved, resulting in direct access to knowledge, information, and decision makers.
- Systematic had the required technical competence.
- The contract supported the shared goals, and all parties were motivated to complete the project on time and budget.

We also identified several areas for improvement:

- Control of subcontractors could have been better.
- It was sometimes difficult for Systematic to obtain needed information because the customer gave other activities higher priority.
- Systematic lacked operational knowledge from future users and was therefore often dependent on the customer.
- Top management on both sides could have been more involved in the project.
- The contract could have been simplified by removing milestones that, from a practical viewpoint, were not needed.

Based on this information, we identified five recommendations for future projects:

- Define a strategy for end-user involvement.
- Aim at common goals for the end users, the customer, and the contractor.
- Establish communication and contact at all levels in both organizations.
- Define only practically useful milestones.
- Consider providing user documentation and training up front.

13.9 CONCLUSION

A gap exists between what we know about IT projects and what is covered in contemporary models for improving customer–supplier relationships. SA-CMM is strongly oriented toward competition, control, and engineering, whereas the SPIRE model is somewhat more balanced. Both models can, however, be improved by systematically applying state-of-the-art knowledge on mechanisms and concepts that facilitate collaboration, trust, and care.

Generally, we agree with the CMM that IT organizations should improve their project-management practice before they focus on customer relations. It makes little sense for a software organization to invite customers into joint improvement initiatives before project-management disciplines are in place. Software development is, however, a complex exchange process that crosses organizational boundaries. As software organizations reach level 2, they must go beyond a traditional focus on internal processes and must include customer relations in their SPI programs.

Too few SPI initiatives take this position seriously. Our diagnosis of Systematic customer relations reveals strengths, weaknesses, and many opportunities for action. Our experiences from this effort support the idea that joint improvement efforts should lead to a useful balance between mechanistic and romantic aspects at all levels of the relationship.

13.10 REFERENCES

Ciborra, C. 1993. *Teams, Markets, and Systems—Business Innovation and Information Technology,* Cambridge, UK: Cambridge University Press.

Ciborra, C. 1996. "Introduction: What Does Groupware Mean for the Organizations Hosting It?" *Groupware & Teamwork*: *Invisible Aid or Technical Hindrance?* New York: John Wiley & Sons.

Dahlbom, B., and L. Mathiassen. 1993. *Computers in Context—The Philosophy and Practice of Systems Design.* Oxford, UK: Blackwell Publishers.

European Community. 1998. *The SPIRE Handbook.*

Ferguson, J., et al. 1996. *Software Acquisition Capability Maturity Model.* Version 1.01. CMU/SEI-96-TR-020. Pittsburgh: Software Engineering Institute.

Kind, P., and J. Ferguson. 1997. "The Software Acquisition Capability Maturity Model." *Crosstalk. The Journal of Defense Software Engineering.* 10:3:13–17.

Mastenbroek, W.F.G. 1993. *Conflict Management and Organization Development.* New York: John Wiley & Sons.

McConnell S. 1998. *Software Project Survival Guide.* Redmond, WA: Microsoft Press.

Ouchi, W.G. 1979. "A Conceptual Framework for the Design of Organizational Control Mechanisms," *Management Science.* 25:833–848.

Robey, D. 1995. "Theories that Explain Contradiction: Accounting for the Contradictory Organizational Consequences of Information Technology." J. I. DeGross et al., eds. *Proceedings from 16th International Conference on Information Systems*. Amsterdam.

Sabherwal, R. 1999. "The Role of Trust in Out-Sourced IT Projects." *Communications of the ACM*. 42:2:80–86.

Williamson, O. 1975. *Markets and Hierarchies: Analysis and Antitrust Implications*. New York: The Free Press.

Winograd, T., and F. Flores. 1995. *Understanding Computers and Cognition—A New Foundation for Design*. Norwood, NJ: Ablex.

Chapter 14

Strategies for Organizational Learning in SPI

Jesper Arent, Morten Hvid Pedersen,
and Jacob Nørbjerg

In this chapter, we look at SPI as an organizational learning process—that is, a process in which an organization's actors build or acquire new knowledge and then use this knowledge to improve both their own practice and the organization's overall performance. Looking at SPI from this perspective moves our focus from issues such as maturity models, KPAs, and documented procedures to the study of knowledge, competence, and learning in SPI.

Successful SPI interventions change how organizations develop and manage software development. Maturity models such as Bootstrap or CMM define goals for change and then assess organizations to determine what they must change to meet the goals. Other SPI literature discusses how organizations can plan and conduct the change process (Paulk et al. 1993; Caputo 1998). However, as contributions to this book and others (Goldenson and Herbsleb 1997) show, it is difficult to sustain successful and ongoing SPI. Better strategies are needed to support the SPI change process, to meet critical challenges, and to avoid pitfalls involved in changing software organizations.

An organizational learning perspective offers valid and useful insights into the improvement process and thus can help you design, plan, and implement successful software process improvements. To illustrate this, we analyze here the four SPI projects described in Chapters 3–6 from a learning perspective. That is, we look at how software engineers, SPI agents, project managers, higher management, and others build and acquire knowledge about better software development and management practices and put this knowledge to practical use in their daily work.

Our analysis shows that each SPI project created organizational knowledge and improved its software development process. In doing so, the projects basically followed one of two learning strategies. The first centers on SPI groups and the implementation of new, documented processes. The second focuses on software development project teams and local changes to each project's work practices. As we discuss later in the chapter, each strategy has particular characteristics and strengths and weaknesses in how it helps you create and sustain organizational learning.

In the following section, we offer an overview of organizational learning and our framework for analysis. We then describe our research approach, followed by an analysis of each SPI case study. Finally, we discuss our findings and areas for further research.

14.1 ORGANIZATIONAL LEARNING IN SPI

There are several broad definitions of organizational learning (see, for example, Garvin 1993). We view organizational learning as the way organizations build, supplement, and order knowledge and routines around their activities and thus improve efficiency by better adapting and developing the broad skills of their workforce (Fiol and Lyles 1985). An organization involved in SPI must thus create, acquire, and transfer knowledge and must modify its behavior to reflect new knowledge and insights. To improve existing software practices, an organization must create new and "better" knowledge and transform this knowledge into habit so that it becomes "the way software is developed around here."

SPI literature offers few discussions of the learning perspective (Baskerville and Pries-Heje 1999; Halloran 1999; Stelzer et al. 1998). However, some SPI researchers have recently explored how organizational learning and knowledge creation can contribute to SPI. Stelzer et al. (1998) discuss how organizational learning principles and techniques contribute to SPI success, and Baskerville and Pries-Heje (1998) propose that maturity models be extended to include knowledge management practices. Stelzer et al. (1998) argue that organizational learning might help design, implement, and improve SPI initiatives and that "we need to assess different strategies for implementing organizational learning in software companies."

Our analysis is based on the theory of organizational knowledge creation described in Nonaka and Takeuchi (1995). From the perspective of Nonaka and Takeuchi, SPI can be viewed as an approach to improving organizational performance that requires knowledge acquisition and distribution on three levels: individual, group, and organization. We use this framework as a basis for analyzing the four SPI case studies.

A Theory of Organizational Learning

Nonaka and Takeuchi's (1995) theory of organizational knowledge creation encompasses individual learning processes, as well as knowledge expansion and dissemination throughout the organization.

According to their theory, new knowledge is created through transformations between tacit and explicit knowledge. *Tacit* knowledge is personal knowledge and experience that is hard to formalize and communicate to others but that can be exchanged through work, observation, and other shared experiences. *Explicit* knowledge is codified knowledge that is "transmittable in formal, systematic language" (Ibid., p. 59) such as models, textbooks, and written procedures. Organizations rely on the tacit, informal knowledge of individuals as well as on the explicit, formal knowledge documented in textbooks, procedures, manuals, and so on.

People learn through a series of conversions between tacit and explicit knowledge. There are four such processes: socialization, externalization, combination, and internalization. In *socialization,* an individual's tacit knowledge is shared with others through such things as work, observation, or imitation. In *externalization*, the tacit knowledge embedded in individual actions and experiences is made explicit through such things as models, descriptions, or metaphors. Externalization is a very important knowledge creation process; it is where ideas or concepts—such as problems and proposed changes—are formalized. Good communication through dialog, listening, and collective reflection supports externalization.

Explicit knowledge from several sources can then be combined into new explicit knowledge. Through this *combination,* existing practices, textbooks, models, and so on, are captured, collected, sorted, and integrated into new descriptions, models, procedures, and so on. Finally, to improve organizational performance, explicit knowledge must be embodied in action and practice. Thus, the new knowledge must be passed back to those who can use it in their work, thereby creating new tacit knowledge. Through this *internalization*, individuals identify, access, and implement relevant knowledge from the organizational knowledge base. In this way, the new practices become "the way work is done."

Learning involves cycling through all four knowledge transformation processes, moving from tacit to explicit to (new) tacit knowledge. Figure 14.1 shows this movement along with the learning processes involved in each transformation.

Knowledge is created by individuals, and individuals learn by creating knowledge. Organizational knowledge creation and learning should therefore be understood as "a process that organizationally amplifies the knowledge created by individuals and crystallizes it as a part of the knowledge network of the organization" (Ibid., p. 59). The theory conceives of this expansion process as a learning spiral that cycles through the four learning processes at ever-higher organizational levels: Individuals share tacit knowledge in group sessions, where they reflect, integrate, and eventually use the new knowledge to improve their practice and performance. Groups then exchange knowledge, share new knowledge with others, and so on. The theory thus distinguishes between learning at the individual, group, and organization levels.

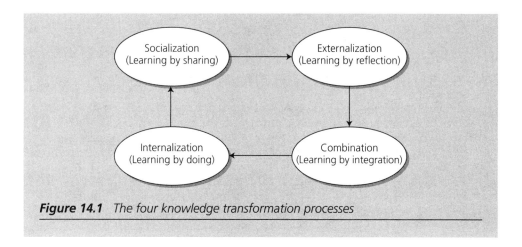

Figure 14.1 *The four knowledge transformation processes*

According to the framework, organizational learning is a continuous cycle that expands through all levels of the organization. When we apply this to SPI it means that first, SPI interventions should be designed and implemented in a way that promotes learning at the individual, group, and organization levels. It is not enough that select individuals learn new practices. To improve organizational behavior, the practices must be embedded in the organization. Second, SPI projects should produce both explicit and tacit knowledge. SPI projects should create an organizational knowledge base—by describing new procedures, standards, and guidelines—*and* institutionalize this knowledge into daily software practices. That is, individuals must identify, access, and use the processes. Third, SPI interventions should use learning processes that expand from the group level to the organization level.

The description of CMM maturity levels implies that SPI-related learning takes place at different organizational levels: Level 1 organizations depend on individual software developers (heroes) to navigate crises; level 2 focuses on improving the project team's ability to manage software processes; level 3 focuses on helping the organization define and improve its overall processes and thus attain a defined capability; and levels 4 and 5 focus on empowering individual software developers to implement continuous improvement. Thus, according to the CMM, learning moves from individuals to projects to the organization and then back to projects and individuals.

In terms of learning in SPI, the target for individual learning is obviously individual software developers and managers as well as those responsible for quality assurance, method support, and so on. As to group-level learning, we should consider both the project teams, which need to acquire and use new practices, and the formal SPI group(s). The SPI literature recommends that organizations establish one or more software process engineering groups (SEPGs) to facilitate and manage the SPI program. SEPG members might be developers who work with SPI part time, or they might come to the group from full-time work with development tools and methods or quality assurance. SEPGs typically are responsible for such things as overall planning and implementation of the SPI project, defining and implementing improved practices, coaching developers in new practices, and building and maintaining a repository of knowledge about new tools and techniques. The SEPG can also assign dedicated process action teams (PATs) to define and implement new and better software processes (McFeeley 1996; Zahran 1998). In this respect, the SEPG and associated PATs become focal points for SPI learning. Hence, group-level learning can be associated both with SPI groups and with software project groups.

In terms of organization-level learning, we follow Snyder and Cummings's (1998) definition: Learning is organizational when (1) it aims at organizational goals, (2) it is shared and distributed among organization members, and (3) its outcomes are embedded in the organizations' systems, structures, and culture.

SPI's ultimate goal is to improve an organization's software practices. To do this, improved practices must become internalized as tacit knowledge across the organization. According to Spender (1996), when this knowledge "has been transformed into habit, made traditional in the sense that no one can explain it, it becomes 'the way we do things around here.' " Such knowledge acquisition is a spiral process, starting at the individual level and moving up through expanding communities of interaction, crossing sectional, departmental, divisional, and organizational boundaries (Nonaka and Takeuchi 1995). This sounds good, but it raises many questions. How do you actually approach organizational learning in relation to SPI initiatives? Where do you start, and whom should you involve? How do you create and expand the necessary knowledge about good practices throughout the organization? To help answer these important questions, we now examine how knowledge was created and diffused in four SPI case studies.

14.2 SPI PROJECT ANALYSIS

Our analysis of the four SPI projects examines key events with the goal of identifying related learning processes and organizational learning. Therefore, we offer only a brief summary of each project, followed by our analysis. Chapters 3–6 describe the projects in detail.

Systematic

Systematic set very ambitious goals for its SPI project (see Chapter 4). Systematic's top management wanted to go from CMM level 1 to level 3 in three years. To reach this goal, Systematic established five PATs, staffed on a volunteer basis by software managers and developers with relevant expertise. The PATs were tasked with developing organizationwide processes for each of the CMM level 2 KPAs.

However, repeated changes to the SPI organization and delays in management approval hindered the writing and implementation of new processes. The first draft versions of new processes (in the project planning and tracking area) were not ready until early 1998. New PATs were formed to finish the other CMM level 2 areas. By the end of 1999, a new business manual containing all the new level 2 processes was up on Systematic's intranet. Some of the new processes had the approval of top management, and others were published in draft form.

The new processes were introduced to all project managers through a training program. In this program, external consultants taught good project-management practices, using the new processes as examples and templates. Project managers interacted while learning the new processes in the training program and applying them thereafter.

Although the company was using the CMM model, it had also been assessed using Bootstrap in August 1997. That Bootstrap assessment placed the company at level 2.00, although it identified the same issues as an earlier CMM assessment. Systematic's follow-up Bootstrap assessment in late 1999 placed the company at level 2.5.

Systematic's SPI project was dominated by experience sharing and collaborative reflecting on current practices in the SEPGs and PATs. As Figure 14.2 shows, expanding learning to other parts of the organization came late and was based on the project-manager training program and, later, on the intranet business manual, which was available to all projects.

Project managers began integrating new knowledge during the project-manager training program and later added learning by doing as they applied the new processes in practice. Furthermore, using the new processes in combination with the ongoing training program promoted continuous learning at the organization level. As part of the training program, the project managers met and shared their experiences with the new processes. Also, toward the SPI project's end, organization-level learning was supported by the publication of the new intranet-based business manual.

However, these new organization-level processes did not grow out of practice but rather were defined by the PATs. It is therefore uncertain whether the new processes represent good (usable) software practice for Systematic overall. To ensure this, further reflection and integration are needed at the organization level. To begin, the company should systematically collect the experiences gained through actual use of the new processes and use this information to modify and enhance the processes.

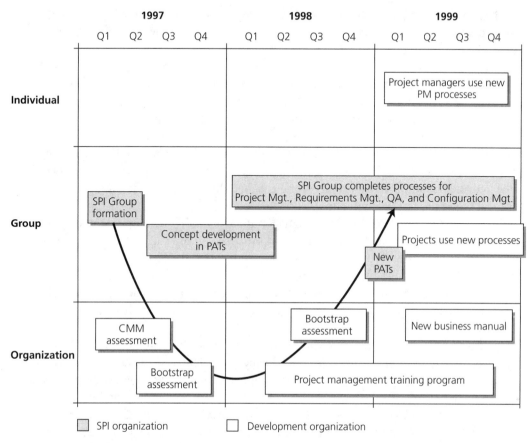

Figure 14.2 *Organizational knowledge creation at Systematic*

Brüel & Kjær

As Chapter 6 describes, SPI activities at Brüel & Kjær dated back several years to the establishment of its Center for Software Process Improvement. A Bootstrap assessment in the fall of 1996 placed Brüel & Kjær at level 2.25, which generally indicates good project-level practices.

Nonetheless, the new SPI group decided to begin its improvement project with a series of interviews with select project managers. Through the interviews, the SPI group collected detailed information about development and management practices, software process problems, and improvement ideas.

The group planned and implemented the ensuing improvement initiatives in close collaboration with project managers and project teams. Each project manager chose one improvement area that he or she considered important for the project and experimented with solutions in cooperation with the SPI group. For example, in the process models area, the SPI group first introduced several alternative process models into a pilot project and then let the manager and team members define and use their own process model. In another improvement initiative, requirements specification, the SPI group trained the pilot projects in several requirements elicitation and specification techniques that had been identified and used in previous SPI initiatives (see Chapters 8 and 18). In both cases, the SPI group followed the projects closely, collected and documented experiences, and coached the developers, helping them adjust and refine processes and techniques as needed.

By the end of 1999, the local SPI manager and the quality manager documented the new development model and requirement processes in the company's quality system. Also, some other projects learned about and introduced the new processes through informal project-manager networks.

A Bootstrap assessment in October 1999 again placed the company at level 2.25. However, the assessment showed less variation among projects and clear progress in the areas that the SPI project had focused on.

As Figure 14.3 shows, Brüel & Kjær's SPI project was dominated by learning by doing, primarily in select project groups. However, the learning processes involved several full learning cycles. Knowledge sharing, reflection, and integration are all seen in the SPI group's interviews with project managers and the use of defect-prevention techniques that had been identified and tested in previous SPI initiatives. The group used the explicit knowledge resulting from these processes to start learning cycles in project groups, where developers were trained in new techniques, used them in practice, shared their experiences with the SPI group, modified their practice, and so on. This produced both tacit knowledge, in changed development project practices, and explicit knowledge, in the addition of new processes to the quality system.

Brüel & Kjær's SPI project improved practice in a few software projects, but the learning was limited to two improvement areas—the development model and requirements specifications—and it has proven difficult to expand the learning processes to other projects. Also, the move to organization-level learning was late and largely incidental. Some new processes have been documented in the quality system, but further dissemination of this knowledge to other project groups has been informal and sporadic; it has occurred largely through the informal project-manager network or personal contact between project managers and the local SPI manager.

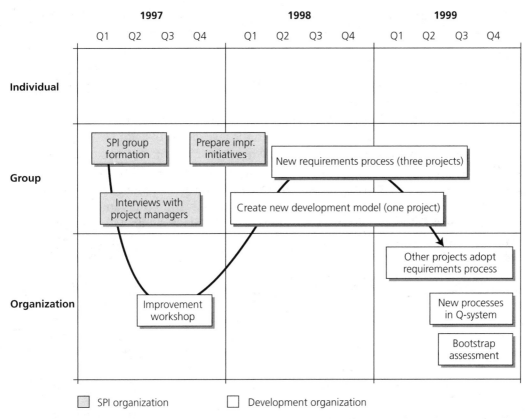

Figure 14.3 *Organizational knowledge creation at Brüel & Kjær*

Ericsson Denmark

In 1997, Ericsson Denmark conducted several parallel SPI initiatives. Most activities were organized by 12 PATs assigned to define new generic frameworks (processes, tools, methods, templates, and so on) related to the six CMM level 2 KPAs and six other areas identified by Ericsson Denmark's internal ESSI program (see Chapter 3).

In late 1997, the SPI project was externally assessed, and that led to a significant change in focus; improvement efforts were to be anchored in development projects and refocused toward the goal of reaching CMM level 2. The SPI group therefore initiated a series of project group self-assessments linked to CMM level 2 key processes. These UltraLight Assessments (ULAs) were repeated monthly during the first half of

1998, and they inspired local and project-specific improvement initiatives. Often, the improvements were simply a matter of documenting existing practices, but sometimes they required other changes, such as appointing and training managers in project quality and configuration. Thus, over a six-month period, project teams gradually changed their practices. A June 1998 assessment placed Ericsson Denmark at CMM level 2 (see Chapters 3 and 10).

After the assessment, Ericsson Denmark's management formed SEPGs in each of the company's four development divisions, with the goal of consolidating level 2 practices at the divisional level and launching further improvement initiatives aimed at CMM level 3. A central SPI group was assigned to coordinate the SEPGs' work. However, because of changing priorities and the restructuring of the other divisions, only one SEPG survived and thus only one division continued the SPI program.

Learning in Ericsson Denmark's SPI project was originally dominated by sharing, reflection, and integration at the group level (the PATs), with no learning in other parts of the organization (see Figure 14.4). The refocusing and change of strategy in late 1997, however, initiated a series of full learning cycles in project groups based on the ULAs. In these cycles, developers shared and reflected on their practices (the as-

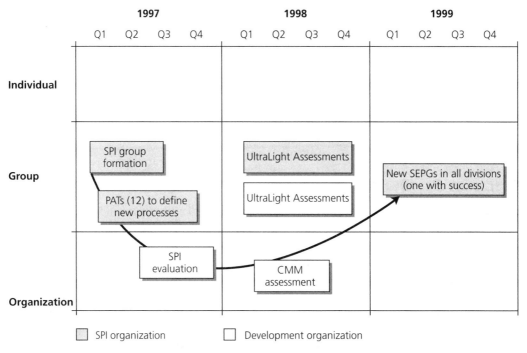

Figure 14.4 *Organizational knowledge creation at Ericsson Denmark*

sessment) and defined and used new processes (integration and learning by doing). The cycles were repeated several times before the CMM assessment and covered all level 2 KPAs.

However, moving the learning process from the project level to the organization level has proven difficult. Following the assessment, Ericsson Denmark attempted this expansion by setting up departmental SEPGs charged with collecting project experiences, creating and implementing departmentwide processes, and exchanging successful level 2 practices with other departments. By the end of 1999, this strategy had succeeded in only one department, and the move to organization-level learning had yet to take place.

Danske Data

In May 1997, parallel maturity assessments placed Danske Data on CMM level 1 and Bootstrap level 1.5 (Iversen et al. 1998). The SPI group then appointed seven PATs to address the issues identified in the assessments. Three of the PATs succeeded in creating outlines of quality meetings, project management, and implementation (the Learn to Implement effort, which focused on diffusion and adoption of methods and tools; see Chapter 5).

As part of the project-management initiative, Danske Data created a Project Manager Competence Center. The PMC Center was founded to educate project managers and support continuous improvements within project management. After various unsuccessful attempts to get project managers to use new processes on their own initiative, the PMC Center's founders started a project-manager training program and developed a self-assessment tool for project managers. The tool is based on the company's own standard of good project-management practices; project managers can use the tool to evaluate their performance after a project ends and to initiate improvement initiatives in their next project (see Chapter 10).

Project-management practice has improved as a result of these initiatives, and a subsequent Bootstrap assessment placed Danske Data at level 2.0.

As Figure 14.5 shows, learning in Danske Data's SPI project was—at the outset—concentrated on sharing, reflection, and integration in the PATs. Apart from some uptake of quality meetings, learning in the organization was limited before the establishment of the PMC Center and the training program. The training program and associated self-assessments were based on the vision established in the project-management standard, which was produced in the PATs and which project managers can tailor to local needs.

The improvement project thus implemented a context to create organizational learning among the project managers through a combination of learning by doing (tailoring and using the new project-management standards) and sharing, reflection,

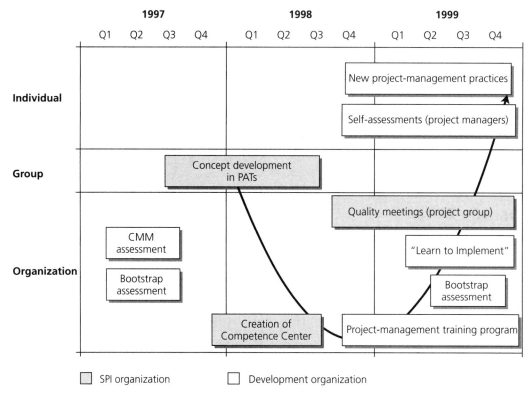

Figure 14.5   *Organizational knowledge creation at Danske Data*

and integration (self-assessments and the training program). It is, however, unclear to what extent learning has expanded beyond the project managers to the group and organization levels. First, it is unclear to what extent the project managers' changed practices can influence developers working on their project teams. Second, the self-assessments take place *after* a project has ended and thus are not integrated with a project's day-to-day work. Finally, even though the training program is a potentially strong vehicle for sharing, reflection, and integration (through discussions among project managers and systematic collection of their experiences), it is unclear to what extent this actually takes place.

14.3 DISCUSSION

As we discussed earlier, learning in SPI means to create and sustain a learning process that expands throughout the individual, group, and organization levels. This learning process should include the creation of both tacit knowledge, through changes in practice, and explicit knowledge, through procedures, guidelines, tools, and templates. In our analysis of the four SPI projects, we identified two distinct strategies for reaching this goal: *exploration,* which aims to investigate new practices and ways of working, and *exploitation,* which aims to capitalize on existing software process knowledge and disseminate it throughout the organization. Table 14.1 summarizes the key characteristics of each strategy.

The exploration strategy focuses on creating tacit knowledge in software projects. Improvement initiatives are defined according to each project's specific needs, and the improved practices are documented and moved into the larger organization only if another project or entity (such as a SEPG) specifically requests them.

The exploitation strategy is centered around SPI groups (SEPG and PATs) and creates knowledge by reflection and integration of existing software process knowledge, such as existing best practices, and processes and procedures from software engineering literature. This information is disseminated throughout the organizations in the form of written procedures.

As we've outlined them here, the strategies are of course archetypes. However, the SPI projects we studied offer more or less clearcut examples of the strategies:

- Systematic's SPI project mainly followed the exploitation strategy. From the outset, the project's ambition was to create common and improved practices at the organization level by developing and organizing a wide dissemination of new standard procedures.

- Ericsson Denmark's SPI project started with a similar strategy—but changed to a more exploratory approach (the UltraLight Assessments) after the first year. Disseminating the new project experiences across levels has been attempted, but with limited success.

- Danske Data's SPI project used both strategies. Some initiatives were driven by exploitation, such as the Learning to Implement project and the design and documentation of new processes, which emerged from discussions in the SEPG and PATs. Other initiatives, such as self-assessments and the project-management standard, were driven mainly by exploration—specifically, by project managers' willingness to learn and experiment with the new standard.

- Brüel & Kjær's approach represents the clearest example of exploration. Improvements were based on the project managers' perceptions of problems and possible solutions and were strongly tied to the development and implementation of new project practices. Some of the improved practices have been documented in the quality system.

Table 14.1 *Key Characteristics of the Exploration and Exploitation Strategies*

	Exploration	Exploitation
Purpose	Improve practice in projects	Document existing organizational knowledge
Principle	Problem-oriented improvements	Process-oriented improvements
Group-level learning	Software project group explores alternative solutions to specific problems	SEPG and/or PATs exploit existing knowledge to define good practiceS within select process areas
Organization-level learning	Software projects share good practices to define good practices for the organization	SEPG and/or PATs integrate existing knowledge into coherent organizational knowledge base available for all projects
Knowledge created	Mainly tacit, in the form of improved (not documented) practices	Mainly explicit, in the form of documented (not changed) practices
Main learning processes at group level	• Sharing • Doing	• Reflection • Integration
Main learning processes aimed at organizational learning	• Sharing • Reflection	• Integrating • Doing
Learning Challenges		
Group-level learning*	What to improve?	Who knows the best practices? How do we transform the best practices into explicit processes?
Organization-level learning	What are the best practices in our organization? How do we transform best practices into explicit processes? Who follows best practices?	How do we integrate good practices into best practices? How do we get all projects to use the new processes?
Tools	• Informal peer networks for spreading experiences • Rotating employees among projects • Light assessments to find areas for improvement	• Process action teams to combine good practices into company standard • Distribute standard process descriptions in quality system • Light assessments to monitor implementation of new processes • Training programs
Enabling conditions	Resources available for experiments at project level	Commitment from top management

* In the exploitation strategy, the "group" is the SPI team and related PATs.

Using our experiences with these projects as a reference, we now offer a more detailed discussion of the exploration and exploitation strategies and the challenges they pose for SPI change agents.

Learning by Exploration

In the exploration strategy, the key learning processes are learning by sharing and learning by doing. These processes focus more on changing practice (creating tacit knowledge) than on documenting practice (creating explicit knowledge). Effective sharing occurs when someone within the project actually performs a good practice and the other group members learn the good practice through observation, imitation, or some similar method. Effective learning by doing occurs when an explicit concept of good practice (from the CMM or an external consultant's suggestions, for example) is used to explore good practices. The strategy is anchored in project groups whose members explore new solutions to their most pressing problems and gradually improve their practice.

In our study, three of the four projects pursued this strategy with an emphasis on learning by doing. Ericsson Denmark and Danske Data used self-assessments as a way to make project managers and team members reflect on and change their own processes, whereas Brüel & Kjær's SPI group trained select project groups to develop and use specific techniques and processes.

As results from all three organizations show, the exploration strategy is successful at the group level. Each company initiated learning processes in individual software projects, in which the project manager—and, to some extent, project teams—learned new ways of working (although it is debatable whether Danske Data's main learning processes emphasized the project groups or individual project managers).

The move to organization-level learning, however, appears to be more difficult. None of the organizations achieved much success in this respect. All project groups at Ericsson Denmark, for example, implemented new processes to meet the CMM level 2 requirements, but the results—in terms of which processes were installed—are intentionally different across projects. With the exploration strategy, implementing common organizational practices requires sharing of and reflection on specific project practices if they are to be successfully transferred to projects throughout the organization. This requires some mechanism to share and collect experiences, to identify the best of the new practices, and subsequently to transfer this knowledge across projects. For example, you might rotate trained developers into different projects so that other project teams can learn through direct experiences such as sharing, teaching, workshops, and so on. Of all the groups, Ericsson Denmark is probably in the best position to do this because all its project groups have established and documented their improved practices, and thus there are a range of good practices to choose from.

Brüel & Kjær's SPI project has created change only in select project groups. Furthermore, the changes do not concern the same process areas; some projects have changed their process model, and others have improved their requirements engineering processes. Here, the challenge is to convince other projects to use the new practices. This effort could be supported by the fact that the SPI group has systematically collected and systematized its pilot-project experience and therefore has a set of written procedures and guidelines available. Also, developers have already expressed interest in this documented experience, and the pilot-project developers know how to apply the new procedures and can help their colleagues. To proceed in this direction, however, Brüel & Kjær must set up a mechanism for integration and sharing across projects.

As our experiences show, the exploration strategy results in quick but uncoordinated improvements and change at the group or project level. The strategy focuses on creating *tacit* knowledge, and therefore the SPI group (or others) must allocate resources to collect and systematize new practices.

The exploration strategy also provides weak support for organizationwide learning. Given this, it must be supplemented with support for experience collection and cross-project exchange through such things as training, workshops, and so on, and a readiness to shift dynamically between learning at the individual, group, and organization levels.

Learning by Exploitation

The dominant learning processes in the exploitation strategy are learning by reflection and integration. These processes are concentrated in the SEPG and/or the associated PATs, but the goal is to create explicit knowledge across the organization in the form of new standard processes and guidelines.

This strategy is good for initiating sharing and reflection on existing practices and for selecting future practices for the overall organization. At Systematic, for example, PAT members learned about practices in different departments and integrated this knowledge into descriptions of new organizationwide best practices. Systematic's experiences point to some of the challenges and risks of the exploitation strategy. First, the strategy delays actual changes in software projects (learning by doing) until the new processes are written. Such delays can be considerable if inadequate resources are allocated to the groups or if the SPI groups refuse to release "imperfect" processes (also known as gold-plating). Failing to produce tangible results can also create frustration and cynicism toward the SPI project. Second, because the exploitation strategy creates new processes from existing practice and experience, there is no guarantee that they will actually be useful when finally implemented.

One way to avoid these risks is to release unfinished or imperfect processes as early as possible, as in the Danske Data example. Here, the project-management standard produced by the SPI group was deliberately general and visionary, rather than detailed and operational, to allow for fast publication and refinement through use.

The exploitation strategy also requires that the SPI organization be prepared to adjust and refine the new processes based on experiences. The SPI group must set up feedback channels and plan to rewrite and republish guidelines. The PATs can be useful in this respect because they already have informal channels for sharing and reflection. Continuous project-manager education, such as that at Systematic, can also create a forum for project managers to share and reflect.

The strength of the exploitation strategy is its ability to produce explicit knowledge in the form of standard processes across the organization by reflecting on and integrating existing practices. Thus, exploitation results in a shared or common foundation for learning in project groups and thus for organization-level learning. However, the strategy can require long lead times before it produces any changes in software development processes and practice.

SPI projects following an exploitation strategy should therefore take steps to avoid gold-plating and long lead times by, for example, releasing semifinished processes, focusing on a few processes at a time, and so on. As with the exploration strategy, you should also be ready to shift between learning at different levels—switching between the organizational focus of PATs, for example, to teaching programs and support of learning and change in individual project groups.

14.4 CONCLUSION

There are several ways to promote learning in SPI; we have identified two strategies. Exploration aims at immediate change by developing new tacit knowledge from changed practices in project groups before disseminating the knowledge (as good practices) throughout the organization. Exploitation postpones changes to practice until explicit knowledge, in the form of organizationwide standard processes, has been created.

Neither strategy is perfect. In fact, the best approach might be a combination of the two. We believe, however, that knowing the strategies along with their characteristic features, strengths, risks, and weaknesses can help an SPI group plan and implement a project tailored to its culture. For example, some organizations might be familiar with the use of written standards and directives and thus might lean toward the exploitation strategy, supplementing it with experiments or pilots in select projects. Other organizations might assign PATs to collect and systematize experiment results at an early stage in SPI-based exploration or might take other steps to strengthen coordination across projects.

Maturity models describe the goals of change in relation to the individual, group, or organization level. However, this does not mean that an SPI group should narrowly focus its change process accordingly. As our analysis shows, learning can and should take place at all organizational levels, regardless of maturity levels. Also, the maturity models' high regard for *written* procedures and guidelines is too limited from a learning point of view; successful learning requires attention to both explicit and tacit knowledge.

We can summarize our experiences and analyses in two brief but important lessons for SPI projects:

- *Never forget the other levels.* Organizational learning requires attention to and interaction among learning processes at the individual, group, and organization level.

- *Never forget the other learning processes.* Organizational learning requires attention to, and interaction among, all four learning processes: socialization (learning by sharing), externalization (learning by reflection), internalization (learning by doing), and combination (learning by integration).

14.5 REFERENCES

Baskerville, R., and J. Pries–Heje. 1999. "Managing Knowledge Capability and Maturity." In Larsen et al., eds. *Information Systems: Current Issues and Future Changes*. Norwell, MA: IFIP/Kluwer Academic Publishers.

Caputo, K. 1998. *CMM Implementation Guide: Choreographing Software Process Improvement*. Reading, MA: Addison-Wesley.

Fiol, C.M., and M.A. Lyles. 1985. "Organizational Learning." *Academy of Management Review*. 10:803–813.

Garvin, D.A. 1993. "Building a Learning Organization." *Harvard Business Review*, July-August:78–91.

Halloran, P. 1999. "Organizational Learning from the Perspective of a Software Process Assessment & Improvement Program." *Proc. HICSS-32*. Los Alamitos, CA: IEEE Computer Society Press.

Herbsleb, J.D., D. Zubrow, D. Goldenson, W. Hayes, and M.C. Paulk. 1997. "Software Quality and the Capability Maturity Model." *Communications of the ACM*. 40:6:31–40.

Iversen, J., J. Johansen , P.A. Nielsen, and J. Pries-Heje. 1998. "Combining Quantitative and Qualitative Assessment Methods in Software Process Improvement." *Proc. of the European Conference on Information Systems* (ECIS 98). Aix-en-Provence, France. 451–466.

McFeeley, B. 1996. *IDEAL: A User's Guide for Software Process Improvement*, CMU/ SEI-96-HB-001. Pittsburgh: Software Engineering Institute.

Nonaka, I., and H. Takeuchi. 1995. *The Knowledge-Creating Company: How Japanese Companies Create the Dynamics of Innovation*. New York: Oxford University Press.

Paulk, M.C., C.V. Weber, B. Curtis, and M.B. Chrissis. 1993. *The Capability Maturity Model: Guidelines for Improving the Software Process*. Reading, MA: Addison-Wesley.

Snyder, W.M., and T.G. Cummings. 1998. "Organization Learning Disorders: Conceptual Model and Intervention Hypotheses." *Human Relations*. 51:7:873–895.

Stelzer, D., W. Mellis, and G. Herzwurm. 1998. "Technology Diffusion in Software Development Processes: The Contribution of Organizational Learning to Software Process Improvement." In T. Larsen and E. McGuire, eds. *Information Systems Innovation and Diffusion: Issues and Directions*. Hershey, PA: Idea Group Publishers. 297–344.

Zahran, S. 1998. *Software Process Improvement: Practical Guidelines for Business Success*. Reading, MA: Addison-Wesley.

PART V

Techniques for Learning to Improve

Chapter 15

Implementing SPI: An Organizational Approach

Susanne Tryde, Ann-Dorte Nielsen, and Jan Pries-Heje

Many IT companies invest significant resources in developing customized methods, tools, and techniques for software development and SPI. Unfortunately, many of these investments never pay off because the changes and improvements are never put into practice. Studies show that even when a company says it has deployed a given method, implementation—the actual use of the method—often fails to take place. There are many reasons for this. In some cases, management loses interest in the project. In other cases, project staff fails to consider the needs of the target user groups or other interested parties, who in turn block or simply ignore implementation. In still other cases, the problem is one of perception. Project staff might believe that diffusion of new methods and technologies happens instantaneously, as when a lump of dye dissolves in a beaker of water. Alternatively, they might think that force and push are required to speed change (Weinberg 1997). In any case, diffusion must be planned and managed carefully to succeed.

In 1997, a Bootstrap assessment (Kuvaja et. al., 1994) at Danske Data revealed that our own SPI tools and methods were not being implemented in projects. After much analysis, our team developed an approach for implementing new methods, tools, and techniques into the larger organization. Our approach is workshop-based and successfully contends with implementation challenges by focusing on both the product and the diffusion process itself. Here, we offer a brief introduction to the problem of diffusion, followed by a description of our Implementation Workshop. We then analyze how our approach worked in practice and present our lessons learned, in the hope that they might benefit your own efforts to implement organizational change.

15.1 DIFFUSION: AN OVERVIEW

In *Diffusion of Innovation*, E.M. Rogers defines *diffusion* as the communication of an innovation through certain channels in a social system over time. He notes that diffusion is a special type of communication because it concerns a new idea and thus involves uncertainty, which is equal to "the degree to which a number of alternatives are perceived." Diffusion, says Rogers, is at root "a kind of *social change,* defined as the process by which alteration occurs in the structure and function of a social system" (1995, pp. 5–6).

According to this definition, diffusion's central elements are (Ibid. p. 10)

- ◆ An innovation
- ◆ Communication channels
- ◆ Time
- ◆ A social system

An *innovation* might be a product, a service, or an idea (Kotler 1988, p. 439). Often, *innovation* is used as a term for a consumer's view of newly introduced products (see, for example, Mowen 1995 or Rogers 1979). According to Rogers, it is not important whether an innovation is objectively new as long as someone perceives it as new.

Communication requires that developers and users arrive at a common understanding by creating and sharing information. Rogers (1995, p. 17) distinguishes between two kinds of communication channels: mass media and personal channels. Mass media includes TV, radio, newspapers, newsletters, and so on, whereas personal communication typically involves person-to-person messages or meetings, either face-to-face or through telephone calls, e-mail, and so on. When it comes to convincing a target group of an innovation's value, personal communication channels are generally most efficient.

Rogers includes a consideration of *time* in his analysis of communication and identifies five adopter categories (Rogers 1995, pp. 254ff).

- ◆ *Innovators* (2.5%) adopt almost everything new simply because it is new.
- ◆ *Early adopters* (13.5%) are often opinion leaders who set the example for others.
- ◆ *Early majority* (34%) includes those who like to adopt new products or services before everybody else but not until they've seen the advantages demonstrated by opinion leaders.
- ◆ *Late majority* (34%) includes skeptics who do not adopt just anything. Typically, those in the late majority will wait, sometimes a long time, for the right opportu-

nity to adopt. A typical late-majority comment might be, "Why should I change when the product I have functions well?"

- *Laggards* (16%) might never adopt a new innovation; if they do, they typically are the last to do so.

As Figure 15.1 shows, Geoffrey Moore (1995, 1998) further developed Rogers's categories by identifying a chasm between the early adopters and the early majority wherein many new high-technology products get caught and come to a standstill. There are also several phase-based models related to the communication and time dimensions. The most prominent model of this sort for describing IT-product diffusion was developed by Cooper and Zmud (1990) and Kwon and Zmud (1987). It includes six phases: initiation, decision, adaptation, acceptance and adoption, routine procedures, and infusion/penetration.

The target group involves a *social system* that in itself sets certain limits on how diffusion can take place. The social system consists of related persons, groups, and departments that include both formal and informal structures. Nonetheless, adoption characteristically occurs one person at a time and can create significant *uncertainty*. Thus, many researchers have focused on the individual's resistance to change (see, for example, Levine 1997) or on the chaos individuals perceive when a foreign element—innovation—enters their world (Weinberg 1997).

All in all, there are a number of descriptive theories and models about diffusion. However, many of the theories focus only on a small, specific part of the diffusion process. Our Implementation Workshop, which we now describe, focuses both on the product (the method, tool, or techniques) to be diffused and on the diffusion process.

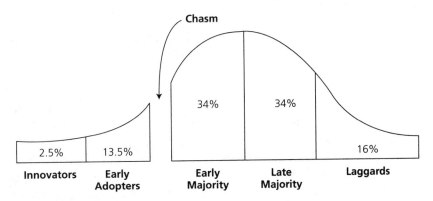

Figure 15.1 *Rogers's five adopter categories with Moore's chasm*

15.2 PROJECT CONTEXT

Danske Data's 1997 Bootstrap evaluation identified seven areas for the company to improve. Six of these areas were completely traditional. The seventh was a recommendation to improve "diffusion and adoption of new methods, techniques, and tools." However, the evaluation was unable to clarify the nature of the problem or offer solutions. It could establish only that Danske Data had developed and made available a wide range of methods and tools, but that few people, if any at all, were using them.

Our workgroup was established to further analyze Danske Data's diffusion and adoption problem. We held two workshops to identify the problems and possible solutions. In April 1998, the company implemented organizational changes aimed at solving many of the structural problems. Thus, our remaining challenge was to ensure that methods, techniques, and tools from specific projects were diffused and adopted throughout the organization.

Our implementation approach was guided by action research, in which researchers cooperate with an organization's employees to create both theoretical and practical knowledge for the organization (Galliers 1992). We based our work on the five phases recommended by Susman and Evered (1978):

1. Specify project infrastructure.
2. Diagnose the problem.
3. Plan action (the Implementation Workshop).
4. Implement actions.
5. Evaluate results (from the Implementation Workshop).
6. Repeat phases 2 to 5 if necessary.

To begin our work, we first studied Danske Data's successes and failures in diffusing new technologies and methods. We quickly realized that attempts to ensure diffusion by adding activities at the end of the project often fail. Instead, such attempts must be started early enough in the project to affect the product itself. We thus decided to create the Implementation Workshop and to hold it right after the product's requirements had been defined. At that point, the project group knows what the product will look like but has yet to prepare specific solutions.

While we were studying the situation at Danske Data, we also read case studies of other organizations' efforts to diffuse and adopt IT. Although the literature did not give us a holistic and action-oriented solution to diffusion and adoption, we were inspired by different authors' analyses of various issues, as the following discussion shows.

15.3 THE IMPLEMENTATION WORKSHOP

Our Implementation Workshop is led by a trained facilitator who steers participants through three phases—analysis, design, and planning—that include a total of six activities (see Figure 15.2). Thus far, we have facilitated more than 10 workshops; most have focused on SPI tools and techniques, although a few have involved more traditional systems development projects.

Analysis Phase

The purpose of analysis is to give facilitators and participants a common understanding of the implementation process and the effort it will require. The analysis consists of two parts. First, we determine our target area by posing and answering questions about the implementation. Inspiration for this part of the analysis comes from Mathiassen and Sørensen (1997). Table 15.1 shows the questions and typical replies.

In the second part of the analysis, we focus on the roles people will play, using a model developed by Jan Pries-Heje and inspired by Checkland and Scholes (1990)

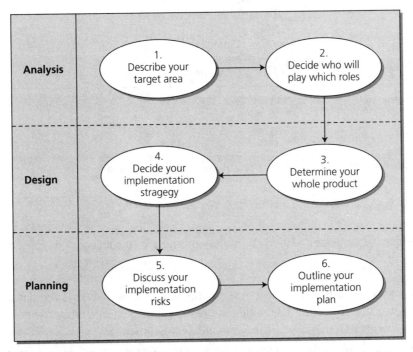

Figure 15.2 *The Implementation Workshop has three phases and a total of six activities*

Table 15.1 *Six Questions that Indicate the Implementation's Target Range*

Questions	Possible Replies
What is your product?	• Method • Tool • Technique
Why should the product be diffused?	• Technology reasons • Requirement reasons
What is the purpose of the product?	• Support of administration • Support of project management • Support of development • Support of management • Support of IT operations

Who must change their activities following product implementation?	• Software developers
	  • Host developers
	  • Client/server developers
	• Experts in specific fields
	  • Database
	  • Economics
	  • Human resources
	• Managers
	  • Project managers
	  • Area managers
	  • Other managers

Who will use the product, and in which order?	• A few individuals • Selected projects • Selected organizational units • The whole organization
What is the desired outcome?	• Everyone in the target group uses the product in a certain way

and Bendix and Andersen (1995). If implementation is to succeed, five roles must be carried out.

- ◆ *Owner:* Owns the product (often is the project's sponsor) and is the person who approves the project and demands the results. The owner is often the boss of the implementation manager or the immediate customer.

- ◆ *Implementation manager:* Manages the implementation project and often is the overall project manager.

◆ *Prime movers:* The product's ambassadors; they are close to the target group and have practical influence over them.

◆ *Target group:* The product's users.

◆ *The environment:* All other interested parties who influence the organizational implementation, such as subcontractors or other projects implementing improvements during the same period of time.

The workshop facilitators offer a detailed description of each role, after which the project group members determine who fills which role in relation to their product.

Design Phase

In the design phase, we focus on how to "package" the product for the target user group. In essence, our goal is to clarify the kind of product needed to improve the odds of implementation success. Next, we select the best implementation strategy, creating a map of important milestones for the implementation plan.

Users typically expect more than a mere technical solution, so our first activity aims to define and package all aspects of the product. We approach this work from

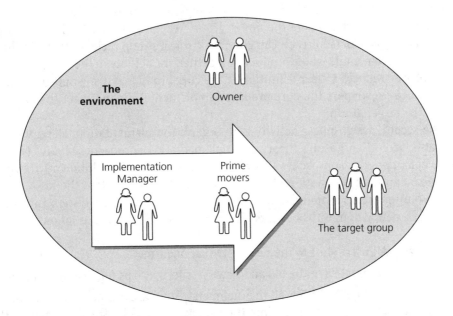

Figure 15.3 *The role model used to identify key stakeholders in the Implementation Workshop*

three product levels: the core product, the whole product, and the expanded product (Moore 1998).

- The *core product* is the developers' idea of what they must prepare to fulfill their promise to customers. For example, a developer preparing a HomeBanking system will typically define the product as the disks containing the program.
- The *whole product* is the customers' idea of what they will get: the core product, plus any related supplementary products that ensure ease of use. For example, a HomeBanking system customer expects to get the program disks along with a quick guide, telephone numbers for technical support, and so on.
- The *expanded product* is any additional services a customer or developer might suggest after the whole product is in operation. For example, customers might request that a tax-calculation service be added to the HomeBanking system.

We thus begin the design phase by brainstorming ideas about the "whole" product. The project group tells us which supplementary products they already plan to develop. We then ask the project group to categorize the core product as either different from or similar to products well known to the target users, and we further ask whether the core product is simple or complex to understand and use. These categorizations often lead to valuable discussions; the project group now begins to look at its product through the eyes of the target group. We have prepared a list of possible supplementary products for each category; the project group picks suitable products from it to supplement its whole product. Altogether, the activity in the first part of the design phase produces a clear definition of the core product and a list of supplementary products to support the core product's implementation and meet the expectations of the target group.

The second design-phase activity is to organize implementation. Here, we take inspiration from Ken Eason's theory on implementation approaches (1988). Eason's theory comprises five approaches. They range from the most revolutionary, in which users abandon their old system one day and adopt the new system the next, to the most evolutionary, in which users gradually introduce the new system into their work over a period of months or years. Eason's five approaches are as follows:

- *Big bang:* All users shift to the new system at one time.
- *Parallel running:* Use of the old and new systems overlaps for a certain period.
- *Phased introduction:* Either all the members of the target group gradually introduce new system functionality into their work process, or a small segment of the target group switches to the new system, followed by a gradual implementation by the rest of the group.

◆ *Trials and dissemination:* The new system is tested by part of the target group, and their results are compared with test results to determine whether the system should be diffused to others or made permanent.

◆ *Incremental evolution:* Individual users test the system to determine its value.

Figure 15.4 shows the five approaches in relation to the dimensions, degree of user participation, and the degree of control. The five approaches are not mutually exclusive, and some can be applied simultaneously. For example, when a new system is going to replace an old one, the systems might run in parallel for some time. During this period, the new system could undergo trials in one part of the target group before it is disseminated and the old system is closed down.

In the workshop, we analyze each of the five approaches, focusing on advantages and disadvantages. For example, user participation increases in each of the five approaches, starting out very low in the big bang approach and demanding high participation in incremental evolution. A similar pattern occurs in relation to control. The big bang approach is very controlled, whereas control decreases little by little in each of the subsequent approaches. Because our workshops are based on the assumption that the product will be formally implemented, the final approaches—trial and dissemination and incremental evolution—are not options. Nonetheless, as we describe

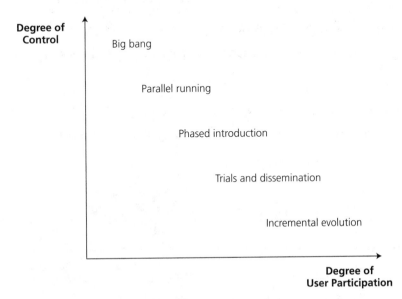

Figure 15.4   *The five implementation approaches used in the Implementation Workshop*

later in Lessons Learned, using Eason's model is very helpful for projects that are just getting under way.

In selecting an implementation approach, the project group gets its main implementation-plan milestones handed to it on a plate. For example, the big bang approach has only one phase (before implementation) and one milestone (implementation complete) because everything must be prepared for the "big bang." To outline the implementation plan according to phases and milestones related to the selected approach, we draw a timeline on a whiteboard and mark the milestones on the line. If possible, we add dates as well (see Figure 15.5). In the end, the design phase gives the project group members a clear idea of how they should carry out implementation on a general level.

Planning Phase

In the planning phase, we analyze risks and create a detailed outline of the implementation that includes the activities identified in earlier phases. Risk analysis lets us ensure that we have not overlooked any potential problems; risk management helps us identify and react to potential problems in time.

We analyze risk in six steps:

1. Identify risks using a standard list of the organization's 10 highest risks.
2. Assess the probability of each risk on a scale from zero to 5.
3. Assess the severity of consequences associated with each risk on a scale from zero to 5.
4. Prioritize risks by multiplying probability and consequence scores.
5. Identify activities to manage the three most important risks.
6. List the risk-management activities for inclusion in the implementation plan.

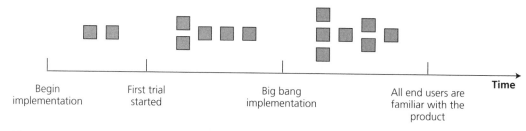

Figure 15.5 *An implementation plan, including milestones and planning activities*

To develop an implementation plan, we apply backward planning as described by Weinberg (1997). That is, we plan in reverse, from the desired results back through interventions to preconditions. The desired result describes the project's ideal status at the last milestone. If more milestones are required, we reverse-plan again to identify them.

Throughout the workshop, participants write all planned activities on small notepads. At this point, we outline our milestones and intermediate states on a blackboard or table top and place all the activity notes on our graph, as Figure 15.5 shows.

15.4 LESSONS LEARNED

We developed our first version of the Implementation Workshop at the end of 1998 and facilitated a trial workshop in February 1999. This resulted in a number of adjustments. We then held two more workshops and made further adjustments after each one. In our fourth trial, we found the workshop acceptable. We then documented it and subsequently made it available to all projects as of May 1, 1999. We have facilitated several workshops, and as of August 1999 had trained a dozen new workshop facilitators. In the process of developing our Implementation Workshop, we learned many lessons.

Use a Detailed Description of the Target Area

We changed the first part of our analysis phase many times. We started with a few who-what-where questions but soon realized that as outside facilitators, we needed more knowledge about the target project if our approach was going to work. We therefore decided on the questions shown in Table 15.1. We also ask the project group members what they think is motivating the project owner or sponsor to initiate the project. Finally, we discuss at length the project's desired outcome. All this typically takes one hour and produces a project description that is detailed enough that facilitators—who are project outsiders—can identify with the project group and its context. Another benefit of this phase is that not all participants always know all the answers to all the questions. Answering the questions together gives the participants the same starting point both for the rest of the workshop and for their continuing project.

Detailed Stakeholder Analysis Is Not Necessary; Role Models Are Better

When we first developed our approach, we used a traditional stakeholder analysis to uncover all stakeholders. In one case, we identified more than 30 stakeholders. Unfortunately, we found no meaningful use for all that information. We now use the role model (see Figure 15.3) as the only stakeholder analysis. In our experiences so far, the role model has covered every major role in every organizational implementation. We have often found, in fact, that one or even two of the roles on actual projects were not being filled by anyone. Thus, in addition to helping analysis, using the role model can help you identify a major potential problem: the lack of actors in important implementation roles.

Don't Overemphasize Implementation Strategy

Literature on diffusion and adoption of IT often considers implementation strategy at length. We began our action research effort with a similar focus. Based on our reading of Bendix and Andersen (1995), we went through a tedious process of deciding on an array of strategies: picking an expert, line management, project change, or process change. This decision, in turn, led to many general recommendations we tried to follow when selecting a strategy for a particular project.

Here's one example: IF the dependency of active accept from the target group is low AND the consequences for the people that are influenced by the change introduced is mainly negative, THEN use an expert-based strategy, and be aware of the huge resistance to change this strategy may create.

However, after having tried this method several times, we realized that we were wasting our time. The advice that emerged from this taxing process was simply too general and was not useful to the actual projects. At that point, we found Eason's model (see Figure 15.4) and we now use it to select an approach rather than a strategy. The benefit of using Eason's model is that it gives project groups an idea of possible phases for their implementation.

Eason's model has worked well in projects that apply the approach very early, just after the project starts. Projects that are well into the analysis or design of a technical solution have less to gain. We thus recommend that you use Eason's model only for projects early in the life cycle.

Determining the Whole Product Is Essential

In the first version of our workshop, we used four dimensions to determine the whole product. However, we found that two of the dimensions (which originally came from Applegate et al. (1992) were overlapping and that one (characterizing the target group) was unnecessary. We thus ended up with only the two dimensions of product complexity and the target group's experience with the technology.

Furthermore, we found it necessary to explain, in detail, what we mean by the "whole product." We often found that the technically oriented people in software projects had a difficult time understanding that a technical solution is not enough.

Our use here of Rogers's five adopter categories—from innovators" to laggards—along with Moore's chasm has been very helpful in explaining this and has made a strong impression on workshop participants.

Discuss Implementation Risks before the Planning Phase

The content of the workshop's implementation phase has not changed since the first draft, but we did switch the activity order. Initially, we started with planning and then tried to identify and analyze risks. However, we found that the workshop participants were quite unwilling to discuss risks after they had outlined a plan. We thus tried doing the risk analysis before the planning, and it worked well. The openness and reflection needed to look into potential problems are better achieved before planning than after.

15.5 CONCLUSION

Danske Data management was very pleased with our focus on organizational implementation. The company now expects all internal projects to participate in the Implementation Workshop. Danske Data has also decided to expand the workshop, offering it to developers implementing products within the Den Danske Bank group.

To our knowledge, our approach to organizational implementation is unique. However, its uniqueness lies not in the six activities one-by-one but rather in the way the parts are combined and cohere. You can, of course, use each of the workshop's parts for different purposes. If you choose to use the whole approach, we recommend holding a one-day, seven-hour workshop with six to eight important stakeholders in the target SPI project.

According to our evaluations, all participants found their workshop time well spent and that the benefits they gained were much greater than their time investment. Participants also said—quite unanimously—that they would never have come up with such a detailed and targeted improvement plan on their own in one day.

To the extent we have been able to check results, it appears that participants are carrying out the activities included in their implementation plans. Nonetheless, it is difficult to say anything definitive until all implementations have been completed for more than a year. The fact that many projects have asked to participate of their own accord also indicates that our Implementation Workshop concept is working.

At this point, our Implementation Workshop appears to be at least a good bid for a solution to part of Danske Data's problem with diffusion and adoption. Our approach can also be used—either in whole or in part—by a project manager from either the development or user side, and by an SEPG or other SPI group.

References

Applegate, L.M., F. Warren McFarlan, and J.L. McKenney. 1992. *Corporate Information Systems Management.* Toronto: Irwin Publishing.

Bendix, J., and O.S. Andersen. 1995. *Forandringsledelse—Kommunikation, Adfærd og Samarbejde.* Copenhagen: Børsens Forlag.

Bødker, K., and J. Basler. 1993. "A Reappraisal of Structured Analysis: Design in an Organizational Context." *ACM Transactions on Information Systems.* 11:2:165-193.

Checkland, P., and J. Scholes. 1990. *Soft Systems Methodology in Action.* New York: John Wiley & Sons.

Cooper, R., and R. Zmud. 1990. "Information Technology Implementation Research: A Technological Diffusion Approach." *Management Science.* 36:2:123–139.

Eason, K. 1988. *Information Technology and Organisational Change.* London: Taylor & Francis.

Galliers, R. 1992. "Choosing Information Systems Research Approaches." In Galliers, R., ed. *Information Systems Research: Issues, Methods and Practical Guidelines.* Oxford, UK: Blackwell Publishers.

Kotler, P. 1988. *Marketing Management: Analysis, Planning, Implementqtion, and Control,* sixth ed. Upper Saddle River, NJ: Prentice Hall.

Kuvaja, P., J. Similä, L. Krzanik, A. Bicego, S. Saukkonen, and G. Koch. 1994. *Software Process Assessment and Improvement: The BOOTSTRAP Approach.* Oxford, UK: Blackwell Publishers.

Kwon, T., and R. Zmud. 1987. "Unifying the Fragmented Models of Information Systems Implementation," In R. Boland and R. Hirschheim, eds. *Critical Issues in Information Systems Research.* New York: John Wiley & Sons. 227–251.

Levine, L. 1997. "An Ecology of Resistance." In T. McMaster et al., eds. *Facilitating Technology Transfer through Partnership: Learning from Practice and Research.* London: Thomson/Chapman & Hall. 163–174.

Mathiassen, L. and C. Sørensen. 1997. "A Guide to Manage New Software Engineering Tools." In T. McMaster et al., eds. *Facilitating Technology Transfer through Partnership: Learning from Practice and Research.* London: Thomson/Chapman & Hall. 257–272.

Moore, G. 1995. *Inside the Tornado.* New York: Harper Business.

Moore, G. 1998. *Crossing the Chasm: Marketing and Selling Technology Products to Mainstream Customers.* London: Penguin/Capstone.

Mowen, J. 1995. *Consumer Behaviour,* fourth ed. Upper Saddle River, NJ: Prentice Hall.

Rogers, E. 1979. "New Product Adoption and Diffusion." *Journal of Consumer Research,* March. 290–301. Reprinted in Ben Enis and Keith Cox, eds. 1985. *Marketing Classics: A Selection of Influential Articles 5th Edition*. Boston: Allyn and Bacon. 164–179.

Rogers, E. M. 1995. *Diffusion of Innovations*, fourth ed. New York: Free Press.

Susman, G., and R. Evered. 1978. "An Assessment of the Scientific Merits of Action Research." *Administrative Science Quarterly.* 23:4:582–603.

Weinberg, G. M. 1997. *Quality Software Management, Volume 4: Anticipating Change.* New York: Dorset House.

Chapter 16

Risk Management in Process Action Teams

Jakob Iversen, Lars Mathiassen,
and Peter Axel Nielsen

Not only is it hard work to design and implement specific improvements, it is also risky business. Much can go wrong in an improvement effort, and mistakes can eventually lead to its failure. The involved actors might not possess appropriate skills and experiences. The design of the new process might not suit the organization or effectively meet requirements. The improvement project might be inappropriately organized, with unrealistic schedules or insufficient management attention. Also, the process action team (PAT) might give too little attention to customers, failing to consider the interests, problems, and motivations of the people and groups that are eventually supposed to use the new process.

To deal proactively with such issues, PATs must manage the risks involved in their efforts. The need for such risk management was the rationale behind Danske Data's development of a practical tool to reduce failures. Using our risk management tool, PATs periodically hold disciplined and tightly structured workshops in collaboration with SPI facilitators. The workshops give the teams a better overview and understanding of their project and its organizational context, and this knowledge helps them to avoid the risks ahead.

We developed our tool in an experimental fashion as part of Danske Data's SPI initiative (see Chapter 5 and Iversen et al. 1999). We first selected a basic form for the risk management tool based on state-of-the-art knowledge of risk management within software engineering. We then systematically analyzed the types of risks and risk resolution actions that are relevant to PATs. These discussions were based on our practical experiences with SPI and on a detailed analysis of risk items and risk resolution actions in the SPI literature (in particular, McFeeley 1996 and Statz et al. 1997). Finally, we tested and refined the tool by applying it in collaboration with several PATs at Danske Data.

16.1 A RISK MANAGEMENT MODEL

Our approach to risk management is based on an underlying model of SPI activities. Figure 16.1 shows the first part of the model and describes the risk areas a PAT faces. The second part of the model outlines the risk resolution strategies that a PAT can apply in response to detected risks. Table 16.1 lists these resolution strategies.

Our model was developed in a stepwise, bottom-up fashion based on several sources. We started by performing a brainstorming session with the SPI practitioners to detect possible risks and risk resolution actions in SPI initiatives. This process led to the identification of 31 risks and 21 actions that we considered relevant to SPI activities. We subsequently classified the individual risk items and resolution actions and then challenged them based on experience and theory reported in the SPI literature (Grady 1997; Humphrey 1989; McFeeley 1996; and Statz et al., 1997). Following this, we added to and modified the lists of risk items, resolution actions, and their classifications. Finally, we presented the model to SPI practitioners for use and then further refined it based on their feedback.

Figure 16.1 shows the situation facing a PAT, characterized by four different areas in which risks might appear:

◆ The *improvement area* is the part of the software organization that will change as a result of the initiative.

◆ The *improvement ideas* are the processes, tools, and techniques that the PAT plans to use in the improvement area.

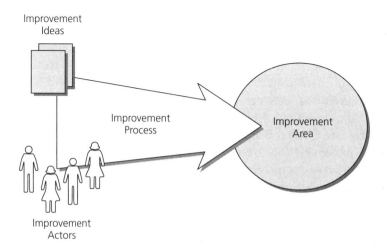

Figure 16.1 *Risk areas for process action teams*

- The *improvement process* is the improvement initiative itself and the way in which it is organized, conducted, and managed.
- The *improvement actors* are the organization members involved in the improvement process.

As an example of each area, we'll consider a PAT charged with introducing configuration management in software engineering projects. The improvement area consists of projects that will use the new or improved configuration management procedures and tools and the people supporting it after it has been institutionalized. The improvement ideas include the descriptions of configuration management that the PAT relies on as well as the actual tools and methods they will implement. The improvement process is the PAT's initiative, the way it is organized, and the involved stakeholders, such as project managers or quality assurance staff. The improvement actors are the PAT members. Individuals interacting with PAT members are *not* improvement actors but rather are stakeholders in the improvement process.

Table 16.1 lists the five risk resolution strategies. These strategies correspond to decreasing degrees of change in the way that PATs act on a risk assessment's result. Each of the resolution strategies is further described by a number of concrete *resolution actions*. Table 16.2 lists these actions in brief, along with their associated risk areas and resolutions strategies. Appendix A (Tables A.2, A.4, A.6, and A.8) offers a more detailed list of resolution actions.

As an illustration of the resolution strategies, consider the following. In the configuration management example, the PAT's mission is to introduce configuration management of all documents (including documentation, code, and so on) in all the company's software engineering projects. The risks of the effort could be reduced by adjusting the mission to include fewer projects (perhaps only large projects, critical projects, or projects in department Y) or to exclude certain types of documents. The

Table 16.1 *Risk Resolution Strategies for PATs*

Resolution Strategy	Concern
Adjust mission	What are the goals of the initiative?
Modify strategy	What strategy is the initiative going to follow?
Mobilize	What alliances and energies can the initiative benefit from?
Increase knowledge	What software-process and improvement knowledge forms the basis of the initiative?
Reorganize	How is the initiative organized, conducted, and managed?

Table 16.2 *Actions Related to Risk Areas and Strategies*

Resolution Strategy	Improvement Area	Improvement Ideas	Improvement Process	Improvement Actors
Adjust mission	• Focus initiative • Specify objective • Create practical results • Focus on business results • Use acceptable solutions	• Consider needs		• Adjust level of ambition
Modify strategy	• Emphasize best practices • Affect expectations • Use facts and experiences	• Create clear visions • Relate to other initiatives • Educate developers • Buy a tool or a method • Adapt standard solutions • Reuse others' successes • Consider alternatives • Use incremental strategy • Solve specific problems	• Adapt strategy to task • Plan visible results • Design effect measures	
Mobilize	• Discuss experiences • Motivate initiative • Exploit incentive schemes • Sell idea	• Discuss means of change	• Get sponsors • Create attention at start-up • Discuss process • Create commitment • Establish collaboration	• Obtain resources • Enter into alliances
Increase knowledge	• Understand practice	• Experiment • Learn from others • Study the state of the art • Evaluate consequences	• Test ideas in pilot projects	• Educate on idea • Educate on SPI • Use consultants

Table 16.2 *Continued*

Resolution Strategy	Improvement Area	Improvement Ideas	Improvement Process	Improvement Actors
Reorganize	• Use measurable goals		• Organize as a project • Establish a contract • Plan initiative • Coordinate with others • Plan implementation early • Communicate • Conduct regular reviews • Make results visible	• Inform about initiative • Build stronger teams • Involve voluntary actors • Drop inactive participants • Incorporate change agents • Find good facilitators

PAT's strategy is to get input on the process from a few key developers and, based on this, select a standard configuration management tool that every project would be required to use. Modifying the strategy might entail involving more (or fewer) developers or gradually implementing the select tool in each project. Mobilizing might involve establishing agreements with an existing method department, production department, or other departments or persons with a vested interest in the effort's results. To increase knowledge, PAT members might attend courses or seminars about configuration management or SPI, for example, or hire knowledgeable consultants. If PAT members have not optimally organized the effort, they might reorganize it by, for example, establishing a formal project, negotiating a project contract with both management and the software engineering projects, or developing a new project plan.

16.2 APPLYING THE MODEL

Our approach is based on the principle that PAT work is dynamic and is characterized by risks that are both overlapping and different from those faced by software engineering projects. The purpose of the approach is to help PATs to avoid catastrophes and achieve satisfactory results. PATs should use the approach regularly, holding workshops every month or two to identify central risks and channel energy toward risk resolution.

Participants in the workshop, or risk session, are the PAT members and other relevant actors. Ideally, all relevant actors can attend, but at least all key actors (project manager, management representative, and so on) should be present. During the session, a facilitator helps participants to discover risks that the team is facing and decide on a primary strategy for alleviating these risks. The approach can be used without outside support. We structure our workshop in four steps as follows.

1. Characterize the situation: To fully benefit from the approach, risk session participants must first be aware of the PAT's situation and the roles that PAT members and others play. We thus display Figure 16.1 on a transparency and ask the actors to interpret the figure and discuss the four risk areas specific to their situation. We then write the agreed-upon interpretation directly on the transparency. If questions arise later as to how specific risk items or resolution actions should be interpreted, we can again display the transparency and use it to focus discussion.

2. Analyze risks: We structure the analysis according to the risk areas. For each of the four risk areas, we present a table of risk items and a table of risk resolution actions on a transparency (see Appendix A). For each risk item, the actors must agree on a score of 0 (low risk), 1 (medium risk), or 2 (high risk). The actors determine scores based on an assessment of both the probability and the consequence of the risk item. We write the scores directly on the transparency. Participants then scan the table of resolution actions to find those actions that might reduce the identified risks (we number the actions based on the action areas shown in Table 16.2). We then mark the target resolution actions with an X. At this stage, we've found that it is better to include too many resolution actions than too few.

   Neither the risk items nor the resolution actions constitute complete lists of all possible risks or actions. They are, however, general enough to provide a reasonably complete picture. If additional risk items are identified in-flight, you can add them to the list and later integrate them into the tables.

3. Prioritize Actions: This step is structured in two parts. First, participants evaluate the risk areas to determine which area carries the highest risk. Next, they prioritize resolution actions to determine which overall strategy will help them best deal with the risks.

   We then summarize scores for the risk items in each risk area and calculate a percentage by dividing the obtained scores by the maximum possible score for each risk area (see Table 16.3). Next, the team establishes priorities by supplementing the discussion of scores with more qualitative insights gained from earlier discussion of specific risk items. Thus, the final priorities need not align with the scores.

Table 16.3   *Prioritizing Risk Areas*

	Sum	Score	Priority (1–4)
Improvement Area	__ / 22 =	__ %	__
Improvement Idea	__ / 20 =	__ %	__
Improvement Process	__ / 22 =	__ %	__
Improvement Actors	__ / 16 =	__ %	__

Having determined on the area that carries the highest risk, we turn our attention to the primary resolution strategies. Table 16.4, on the next page, shows the five resolution strategies. The resolution actions listed in the table are the same as those in the four action tables (Tables A.2, A.4, A.6, and A.8) arranged now according to their related resolution strategy rather than by risk area. The X's indicate the area that the action was originally listed under.

4. Take action: The final step in our approach is to take action. We do this primarily by adjusting the PAT's plan, but we might also establish special task forces to handle specific problems, reorient the initiative, request more resources, and so on. At this stage, the PAT members should be fairly open-minded and should consider their chosen strategy broadly. For example, if the primary strategy is to adjust the mission and the only resolution actions selected were "Focus the initiative" and "Adjust level of ambition," other actions will likely be necessary to adequately adjust the mission. Such actions could be listed under "Adjust mission" or other strategies, or they might be derived from the specific experiences and insights of the involved actors.

16.3 EXPERIENCE AND ADVICE

Our risk management approach has been used successfully in several PATs, with one of us acting as facilitator. Based on this experience, we have formulated some advice for applying our approach.

All four risk areas (shown in Figure 16.1) have proven to be both necessary and meaningful during risk analysis. It is, however, important that PATs spend sufficient time projecting the risk areas onto their situation. PAT members typically understand the abstract meaning of the four areas, but facilitators must continually remind them

Table 16.4 *Prioritizing Strategies*

Strategy	Actions	Impr. \Area	Impr. Ideas	Impr. Proc.	Impr. Actors	Ind. Weight	Grp. Sum	Grp. Weight
Adjust Mission (1)	Focus the initiative	X						
	Specify the objective	X						
	Create results that are conceived to be usable	X						
	Focus on business results	X						
	Use culturally acceptable solutions	X						
	Consider identified needs for improvement		X					
	Adjust the level of ambition				X			
Modify Strategy (2)	Document and emphasize best practice in the improvement area	X						
	Affect the expectations towards the initiative	X						
	Base the initiative on facts and experiences	X						
	Create clear and shared visions		X					
	Identify and solve specific problems		X					
	Use an incremental improvement strategy		X					
	Consider alternative improvement ideas		X					
	Reuse others' successes		X					
	Adapt well-known standard solutions		X					
	Buy a tool or method		X					
	Educate actors in the improvement area		X					
	Take advantage of the relationships to other improvement initiatives		X					
	Adapt the strategy to the task			X				
	Plan visible results every 6-9 months			X				
	Design effect measures			X				
Mobilize (3)	Initiate discussions about experiences and problems in the improvement area	X						
	Create an understanding of the necessity of the initiative	X						
	Exploit and adapt incentive schemes	X						
	Sell the idea	X						
	Initiate discussion about possible means of change		X					
	Get sponsors			X				
	Arrange an event to create attention at project start-up			X				
	Initiate discussions about the improvement process			X				
	Create and maintain management commitment and backing			X				

Table 16.4   Continued

Strategy	Actions	Impr. \Area	Impr. Ideas	Impr. Proc.	Impr. Actors	Ind. Weight	Grp. Sum	Grp. Weight
Mobilize (3)	Establish and maintain collaboration with the improvement area			X				
	Obtain resources for actors				X			
	Enter into alliances				X			
Increase Knowledge (4)	Understand and document the current practice in the improvement area	X						
	Evaluate the consequences of the improvement area		X					
	Study state-of-the -art		X					
	Take advantage of experiences from other organizations		X					
	Experiment		X					
	Try out improvement ideas in pilot projects			X				
	Educate the process action team in the improvement idea's professional foundation				X			
	Educate the process action team improvement work				X			
	Use consultants				X			
Reorganize (5)	Formulate measurable goals		X					
	Organize the improvement initiative as a project			X				
	Establish a contract with management regarding the improvement initiative			X				
	Plan the improvement initiative			X				
	Coordinate with other improvement initiatives			X				
	Plan implementation from the outset			X				
	"Communicate plans, problems, progress, and results"			X				
	Conduct reviews at regular intervals			X				
	Make the results visible			X				
	Get good facilitators				X			
	Incorporate experienced change agents				X			
	Exclude participants who do not contribute				X			
	Involve voluntary actors from the improvement area				X			
	Teambuilding				X			
	Inform about the group's work				X			
	Number of chosen actions							

of the concrete interpretations. In our experience, getting teams to be clear about the scope of their improvement projects proved most troublesome.

Our teams found the five risk resolution strategies to be meaningful and to cover all types of possibly relevant actions. The teams liked the idea of one summarizing strategy, especially because it is possible to trace back through the lists and see which specific risks are actually covered by the final risk resolution strategy.

To get the most benefits from our approach, the facilitator must insist on discussing all questions in the risk item tables. This helps focus attention on questions that would otherwise be avoided, either because they are too painful to discuss or simply because they seem difficult, cumbersome, or trivial to resolve.

Having been taken through numerous, detailed questions regarding the risk areas, our teams were relieved to find overview and simplicity on the other side. We found that the schemes for establishing a risk area overview and arriving at a primary risk resolution strategy were good tools for focusing participants' attention. At the same time, their decision about how to prioritize risk resolution strategies was well informed by the insights obtained during the detailed analysis.

Our proposed approach does not in itself create a useful result; much depends on how the approach is applied. Given this, we offer the following basic advice.

- Be specific. The underlying model is generic, and you must constantly remind all participants of the concrete interpretation of the four risk areas and the practical implications of the five risk resolution strategies.

- Document additions, alterations, and interpretations. During the risk sessions, many items are interpreted, some items might be added, and others might be altered. To keep track of the valuable information that arises in discussions, you should annotate the four risk item tables with specific interpretations of meaning and scope.

- Apply the approach several times during a project. Risks are bound to change as a project unfolds over time. The initial risk assessment is valuable, but you can achieve additional benefits by reapplying the approach after a project gets well under way, enters a crisis, or finds itself in shallow waters.

- Use a facilitator to enforce discipline and clarity. A facilitator is crucial in that he or she can detach from the situation, ask silly questions, know the approach well, know when to deviate, and, most of all, know how to keep clear of typical pitfalls.

16.4 CONCLUSION

Our approach identifies and addresses delicate, troublesome, and dominating risks in real-world software process improvement. Such risks exist and can be painful to acknowledge. However, the consequences of unrecognized risks can be even more painful, and sometimes devastating. It is therefore not surprising that several sources in the literature agree that it is important to handle risks in SPI (Grady 1997; Humphrey 1989; McFeeley 1996; and Statz et al., 1997).

The role of facilitator is indispensable in our approach. Each of us has played this role, and, based on this experience, we recommend that you choose facilitators who are knowledgeable and experienced with both SPI and risk management, but who are neither PAT members nor their managers. In this way, the facilitator can concentrate on the role of facilitating the process without worrying so much about the actual content of the workshop. In addition, the participants can be assured that management will not hold the discussions against them.

So far, our risk approach has had a positive impact on Danske Data's SPI efforts because all the participating PAT members have gained a much better understanding of the significance and challenges involved in their change initiative. In addition, conducting the workshop has inspired the PATs to modify their plans to accommodate the workshop results. Nonetheless, there are several areas where our approach might be further developed, including extending the lists of general risk items and resolution actions, encompassing dynamic and company-specific lists of risk items and actions, increasing its overview by juxtaposing relevant risk items and actions, and adjusting the approach so that it might be more easily used for unfacilitated self-assessments. Another interesting possibility might be to develop a similar risk management approach that could be used in the SPI group itself.

Risk Management in the Literature

Risk management techniques generally use some kind of logic or heuristics to link situations to risk resolution actions based on several risk factors. There are three general possibilities for doing this. First, you could list a number of risk factors and then for each factor offer several possibly relevant resolution actions. This approach was applied by Alter and Ginzberg (1978) and by Boehm (1991). Second, you could characterize several situations and then for each situation propose a suitable combination of resolution actions, as demonstrated by McFarland (1982). Third, you could use a stepwise approach in which an analysis of specific risk items leads to identification of a useful intervention strategy. Davis described an example of this (1982).

We based our approach on work by Davis and used his model as a guiding example. The model supports a stepwise analysis process in which participants discuss their situation from different viewpoints. Moreover, it supports participants in understanding risks and strategies for intervention at a general level while at the same time providing a detailed picture of all the relevant risks and actions.

Our approach for assessing risks and prioritizing actions to alleviate or circumvent the risks and their consequences can be seen as a supplement to the approach suggested by Statz et al. (1997). Their approach addresses SPI initiatives as a whole as well as individual PATs, whereas our approach focuses solely on the PAT level. Their approach is based on 13 categories of risks and a total of 63 specific risk items, but it does not include a model of possible risk resolution strategies. One of their model's strengths is that it supports systematic data collection across organizations, thereby helping its users focus on the most common risks in SPI efforts. In creating our model, we used the Statz model as a guide in designing the specific questions related to each of the four risk areas.

REFERENCES

Alter, S., and Ginzberg, M. 1978. "Managing Uncertainty in MIS Implementation." Sloan Managment Review. Fall.

Boehm, B. 1991. "Software Risk Management: Principles and Practices." IEEE Software. 8:1.

Davis, G.B. 1982. "Strategies for Information Requirements Determination." IBM Systems Journal. 21.

McFarland, W. 1982. "Portfolio Approach to Information Systems." Journal for Systems Management. January: 12–19.

Statz, J., D. Oxley, and P. O'Toole. 1997. "Identifying and Managing Risks for Software Process Improvement." Crosstalk—The Journal of Defense Software Engineering. 10:4:13–18.

Action Prioritization Procedure

To determine the priorities of the five strategies, we use a transparency of Table 16.4 to carry out the following operation.

1. Put a circle around the Xs that represent resolution actions that were X-marked during the analysis. To make things easier, you can use a text highlighter to emphasize the rows with circled Xs. Count the number of circled Xs along each column. This can help you see whether the selected actions provide a reasonable coverage of the highest risk areas. If not, it might be useful to go back and add more actions to some areas.

2. Let each participant distribute the weights 10, 8, 6, 5, 4, 3, 2, and 1 on the highlighted actions. Each weight can be used only once, and all weights must be used. If fewer than eight actions were highlighted, use only the higher weights. Write the weights on the transparency for each actor in the column labeled "Ind. Weight."

3. Calculate the sum of the individual weights, and record this in the column labeled "Grp. Sum."

4. The participants now discuss how to distribute the weights 10, 8, 6, 5, 4, 3, 2, and 1 on those actions that were given a calculated sum in step 3. Again, qualitative insights play an important role, and the final weights (entered in the column labeled "Grp. Weight") need not follow the calculated "Grp. Sum."

5. Based on an overall, qualitative discussion, participants can now prioritize the five resolution strategies from 1 (most important strategy) to 5 (least important strategy).

Alternating between making individual judgments (step 2) and group decisions (steps 4 and 5), creates a fairly balanced decision process.

16.5 REFERENCES

Grady, R.B. 1997. *Successful Software Process Improvement*, Upper Saddle River, NJ: Prentice Hall.

Humphrey, W.S. 1989. *Managing the Software Process*. Reading, MA: Addison-Wesley.

Iversen, J.H., L. Mathiassen, and P.A. Nielsen. 1999. "Managing Risks in Software Process Improvement." *Seventh European Conference on Information Systems* (ECIS 99), Copenhagen, Denmark.

McFeeley, B. 1996. "IDEAL: A User's Guide for Software Process Improvement." CMU/SEI-96-HB-001. Pittsburgh: Software Engineering Institute.

Statz, J., D. Oxley, and P. O'Toole. 1997. "Identifying and Managing Risks for Software Process Improvement." *Crosstalk—The Journal of Defense Software Engineering*. 10:4:13–18.

Chapter 17

Principles of Metrics Implementation

Jakob Iversen and Karlheinz Kautz

Metrics programs are a vital part of every serious SPI endeavor. Despite reports on successful metrics implementation (Fenton and Pfleeger 1997; Dekkers 1999; Weinberg 1993; and Carleton et al. 1992), most companies experience great difficulty implementing a metrics program as part of their SPI activities. Does this mean that the many experts writing books and issuing recommendations are wrong? Likely not. The truth more likely resides in the complexity and uncertainty involved in implementing metrics as part of an SPI initiative.

Our goal is not to disregard the existing recommendations and advice but rather to amend these recommendations with observations of our own, captured in nine principles and prefaced by the overall recommendation that any individual recommendation should be tailored to the local situation.

Various writers have identified key elements of metric program implementations. Grady and Caswell (1987) derive their suggestions from experiences at Hewlett-Packard, a very large U.S.-based IT provider. Rifkin and Cox (1991) analyzed the 11 best measurement programs in the United States, among them programs at NASA, Contel, and Hewlett-Packard. Pfleeger (1993) offers 10 lessons learned—again from Contel, a large telecommunication company—and Dekkers (1999) offers her seven "secrets" for success based on consulting work in the United States. The implementation advice offered by these authors largely overlaps. As an example, we summarize the works of Rifkin and Cox and of Dekkers in Table 17.1 and Table 17.2, respectively.

Table 17.1   *Recommendations for Successful Metrics Programs (Rifkin and Cox 1991)*

Pattern Type	Recommendation
Measure	• Start small • Use a rigorously defined set • Automate collection and reporting
People	• Motivate managers • Set expectations • Involve all stakeholders • Educate and train • Earn trust
Program	• Take an evolutionary approach • Plan to throw one away • Get the right information to the right people • Strive for an initial success
Implementation	• Add value • Empower developers to use measurement information • Take a "whole process" view • Understand that adoption takes time

Such guidelines and frameworks are useful, but to be successful, an organization should tailor a method to fit its particular situation rather than follow it step-by-step. Chief among these considerations is that of an organization's culture. Although all experts stress this, one of the limitations of much advice about metrics implementation has been its tendency to focus on issues related to large U.S. companies. By doing so, the advice disregards the numerous software companies that do not have thousands of software developers. In Europe, for example, small and medium-sized com-

Table 17.2   *Secrets of Highly Successful Measurement Programs (Dekkers 1999)*

The Seven Secrets

1. Set solid objectives and plans for measurement.
2. Make the measurement program part of the process, not a management "pet project."
3. Gain a thorough understanding of what measurement is all about—including benefits and limitations.
4. Focus on cultural issues.
5. Create a safe environment for reporting true data.
6. A predisposition to change.
7. A complementary suite of measures.

panies are predominant (Münch et al. 1996). In addition, by drawing on the experiences of U.S.-based companies, not all the advice will necessarily fit in other cultures. In general, for example, Scandinavians are very egalitarian; decision making is slow because it is based on extensive peer discussion. In the United States, hierarchical decision making and direct orders dominate (Hofstede 1983). One of the major differences between Scandinavian and U.S. organizations is the level of personal empowerment and autonomy enjoyed by individual programmers and project groups (Siakas and Balstrup 2000). Thus, a metrics program in a Scandinavian organization is far less likely to succeed if the developers perceive that the bureaucratic inconveniences involved in reporting data are not sufficiently offset by benefits either for the programmers directly or for the project or organization. Simply telling Scandinavian developers that things should be done in a certain way is bound to fail. This line of thinking may also benefit metrics managers at large U.S.-based companies, because U.S. culture is likely to move in the direction of increased empowerment and autonomy. Also, the many small companies starting up based on Internet development, wireless communication, and other fast-paced technologies are certainly candidates for these guidelines.

We have assisted with and analyzed the implementation of different metrics programs in several Scandinavian organizations. In relation to U.S. companies, the organizations we studied are small, although from a European perspective they vary from large to very small. Based on our experiences, we have formulated nine principles that increase the likelihood of successful metrics implementation (Table 17.3). Our

Table 17.3 *Summary of Our Principles*

Area	Principle
Knowledge	1. Use improvement knowledge.
	2. Use organizational knowledge.
Organization	3. Establish a project.
	4. Establish incentive structures.
Design	5. Start by determining goals.
	6. Start simple.
Communication	7. Publish objectives and collected data widely.
	8. Facilitate debate.
Usage	9. Use the data.

principles do not cover all aspects of metrics implementation, and following them does not guarantee that your metrics implementation will succeed. As with all general principles, ours must be carefully tailored to your specific metrics project. We offer advice on how to do this later in the chapter. First, however, we discuss our nine principles in relation to two projects. The first was an SPI project at Danske Data (see Chapter 5), and the second was an independent project involving three small companies. We now briefly describe the projects, followed by an elaboration of the principles in relation to their particular and very different contexts.

Advanced Guidelines

Our principles are pragmatic and might be criticized for lacking a highly developed theoretical foundation. But this is exactly the point. Given that measurement is an essential component of improvement, we agree with former SEI director Larry Draffel (1994) that it is more important to initiate data collection and analysis than to wait "until we get the 'right' measures." Of course, metrics must be technically correct and meaningful, and theory should neither be ignored nor inspire fear. The question is one of priorities, and in our view, practical application and usefulness to the company take precedence over technically and theoretically correct but complex solutions.

After you have launched your initial metrics program and gained experience, you might want to move your program in new directions. At that point, theory and advanced advice make sense and academic definitions are more likely to be intelligible and even invaluable. Examples include important definitions of measurement itself, such as those offered by Fenton and Pfleeger (1997). They define measurement as "the process by which numbers or symbols are assigned to attributes of entities in the real world in such a way as to describe them according to clearly defined rules" and as "a mapping from the empirical world to the formal, relational world." Furthermore, they explain that "a measure is the number or symbol assigned to an entity by this mapping in order to characterize an attribute." For helpful guidance in advanced rules for mapping and the conditions for representing data to ensure meaningful measures, we recommend Fenton and Pfleeger's 1997 book *Software Metrics—A Rigorous and Practical Approach*.

In this chapter, we also purposefully avoid other theoretical issues in favor of more pragmatic concerns. For example, we do not discuss such things as the distinctions between direct and indirect measurements of dependent and independent attributes. Nor do we cover measurement scales and scale types. Nonetheless, these issues are certainly important, and, even though we view them as overly academic for smaller metrics programs, they can be helpful for more sophisticated and complex programs.

These more theoretical issues supplement rather than interfere with our principles, which are applicable whether you use a purely metrics-driven improvement approach such as the ami method (Pulford et al. 1996) or whether your improvement is based on a well-known assessment and improvement approach such as CMM (Humphrey 1989), Bootstrap (Kuvaja et al. 1994), or SPICE (El Emam et al. 1998).

17.1 SAMPLE METRICS PROGRAMS

Table 17.3 shows our nine principles organized into five areas: general knowledge about improvement and the program's context, and the program's organization, design, communication, and usage. We identified these principles based on our literature survey and experiences developing and introducing metrics programs. We applied the principles in an SPI case study (Iversen and Mathiassen 2000) and verified them in an analysis of an independent project involving three small companies (Kautz 1999).

Although the second project was not part of the SPI project, we include it here for three reasons. First, of the four companies in the SPI project, only Danske Data actively pursued a metrics program. By including an external case, we compensate for what would otherwise be too narrow a view of metric program challenges. Second, the three external companies we discuss are very small: Each had fewer than five system developers and almost no administrative overhead. Including them here lets us discuss the applicability of our principles in relation to small companies, as well as to the relatively large Danske Data. Given the increasing presence of small, start-up software companies, including them in improvement discussions is all the more relevant. Finally, one of us was a consultant on the external project, giving us easy and extensive access to relevant data and knowledge (Kautz 1998, 1999).

Danske Data

Danske Data started its metrics program with the goal of showing a 10% increase in efficiency based on changes introduced by its SPI project (see Chapter 5 and Iversen and Mathiassen 2000). To accomplish this, we introduced a program to measure six factors: project productivity, quality, adherence to schedule, adherence to budget, customer satisfaction, and employee satisfaction (see Table 17.4). We closely followed the metrics program for almost three years.

Our plan was to collect data on all finished projects quarterly and then publish a report based on the data. Because the CEO defined the 10% goal for SPI, we targeted the program primarily toward senior management. Our intention was to minimize disruption of the development projects and collect as much data as possible automatically. We initiated the Danske Data metrics program in March 1997; the first report was published in September 1999.

From the outset, our goal was to measure the six indicators shown in Table 17.4. The idea was to include an array of measures so that results would be better balanced and dysfunctional behavior would be less likely, and thus have less impact.

The major hurdle we faced was to make sure that our data quality was such that senior management could confidently make the reports public within the organization. One of the problems we faced was in our attempt to count function points au-

Table 17.4 Indicators in the Danske Data Metrics Program

Factor	Definition
Project productivity	Resources used to develop the system relative to its size in function points
Quality	Number of error reports both absolute and relative to size in function points
Adherence to schedule	Variation from agreed time of delivery both absolute and relative to size in function points
Adherence to budget	Variation from estimated use of resources
Customer satisfaction	Satisfaction with the development process and the implemented solution (multiple-choice questionnaire)
Employee satisfaction	Satisfaction with the development process (multiple-choice questionnaire)

tomatically. We had to abandon this after several tries because the results did not seem to reflect reality. Another problem was that questionnaires to measure customer satisfaction covered questions related to both contractual agreements and the project as a whole, whereas respondents were users who were involved only in acceptance tests.

Three Small Companies

Each of the three companies develops one main project: Company A develops a system for stochastic modeling and analysis; Company B, a system simulating oil reservoirs; and Company C, a system for managing pension funds and their members. All three companies were less than five years old when they started their improvement projects, none had more than five employees, and all employees were system developers. Because of a growing demand for variants of their products, each company was having problems controlling source code versions and wanted to introduce configuration management. For each company, resources were scarce and they therefore joined forces and designed a joint project for which they received support from the European Union's European Systems and Software Initiative (ESSI) program.

The ESSI program required that each company use metrics to verify and validate the effect of the improvement actions. Originally, neither the project leaders nor the developers were convinced of the benefits of a metrics program. However, as they worked with the new configuration and change-request management routines, this distrust gradually faded and team members developed a shared understanding of metrics and opinions as to what might be interesting measures.

In each company, the metrics program served a different, dedicated purpose. This was a major factor in employees' successfully adopting their metrics program. Because the programs were tailored to each situation, measures were clearly visible and resulted in improved planning and performance, improved working conditions, and higher customer satisfaction (see Table 17.5). One company measured the number of fixed change requests delivered on time and the time used in review meetings and found that the number of change requests delivered on time had increased from 45% to 77%, and that review meeting time had shortened by a factor of 4. Another company found that the average time spent on a change request was twice what was expected. Although they were disappointed, they considered the figure to be accurate, and that let them plan better and offer customers more realistic information. Although such data contains a certain imprecision and inaccuracy—underlining how carefully metrics should be used—the involved companies were confident that the metrics indicated interesting tendencies. At the projects' end, they all planned to improve their metrics programs and continue measuring.

Table 17.5 *Results of the Metrics Programs for the Three Small Companies*

Company A
Chief developer's library development effort decreased.
Library development effort by other staff increased from 8% to 16%.
Efficiency did not decrease.

Overall result: Improved planning and greater flexibility in work organization.

Company B
The number of fixed requests delivered on time increased from 45% to 77%.
The time spent on code merging was reduced by more than a factor of 4.
The weekly review meetings were shortened by a factor of 4.

Overall result: Improved planning and performance, improved working conditions, higher customer satisfaction.

Company C
The number of change requests increased considerably.
The time spent on change request handling was determined more precisely.
The preparation time for releases was reduced drastically.

Overall result: Improved planning and performance, improved working conditions, higher customer satisfaction.

17.2 PRINCIPLES IN ACTION

We now describe the principles in each of the five target areas and illustrate their application with concrete examples.

Knowledge

When implementing metrics, you must draw on different kinds of knowledge. To be successful, it is important that you bring in knowledge about SPI and organizational change as well as knowledge about the organization in which the metrics program will be implemented (see also Chapter 12).

Principle 1: Use Improvement Knowledge

To successfully develop and deploy metrics programs, organization members and members of the improvement and measurement teams must have or acquire the requisite knowledge. Participants should of course learn about the state of the art of software metrics, but that in itself is not enough. Metrics implementation is a complex form of organizational change. For it to be successful, metric implementers must be knowledgeable about and experienced in SPI, software development, software engineering, and the process of organizational change itself.

Because none of the small companies knew about SPI or metrics, we provided basic education on both. The three companies' joint improvement initiative was guided by the SPICE approach (El Emam et al. 1998). For the metrics program, we were inspired by both the GQM paradigm (Basili and Rombach 1988) and the ami method (Pulford et al. 1996), but executed both in a very lean manner. Instead of developing a comprehensive metrics program, we collaborated with practitioners to develop simple metrics programs that were quantitative but small in scale. We provided guidance in defining metrics and collecting data and also helped practitioners prepare documents and reports. It is important to note that we provided only assistance and not prescriptions. The practitioners themselves accomplished the changes and implemented the new practices.

The story at Danske Data was much the same: Practitioners had no prior knowledge of SPI or metrics. Instead, researchers and consultants stepped in, providing literature and offering lectures and general advice. Also, one of the other SPI companies had previously worked with a metrics program that it had abandoned; some of the program's principles were transferred to Danske Data. All this helped the metrics group to gain the necessary knowledge and experience. Again, however, we merely provided practitioners with the knowledge and then let them use it to make decisions about how to implement the metrics program.

Principle 2: Use Organizational Knowledge

Many metrics programs fail because of limited understanding of the program's organizational context. There is a difference between the work procedures described in handbooks and the actual work practices. For a metrics program to succeed, the various actors must understand why they are collecting particular data. It is also helpful to understand the organizational politics. One way to achieve this understanding is to involve as many of the employees affected by the intended changes as possible.

In the three small companies, we collected organizational knowledge by analyzing current practices and interviewing developers at the start of the project. Among the issues we focused on were how different system versions were managed, how change requests were handled, and how resources were managed and registered. This approach gave us valuable input for developing the routines for handling configuration management and change requests. It also provided the knowledge we needed to define metrics and gather data.

The most important result of our analysis was to keep the metrics simple so that they would not interfere with the organizations' creativity and flexibility. We also decided to aggregate the figures using existing data, which was easily accessible from the established configuration item libraries and change request databases. This served to assuage existing doubts and deliver promised benefits while also decreasing the burden on developers, who were not accustomed to collecting data about their daily work.

At Danske Data, we held no special activities aimed at increasing our research team's general understanding of the organization in relation to the metrics program. Instead, we relied on the practitioners' existing organizational knowledge, a reasonable decision given the SPI group's broad base in the organization. Several members were also project managers on development projects and thus were in daily contact with other project managers and developers. This gave them insight into how people were feeling about the initiative throughout the organization. As with Principle 1, where practitioners gained SPI and metrics knowledge along the way, our team gained knowledge about Danske Data as the project progressed. As the project progressed, the difference in knowledge between researchers and practitioners was greatly minimized in these areas.

Program Organization

Many metrics programs are established without a formal structure. However, if your program is to have significant impact, you must address the organization of the program itself as well as the supporting incentive structure.

Principle 3: Establish a Project

Metrics programs are not free. To increase attention and visibility and to validate expenditures, the initiative should be set up as a formal project with responsibilities for planning and reporting progress and with explicit success criteria. It is also important to plan how metrics will be gradually introduced into projects.

Initially, the Danske Data metrics program was a focused but informal effort. Within a few months we had established the program's foundation and began to collect data. During this phase, practitioners found the metrics work interesting and were committed to successfully implementing the program. However, when the program later became riddled with problems, the loosely structured organization proved inadequate. It was evident that we needed a dedicated improvement project if we were to succeed over the long term. This second effort was carefully planned and staffed, and we established clear goals and success criteria. One of the goals of the improvement project was met after six months when the metrics' quality had increased such that we could publish results in the organization. We also evaluated how many data elements were missing or unreliable and made it a specific goal to decrease such numbers. Establishing a formal project also made the program far more visible and made it much easier for participants to argue for adequate resources.

In the three small companies, the metrics program was part of a defined improvement project, and we introduced it to participants in clearly marked work packages with formally required deliverables. One senior developer acted as a local project leader, and another was the overall project manager. The project's day-to-day work and management were coordinated in weekly meetings among project leaders, where both formal and informal matters were discussed. The request for documented deliverables enforced a certain discipline and product orientation on the practitioner team. According to the project members, without such demands they would have put much less in writing and thus would have had less stored for future actions. The local project leaders were also principal project members and were responsible for establishing the metrics and collecting the measurement data. In each company, at least one additional developer was also involved in providing some metrics data. Thus, despite the inherent demands of daily business, the metrics program was taken seriously from the start.

Principle 4: Establish Incentive Structures

Those who report metrics data must see some advantage in the program. Ideally, the program's results will directly benefit developers in their daily practice. However, in some cases, a more indirect approach using such things as bonuses and awards can facilitate the uptake of the metrics program. If carefully designed, such incentives can provide an efficient kick-start for metrics implementation.

Along with providing advantages, you must avoid saddling participants with disadvantages and extra burdens. When tools and procedures either counteract efficient data collection and reporting or are not properly integrated into the developers' normal work practice, you are far less likely to attain sufficient data quality.

At Danske Data, we offered incentives to improve data quality. All projects were required to record data in the online project- and hour-registration system. However, no one did this completely or accurately, mainly because they saw no immediate use for the data they provided. We achieved a marked improvement in data quality by better informing project managers about what data they should report, how they should report it, and why it mattered, as well as showing them results based on the data. Moreover, when one division offered the division managers and project managers a bonus for complete and accurate data reporting, data quality increased dramatically for subsequent projects.

One reason such a bonus system was needed was because an "adverse" incentive was also in place. Originally, the system for registering project data and work hours was useful only in the accounting department's daily work. Project managers saw little value in entering the data. They also felt that the data requested made it impossible to provide a full understanding of a development project. For example, they could enter only one estimated completion date, and this meant that when they re-estimated projects, only the new estimate or the old one could be retained. With no clear guidance on how to cope with this situation, many project managers simply refrained from entering any data at all. These problems have been recognized and a recent improvement initiative has been established to alleviate them and to remove the adverse incentives.

In the three small companies, no explicit bonus or reward system was introduced or needed because developers directly experienced metric program benefits. In one company, employees stated that working conditions had improved and that the correctness and integrity of its software products had increased. Also, because fewer errors were reported from individual customers after delivery, higher customer satisfaction could be documented. In the other two companies, employees said that the process of recording data made their work experience much more professional and motivating.

Program Design

Just as the metrics effort needs to be organized, so the content—the metrics themselves—must be organized and designed. We offer two principles to help with metrics design: determine the goals of the program and avoid being overly ambitious when you start.

Principle 5: Start by Determining Goals

Successful metrics implementation requires clear goals from the outset. Without such clarity, the effort can be difficult to manage and decisions on which measures to choose will be made blindly. One goal-based approach to metric program design is the Goal Question Metrics approach (Basili and Weiss1984). No matter which method is used, it is important that the goals and the derived metrics be meaningful to those who deliver and use the data.

In the case of the three companies, project objectives were formulated at the very beginning as requested by the ESSI program. The objectives were to (1) formalize and document procedures for configuration management in each company, (2) choose and implement configuration management software, and (3) establish a metrics program to measure the impact of the new process. There were three expected outcomes. First, improved procedures for configuration management for source code were expected to reduce time spent on producing new versions and releases, correcting errors, and handling changes. Second, improved procedures for documenting source code were expected to let all developers work in all product areas and thus facilitate the extension of development teams. Finally, improved procedures for testing source code should reduce the number of errors in the delivered products.

Given these objectives and outcomes, the companies then decided which measures were most critical for them. Company A wanted to let all developers work on all parts of its product, thus reducing reliance on the chief developer. Company B wanted to increase the number of accepted change requests handled in a given time frame. Company C wanted to reduce the time it took to handle customer change requests and finalize releases for shipping. With these clear objectives, the employees collected the necessary data.

At Danske Data, the original goal was to show 10% improvement in productivity. However, this broad goal was difficult to translate into meaningful measurement activities. Defining the six factors in Table 17.4 helped somewhat, but these were essentially chosen to broaden the metric program's horizon rather than support the stated goal. In addition, ownership of the metrics program was problematic. Although the CEO had stated the 10% goal, he had, in fact, not requested a metrics program. When the metrics group started its work, we felt that they were fulfilling a management vision, but when the results started coming in, management did not seem enthusiastic.

One of the key problems at Danske Data was that the metrics program was defined before any improvement initiatives were launched. Thus, the metrics were not very well suited to giving information about the effect of specific improvement initiatives. Instead, they were directed more at the general state of the development process.

Principle 6: Start Simple

Systematically collecting data to use as a basis for decision making is a difficult and complex undertaking. We therefore recommend that you start with a small set of metrics. Sometimes, even a single measure is enough to assess the fulfillment of defined goals if you choose the right metrics. Another approach is to use existing data or to collect data automatically, thereby minimizing disturbance in the development organization. In any case, the list of metrics and their definitions must be adapted to both the organization's conditions and the metric program's defined goals.

In the three small companies, we started the metrics program with a description of expected results. Each company decided to measure what it individually considered most critical, and, accordingly, we developed simple, quantitative, small-scale programs. We aggregated figures from existing data, which were easily accessible from the established configuration item libraries and change request databases. For each company, one metric was defined to suit the particular goals—that is, to get an indication of whether the new practices and tools let all developers work on all products, supported the delivery of accepted change requests within the estimated time frame, or influenced the time required to handle customer change requests and finalize releases for shipping, respectively. In all three companies, we collected data with as much rigor and care as possible to secure credibility and precision.

When we initiated the Danske Data metrics program, the goal was ambitious: to measure six fairly complex factors (Table 17.4) and require all projects to report data from Day One. This was an enormous undertaking and, as of yet, not all the factors have been measured, and some have even been officially abandoned. This created a great deal of frustration in the metrics program team. Another project attempted to automatically compute function points (Albrecht 1979) to measure developer productivity. The project spent two person-months establishing the routines for collecting this information. Then, however, after counting function points in several application systems, it was difficult to see any relationship between the perceived system complexity and the counting procedures' results. The function point metric was thus abandoned. As a consequence, it became impossible to measure productivity because there was no longer any measure of the output from the software development process.

Communication

Measuring the performance of professionals is not an exact science, and some interpretation of the numbers is necessary. This can give rise to negative feelings toward the metrics program. You can counter this by communicating openly about the program's objectives and results as well as by facilitating discussions about the validity and reliability of the measurements.

Principle 7: Publish Objectives and Collected Data Widely

It is important to communicate the objectives of the metrics program widely and to publish the results broadly, including as many relevant people as possible. However, it is also important to protect individuals and not relate the metrics results to performance evaluations. Otherwise, data integrity is likely to be compromised because workers would attempt to ensure that their numbers looked good.

Measurements provide views of sensitive issues. Given this, you must ensure that the results you make public are based on data that are sufficiently valid and reliable and can thus support fruitful discussion. Metrics are likely to reveal unpleasant things about the software operation. Being able to use these results to improve the organization—rather than figure out who is to blame for problems—is an important part of the cultivation involved in implementing metrics programs.

In the three small companies, we made no extra efforts to publish the metrics data. Measurement data were published and distributed during weekly coordination meetings that included all developers. In these meetings, developers discussed both formal and informal matters and openly communicated about the metrics program's development and results. Thus, no additional roll-out of the results was necessary. In addition, the metrics data—including data that showed no direct improvement—were reported to the ESSI program and made publicly available to software practitioners and academics through articles published in the journal *Software Process—Improvement and Practice* (Kautz 1998) and *IEEE Software* magazine (Kautz 1999).

At Danske Data, we initially intended to publish the measurement findings each quarter. However, it took us more than two years to get the first measurement report published. Management withheld earlier reports because they felt the data validity was insufficient. During this period, the metrics group recognized that one obvious way to improve the program was to get the numbers published so that those responsible for providing the data could see some value in doing so and could provide direct feedback on the program itself.

Even though the reports were not made public in an official report, we communicated the collected data through other channels. For example, our metrics group staged a road show to take measurement results to managers and developers in different divisions and locations. The road show stirred interest and debate during the presentation sessions, even though the results were completely anonymous and we presented them only at a high level of abstraction. The road shows were successful enough to convince the metrics group that the best way to improve the metrics program was to communicate widely about the collected data. This insight increased our frustration at being unable to make the reports public.

Principle 8: Facilitate Debate

Beyond merely publishing objectives and gathered data, you should have a forum for discussing the metrics program and its results to prevent the formation of myths about the material you collect and how it will be used. You might, for example, have an electronic message board, hold measurement meetings, or put the metrics program on the agenda of other meetings.

In all three small companies, metrics were discussed in the weekly coordination meetings as well as in meetings with individuals and as part of normal workdays. Developers often had concrete questions arise as they applied new routines in their daily work. Their feedback and experiences led us to continually evaluate the procedures, and we discussed and refined the routines and the metrics program accordingly. The project leaders, who served both as mentors and as champions for change, were responsible for keeping descriptions up to date. Their prompt reaction to employees' proposals added further support to what was a smooth introduction process.

At Danske Data, public debate about the metrics program was hampered by the lack of public data. Because people had no actual results to talk about, the program was either ignored or the topic of hearsay. The SPI group did establish an electronic discussion board to instigate debate on all SPI initiatives in the organization, but it was rarely used. Some discussion based on actual data did take place with the senior management group when we delivered the reports to them to approve for publication. However, these discussions did not extend beyond the official meetings. In addition, some project managers felt that the data reporting system was inadequate and discussed improvement possibilities with the metrics group. Based on these discussions, we issued more thorough descriptions of how to fill out the relevant fields. This resulted in a better understanding among project managers about the significance of the various measurement variables, and it subsequently led to better data quality.

Data Usage

After the data have been collected, they must be used to implement changes for improvements or at least to increase understanding about how the organization works. If those who provide the data do not see them being applied, they are not likely to use many resources for supplying further data, thus causing deteriorating data quality and jeopardizing the whole improvement effort.

Principle 9: Use the Data

Metrics results must be used to gain insight into the software process and to correct its problems. Failing this, the metrics program will soon degenerate into a bureaucratic procedure that merely adds to software development overhead. If no consequences are forthcoming from poor measurement results, the metrics program is unlikely to succeed. However, in creating solutions based on data, you must keep in mind that the entities involved in software development cannot be measured with absolute precision. Given the data's inherent imprecision and inaccuracy, it is important that you don't overinterpret the data. That said, being able to recognize trends from imprecise or incomplete data sets is more helpful than having no data at all.

The three small companies used the data in different ways. In Company A, the data showed that the chief developer spent fewer hours on development tasks and used the time saved for business administration. This was a positive byproduct of the improvement project. The data also showed that the number of hours that the chief developer spent tutoring other developers on the task had not changed. The tutoring hours remained constant despite improved documentation. Thus, the company aims were not supported in this case. However, the results were used for planning further work and new projects with respect to the required resources. In Company B, the time spent merging the code after changes had been made was reduced to less than one-third, from 90 to 20 minutes on average. A similar reduction was observed for the weekly review meeting of the test runs, from 120 to 30 minutes on average. This allowed for extra testing time. Finally, in Company C, more precise examination and additional coding doubled the average time spent on a request. This figure was not surprising; the company considered it more realistic and could thus better plan and inform the customer about delivery of error corrections. Discussions with customers confirmed this; they were happier with the company's service and software as a result of accurate estimates of error correction and an increased number of corrected errors. In all three companies, the metrics data were thus used to continuously improve planning, performance, and working conditions, and that led to higher customer satisfaction.

When we left Danske Data's metrics group in 1999, the full metrics program was not yet in active use. One reason for this was the lack of program ownership. No one actively requested the data. The metrics group was convinced that they were in a vicious circle. The data reported were of poor quality because those who reported them did not see much advantage in supplying accurate data in a timely manner if the data were not used. At the same time, the poor data quality made management wary of making the results public. After the metrics report was finally made public in September 1999, the metrics group felt much more optimistic about the future of the program.

17.3 DISCUSSION AND CONCLUSION

Even though the companies described here were aware of and adhered to many of our principles, they still had problems implementing a successful metrics program. This was especially true for Danske Data. There are several explanations for this.

First, implementing a metrics program requires an organization to adapt its culture and practices to a new way of thinking in which decisions are based on measurable phenomena rather than intuition and personal experience. Second, because measurements are taken while the organization is improving, it is difficult to establish a baseline for the improvements. At Danske Data, the goal was to show that a three-year SPI effort would yield a 10% increase in productivity. However, during implementation of the metrics program, the organization changed considerably, increasing its software development staff from about 300 to about 500 people and expanding the number of development sites from three to five locations. In the same period, several improvement initiatives were launched that significantly changed the software development process as well as the productivity levels. This made it difficult to establish a baseline productivity level to evaluate improvements against. Thus, there was no way to verify a 10% productivity increase.

As our experiences show, establishing a successful metrics program requires more than predefined checklists and guidelines; principles must be adjusted to suit a particular organization's context and culture. Applying software technologies in organizations is a complex undertaking (Bjerknes 1992; Wastell 1992; and Walsham 1993), and debate is ongoing as to how and when to apply metrics and which metrics to apply for evaluation (Humphrey 1989; Paulish and Carleton 1994; Brodman and Johnson 1995; Fenton and Pfleeger 1997; Kautz 1999). Our principles are certainly a good starting point, but they are interrelated in a complex and somewhat unpredictable way, and how you apply them depends heavily on the application context. However, we do have some general advice based on our experiences.

As was the case in the three small companies, metrics program success is most likely when the overall environment is fairly stable and measurement does not place a significant burden on practitioners' time. In the three companies, practitioners did not experience the work-process measurements as an impediment to their creativity and flexibility. On the contrary, a systemic approach to process improvement using metrics supported practitioners' creativity, and they found it to be both motivating and vital to their professionalism. Appropriate metrics were experienced not as a personal threat but rather to help practitioners monitor their processes for further improvement. It may seem difficult to identify data for quantitatively measuring software process improvements, but using simple, existing metrics that are relevant to your organization can be a good starting point.

Finally, to ensure the continued success of a metrics program, you should continually evaluate and improve it. In doing so, it is possible to detect when you need to add new metrics, find new ways to collect them, and so on. You can evaluate your program in any one of several ways, including conducting interviews and surveys. Although we have not thoroughly analyzed or applied this idea, we might state it as a 10th principle: *Evaluate your metrics program to further improve.*

Our principles are directed both at measurement in the small, as we have shown in our measurements of single characteristics in the small companies (Kautz 1999), as well as for larger endeavors involving companies with several hundred software developers (Iversen and Mathiassen 2000). We have also shown that the principles are suitable for measuring "hard" engineering issues, such as those in the three small companies, and "soft" human issues at such as those at Danske Data. The crucial point is to adjust the principles to the environment and the situation at hand.

17.4 REFERENCES

Albrecht, A.J. 1979. "Measuring Application Development." *Proceedings of the IBM Applications Development Joint SHARE/Guide Symposium*. Armonk, NY: IBM. 83–92.

Basili, V.R., and D.M. Weiss. 1984. "A Methodology for Collecting Valid Software Engineering Data." *IEEE Transaction on Software Engineering*. 10;6:728–738.

Basili, V.R., and H.D. Rombach. 1988. "The TAME Project: Towards Improvement-Oriented Software Environments." *IEEE Transaction of Software Engineering*. 14:6:758–773.

Bjerknes, G. 1992. "Dialectical Reflections in Information Systems Development." *Scandinavian Journal of Information Systems*. 4:55–78.

Brodman, J.D., and D.L. Johnson. 1995. "Return on Investment from Software Improvement as Measured by U.S. Industry." *Software Process*[em]*Improvement and Practice*. Pilot Issue: 35–47.

Carleton, A.D., R.E. Park, W.B. Goethert, W.A. Florac, E.K. Bailey, and S.L. Pfleeger. 1992. "Software Measurement for DoD Systems: Recommendations for Initial Core Measures." SEI-92-TR-19. Pittsburgh: Software Engineering Institute.

Dekkers, C.A. 1999. "The Secrets of Highly Successful Measurement Programs." *Cutter IT Journal*. 12:4:29–35.

Draffel, L. 1994. "Professionalism and the Software Business." *IEEE Software*. July:8.

El Emam, K. et al. 1997. *SPICE—The Theory and Practice of Software Process Improvement and Capability Determination*. Los Alamitos, CA: IEEE Computer Society Press.

Fenton, N.E., and S.L. Pfleeger. 1997. *Software Metrics—A Rigorous and Practical Approach*. Boston: PWS Publishing Company.

Grady, R.B., and D. Caswell. 1987. *Software Metrics: Establishing a Company-Wide Program*. Upper Saddle River, NJ: Prentice Hall.

Hofstede, G. 1983. "The Cultural Relativity of Organizational Practices and Theories." *Journal of International Business Studies*. Fall:75–89.

Humphrey, W.S. 1989. *Managing the Software Process*. Reading, MA: Addison-Wesley.

Iversen, J.H., and L. Mathiassen. 2000. "Lessons from Implementing a Software Metrics Program." *Proceedings of the HICSS-33 Conference*. Los Alamitos, CA: IEEE Computer Society Press.

Kautz, K. 1998. "Software Process Improvement in Very Small Enterprises: Does It Pay Off?" *Software Process—Improvement and Practice*. 4:4:209–226.

Kautz, K. 1999. "Making Sense of Measurements for Small Organizations." *IEEE Software*. 16;2;14–20.

Kuvaja, P., et al. 1994. *Software Process Assessment & Improvement—The Bootstrap Approach*. Oxford, UK: Blackwell Publishers.

Münch, K., et al. 1996. "ESPITI Final Evaluation Report." Report D 6.3.2/P-WP 6. Karlsruhe, Germany: Forschungszentrum Karlsruhe.

Paulish, D.J., and A.D. Carleton. 1994. "Case Studies of Software Process Improvement Measurement." *Computer*. September:50–47.

Pfleeger S.L. 1993. "Lessons Learned in Building a Corporate Metrics Program." *IEEE Software*:10:3.

Pulford, K., et al. 1996. *A Quantitative Approach to Software Measurement—The ami Handbook*. Reading, MA: Addison-Wesley.

Rifkin, S., and C. Cox 1991. *Measurement in Practice*. Pittsburgh: Software Engineering Institute.

Siakas, K.V., and B. Balstrup. 2000. "A Field Study of Cultural Influences on Software Process Improvement in a Global Organisation." *Proceedings of the EuroSPI 2000 Conference*. Bray, Ireland: ISCN.

Walsham, G. 1993. *Interpreting Information Systems in Organizations*. New York: John Wiley & Sons.

Wastell, D.G. 1992. "The Social Dynamics of Systems Development: Conflict, Change, and Organizational Politics." In S. Easterbrook, ed. *CSCW: Cooperation and Conflict*. London: Springer Verlag.

Weinberg, G.M. 1993. *Quality Software Management: First-Order Measurement*. New York: Dorset House.

Chapter 18

Better Requirements

Jan Pries-Heje and Otto Vinter

The difficulty of defining and executing improvement programs is well known and gives rise to many questions. Are we improving the right processes? How can we overcome resistance to the program? How can we ensure that improvements are diffused and adopted throughout the organization?

At Brüel & Kjær, we developed a program for improving our requirements engineering process that can serve as a guide to other companies as they set out to improve their own processes. Our program is based on action research. Bob Galliers (1992) describes action research as an approach that lets researchers create new theoretical knowledge along with new methods that have practical value for the organization.

Our program has three phases: the analysis phase, the focused pilot phase, and the broad dissemination phase. These phases evolved from principles recommended by Susman and Evered (1978). Their method contains the following five steps (steps 2 and 5 are repeated when necessary).

1. Specify project infrastructure.
2. Diagnose problems.
3. Plan actions.
4. Implement actions.
5. Evaluate results.

We performed infrastructure specification (step 1) when we wrote our proposal requesting ESSI funding to improve our requirements-engineering process.[1] Our

---

1. We received funding for our Methodology for Preventing Requirements Issues from Becoming Defects—the PRIDE project—from the European System and Software Initiative (ESSI). The final project report is in Vinter et al. 1999.

problem diagnosis (step 2) was based on analyzing problem reports and identifying the main causes for requirements-related problems (see Chapter 8). This step constitutes our *analysis phase*.

Our action planning (step 3) involved finding and committing two pilot projects to try out our techniques; it constitutes our *focused pilot phase*. After the pilot projects were complete, we initiated our *broad dissemination phase* to diffuse and formalize the requirements engineering process. This involved four additional projects.

Our implementing action (step 4) occurred over the course of the six projects (two pilot projects and four follow-up projects). We monitored the projects closely and interviewed project participants before, during, and after they used the techniques. Finally, we evaluated our results (step 5) and analyzed material based on our interviews and observations. We then finalized the training material and the ISO 9001 procedures.

We now describe each of our three phases in detail. We first describe the analysis phase and explain how we found an optimum set of requirements specification techniques. Next, we explain the focused pilot phase and the concepts underlying the main techniques that the projects used, followed by a discussion of the dissemination phase. Finally, we discuss how other companies might use our techniques to initiate their own improvement program.

18.1 THE ANALYSIS PHASE

The analysis phase consists of three activities:

1. Gather up-to-date information and diagnose problems.
2. Identify techniques for solving the problems.
3. Prioritize the techniques using cost/benefit analysis.

Gather Information

Any analysis requires information to analyze. Such information might come from an assessment (see Chapter 11), from studies of literature, or, as in our case, from problem reports (see Chapter 8).

Brüel & Kjær's software development process was widely seen as unsatisfactory. Many projects had schedule overruns, and products were often shipped with bugs. Even when management appointed task forces to improve product quality, problems were still reported from the field. The general opinion was that the main problem was insufficient testing before release.

However, a rigorous analysis of problem reports from previous projects (using Beizer 1990), pointed out an additional major problem: requirements engineering. In fact, more than 50% of all Brüel & Kjær problem reports were classified as requirements-related (Vinter et al. 1999).

Specifying and managing requirements is a key issue in software development. In CMM, for example, requirements management is one of six KPAs that you must master to escape chaos and move from level 1 to level 2. As another example, quality guru Phil Crosby defines quality as conformance to requirements, and thus requirements "must be clearly stated so that they cannot be misunderstood" (1980, p. 15). Numerous other researchers also emphasize the importance of truly understanding customer needs and demands so that you can formulate requirements that reflect actual needs. As Lauesen (1999) puts it, requirements specification "is one of the most difficult, yet important areas of systems development" and yet "little guidance is available for the practitioner." It is precisely this guidance that we hope to offer.

Identify Problem-Solving Techniques

While analyzing and categorizing the problem reports, we simultaneously carried out a survey of the literature on requirements elicitation, specification, and use (see Davis 1993; Thayer and Dorfman 1997; Sommerville and Sawyer 1997) and found several techniques recommended for achieving better requirements.

Next, during problem-report analysis we tried to imagine ways to prevent each bug. We began with our list of known techniques and added to it if none of the listed techniques could prevent the bug in question. We also considered and later dropped many well-known techniques because they seemed useless in relation to actual bugs. Many of the more useful techniques were commonsense procedures that we moved up from the design phase to the requirements phase and then formalized. Used in this context, such techniques seem to contribute significantly to product quality.

Prioritize Techniques

Next, we performed a cost/benefit analysis of the techniques by estimating the hit rate of each technique for each error report. Because we had no data on the actual benefits of preventing a specific bug, we used the time-to-find-and-fix as the benefit. We estimated each technique's savings by multiplying this benefit by the hit rate, accumulating over all error reports, and then subtracting the cost (time) of using the technique. Using this cost/benefit analysis, we produced a prioritized list of 13 techniques.

18.2 THE FOCUSED PILOT PHASE

The focused pilot phase consists of three activities:

1. Let one or two pilot projects select techniques to implement.
2. Train the teams in the techniques.
3. Follow up with the teams and evaluate how they use the techniques.

From a managerial viewpoint, it might seem faster to forgo pilot projects and simply enforce the use of optimized techniques across the organization. However, that kind of dissemination often fails. As Gerald Weinberg (1997, p. 3) puts it, "Attempts to change software organizations commonly fail because of inadequate understanding of change dynamics." Weinberg calls management-enforced change the "Hole-in-the-Floor" model. To understand this model, imagine an organization as a house with two floors. At the lower level we have the people doing the work. At the upper level we have the planners developing perfect things. In this model, change is a matter of management drilling through the floor between the levels and dropping change through the hole to the level below. However, according to Weinberg, this model of instant change fails in reality because the model's assumptions are wrong: Forcing people to use techniques would probably create more resistance to change than actual change.

Behavior is changed one person at a time, project by project. Because our project teams typically consist of three to five people, we limited our implementation efforts to two carefully selected projects. This choice proved extremely useful in disseminating the techniques throughout the organization: Project members spread the word about improvements in an unplanned but very effective way. Based on our experience, we recommend that you start with a focused pilot phase before you perform a broad dissemination.

Select Techniques

To ensure each pilot project's commitment to the techniques, we applied the theory of planned behavior (Ajzen 1991). According to this theory, "People's behavior is strongly influenced by their confidence in their ability to perform" (p. 184). Furthermore, empirical analysis shows that when people adopt new techniques, personal considerations tend to overshadow "the influence of perceived social pressure" (p. 189).

Given this, we first held a one-day introduction to our methodology and the top 13 techniques; then we interviewed project participants individually to get their opinions on each technique. We then summarized the analysis and presented the results to the teams. Based on the results, each team selected five techniques, for a total of seven different techniques.

Selected Requirements Engineering Techniques

The project teams selected seven techniques:

- Scenarios: Relate demands to use situations, and describe the essential tasks in each scenario.
- Usability test of functional prototype: Ensure that the system meets users' day-to-day needs by developing and user-testing a functional user-interface prototype.
- Consult product expert: Let a product expert check screens for deviations from earlier product styles.
- External software stress test: Test to ensure that external software fulfills the requirement expectations, emphasizing extreme cases.
- Orthogonality check: Check requirement specification to ensure that users can apply operations and features whenever they are useful.
- Initial value check: Check to ensure that it is clear which attributes should appear when a screen is opened or an object is created.
- Performance specifications: Ensure that the requirements specification contains performance goals for each requirement.

Train Teams to Use Techniques

We developed a two-day workshop to train project teams in the techniques they selected. Our focus was on preparing them to apply the techniques. We therefore structured the course so that project team members could try the techniques on problems related to their work. In one case, for example, a four-member project team developed a paper mockup for their upcoming project and then usability-tested it with a person from another group.

Follow Up and Evaluate Use

Throughout the focused pilot phase, we conducted a series of interviews with team members to assess their attitudes toward the techniques.

Interview Guide

For each technique, we asked team members the following questions:

1. Have you used this technique?

    If no: 1. Why not?

    If yes: 1. What was your experience with using the technique?

                2. Can you give us an example of how it was successfully used?

                3. Do you still consider this technique useful and efficient?

                4. Did the workshop give you enough knowledge to use the technique successfully?

                5. How much extra time did it take to use this technique (compared with either not using it or with using a different technique in earlier projects)?

We interviewed a majority of the team members at four major pilot-project milestones: immediately after training, after scenarios were developed, after usability tests, and after the product release.

Team Members Respond

Here are some typical reactions to two techniques used by the pilot project teams.

Scenarios

"I am in fact deeply surprised. The scenarios made it possible for us to see the workflow through the system in a very concrete way."

"In the beginning of the project I was quite skeptical. I thought it would take too much time. But now I think that we get a much more realistic and exciting requirements specification as a result of the scenarios. It will also make it much easier to make a prototype."

"It has been an exciting experience to use scenarios. Once we had the scenarios, the requirements popped up by themselves."

Screen Mockups/Usability Test

"It only took a week to develop the original prototype in Visual Basic, and we performed the modifications from the first set of tests to the next overnight in a hotel room."

"The closer we got to the real users, the clearer we were on the actual tasks that they performed."

"We got more information out of the tests than we are able to incorporate in the product. We found features that we had never thought about, as well as features that were irrelevant to the users."

Both pilot projects completed the scenario technique as prescribed. However, after they'd written the scenarios, the teams could not wait for a functional prototype to be developed. Instead, in only two weeks they developed a prototype using a screen mockup to show navigational facilities. One team did this in Visual Basic; the other used the Bookmark feature in MS Word 6.

Of the remaining three techniques, both teams failed to apply one technique and applied the other two techniques incompletely. Based on this, we realized that introducing so many new techniques at once was too ambitious. Two new techniques was all the teams were able to perform properly.

At this point, one of the projects got a new project manager, who didn't believe in the techniques. He discarded the prototypes and designed the user interface to resemble a product he was familiar with. Product development continued from there. We had little opportunity to study the project further; we know only that the team overshot its budget significantly and didn't complete the project on time.

Although the requirements engineering process took longer than we expected, the specification and design phases were shorter than expected and thus there was no critical delay overall on the other project. Following the pilot phase, the project continued product development according to Brüel & Kjær's standard software development procedures.

After the product was released, we analyzed the problem reports in the same way we had done before. We found a significant reduction in error reports and an impressive reduction in usability-related requirements issues for each new screen. However, the greatest impact of the requirements engineering techniques was on users' perception of product quality. The product steadily sells more than twice as much as the team's earlier product.

18.3   THE BROAD DISSEMINATION PHASE

The broad dissemination phase consists of four activities:

1. Disseminate pilot-project results.
2. Diffuse knowledge about techniques.
3. Support projects in using techniques.
4. Evaluate how projects use techniques.

Disseminate Results

After our final evaluation of the pilot project, we presented our findings within Brüel & Kjær and also outside the company. We invited software developers from all major development projects to at least one presentation of the results. Furthermore, we posted all intermediate documents and presentation materials on the company intranet. Following this, we received many requests for copies of the training material from the pilot phase, especially material related to the scenarios.

Several projects then contracted with us to train them in the techniques. We trained four project teams in the second round of improving requirements specification. Based on the convincing results from the pilot projects, the new project teams were motivated to change and knew which techniques they wanted to use. As a result, we could move right into the training stage.

Diffuse Knowledge about Techniques

Again, we held a two-day workshop for project team members. This time, however, we did not include the techniques that did not work well in the pilot phase; our course focused solely on scenarios, prototyping, and usability testing. Furthermore, we discouraged the teams from creating fully functional prototypes. That is, we gave them examples of simple, early development stage prototypes and emphasized how much they could achieve using them, offering examples from the pilot projects.

Support Technique Use

In the pilot phase, we interviewed the project members several times. During these interviews, they asked us questions that helped them better understand and apply the techniques. However, we didn't directly interact with the projects while they were using the techniques.

In the dissemination phase, we decided to keep close, continuous contact with the projects. We did this for two reasons. First, in the pilot phase, some techniques were not used correctly. Second, we hoped to avoid a repeat of the pilot phase situation in which a project manager abandoned the techniques.

We arranged to meet regularly with each team during the analysis and requirements-specification phases. At these meetings, we listened to team members and offered to mentor them in using the techniques, thereby ensuring that they were applied in the best possible way. In doing this, we ensured that the projects stayed on track and did not cut corners in applying the techniques because of other problems in the project. Although we initially planned to meet monthly, we actually held meetings every two weeks or so.

At the meetings, we used a standard agenda, discussing the following:

1. Project status and activities planned for the near future
2. Experiences, problems, and success with the techniques

3. Issues or areas that needed our support

4. When to hold the next meeting

Each meeting typically took two hours, and we also spent, on average, about four hours per team in between-meeting support.

Our direct interactions were a success. All four projects completed the requirements phase using the techniques. One of the projects was later canceled for internal organizational reasons. Two other projects were significantly rescoped, but the scenario results and usability test experiences remained valid and were used in product development.

Evaluate Use of Techniques

After the four projects had used the techniques, we again interviewed project participants. Next, we analyzed the interview transcripts from all six projects using techniques for sequential case analysis (Miles and Huberman 1994). Based on our results, we evaluated our experience with the techniques. Following is a summary of what we found.

Our requirements engineering process improved significantly. The techniques we introduced are now standard practice in our company and are supported with training material and documented in ISO 9001 procedures. Developers' reaction was very positive, and both product quality and sale figures increased.

Although we originally intended to try several requirements engineering techniques, in the end our efforts were focused on scenarios and usability tests on early prototypes. These techniques proved to be effective for several reasons. First, we could teach a team of developers to use the techniques in two days. Second, the techniques required neither expert knowledge nor support to achieve significant benefits. Finally, as we noted earlier, developers were extremely satisfied with the results they achieved.

In interviews, developers were enthusiastic about the opportunity to have closer contact with potential customers and users. This contact gave them a wealth of domain knowledge, which in turn let them develop better and more user-friendly products. They also said that the techniques helped them more thoroughly perceive the real needs of potential customers and users.

Developers also repeatedly mentioned improvements in internal communication and coordination. In particular, they noted that there were far fewer exhausting discussions about how to interpret user requirements and needs. Time spent discussing different implementations also decreased because they could simply refer to a scenario or a specific validation of a prototype idea, which without dispute served as a common reference.

Because we conducted a pilot phase first, we were able to demonstrate the techniques' success to both developers and management. The pilot project's impressive results motivated other projects to use the techniques. It was never necessary to "sell" the techniques at Brüel & Kjær to get development teams to use them.

Finally, our direct and regular interaction with the project teams was an extremely effective tool for ensuring that the techniques were used—and used properly. This interaction ensured that the teams' experience in using the techniques would produce the expected results.

18.4 HOW CAN OTHER COMPANIES IMPROVE?

Clearly, Brüel & Kjær gained much from this process improvement, and we believe other companies can benefit from our program. Although we do not have statistics to support this claim, we have presented our results to experienced developers outside our company, and several have been inspired to start similar improvement efforts. Also, we believe our program has applicability beyond improving requirements engineering. For example, it could be used to improve project management, risk management, quality assurance, and so on. However, to prove this, further research and investigation are needed.

In developing the phases and their activities, we have tried to be as general as possible. The result is a generalized overview of our program's three phases and 11 activities. We added an activity—"support use of techniques in projects"—in the focused pilot phase. Although we did offer informal support for the pilot projects, we added systematic mentoring and regular support meetings in the broad dissemination phase. Today, we would definitely offer this formal support and mentoring in the pilot phase, too.

Action research embodies a strategy for studying change in organizations. This strategy consists of formulating a theory and an intervention strategy and then taking action to introduce change into the target organization. Action research was our guiding strategy for formulating our improvement program framework. We gained theoretical knowledge on effective requirements engineering techniques and then successfully put them to practical use in our organization.

Could we have used other research approaches? Action research is only one of several qualitative research methods used in the field of information systems. Worldwide, action research is eclipsed by more traditional social-science methods such as case studies, experiments, and sampling surveys (Galliers, 1992). However, none of the other research methods is well suited to introducing change in the course of a study. Thus, action research should be very important for the study of SPI because it is oriented toward change, especially when participation and organizationwide change are required. We believe that our study bears this out.

Overview of Framework for the Improvement Program

Our program has three phases and 11 activities.

ANALYSIS PHASE

1. Gather up-to-date information and diagnose problems.
2. Identify techniques for solving the problems.
3. Prioritize the techniques using cost/benefit analysis.

FOCUSED PILOT PHASE

1. Let one or two pilot projects select techniques to implement.
2. Train the teams in the techniques.
3. Support use of techniques in projects.
4. Follow up with the teams and evaluate how they use the techniques.

BROAD DISSEMINATION PHASE

1. Disseminate pilot project results.
2. Diffuse knowledge about the techniques.
3. Support projects in using the techniques.
4. Continuously evaluate how projects use the techniques.

18.5 REFERENCES

Ajzen, I. 1991. "The Theory of Planned Behavior." *Organizational Behavior and Human Decision Processes*. 50:179–211.

Beizer, B. 1990. *Software Testing Techniques*, second ed. New York: Van Nostrand Reinhold.

Crosby, P. 1980. *Quality Is Free*. New York: Mentor.

Davis, A.M. 1993. *Software Requirements: Objects Functions & States*. Upper Saddle River, N.J.: Prentice Hall.

Galliers, B. 1992. "Choosing Information Systems Research Approaches." Galliers, R., ed. *Information Systems Research: Issues, Methods and Practical Guidelines*. Oxford, U.K.: Blackwell Publishers.

Lauesen, S. 1999. *Software Requirements: Styles and Techniques*. Copenhagen: Samfundslitteratur.

Miles, M.B., and A.M. Huberman. 1994. *Qualitative Data Analysis: An Expanded Sourcebook*, second ed. London: Sage Publications.

Sommerville, I., and P. Sawyer. 1997. *Requirements Engineering: A Good Practice Guide*. New York: John Wiley & Sons.

Susman, G., and R. Evered. 1978. "An Assessment of the Scientific Merits of Action Research." *Administrative Science Quarterly*. 23:4:582–603.

Thayer, R.H., and M. Dorfman, eds. 1997. *Software Requirements Engineering*, second ed. Los Alamitos, CA: IEEE Computer Society Press.

Vinter O., S. Lauesen, and J. Pries-Heje. 1999. "A Methodology for Preventing Requirements Issues from Becoming Defects." ESSI Project 21167. Final Report. Nærum, Denmark: Brüel & Kjær.

Weinberg, G.M. 1997. *Quality Software Management/Volume 4: Anticipating Change*. New York: Dorset House.

Appendix A

Risk and Action Tables

A.1 IMPROVEMENT AREA

Table A.1 Risk Items Associated with the Improvement Area

Risk Items	0–2
Are the improvement area's processes and actors clearly delimited?	
Is current practice in the improvement area well understood?	
Are the problems acknowledged among the actors in the improvement area?	
Is there a desire to change among the actors in the improvement area?	
Do the actors in the improvement area have realistic expectations about the improvement initiative?	
Is adequate attention and energy in the improvement area directed toward the improvement initiative?	
Are traditions and cultures homogenous in the improvement area?	
Is interest in the initiative shared and similar throughout the improvement area?	
Are the actors in the improvement area open to new ways of thinking?	
Will the actors in the improvement area benefit from the improvement?	
Does the PAT enjoy recognition and trust from the actors in the improvement area?	
Total risk for improvement area	/22

Table A.2 Risk Resolution Actions Associated with the Improvement Area

Risk Resolution Actions	X
Focus the initiative (1)	
Specify the objective (1)	
Create results that are perceived to be useful (1)	
Focus on business results (1)	
Use culturally acceptable solutions (1)	
Document and emphasize best practices in the improvement area (2)	
Initiate discussions about experiences and problems in the improvement area (3)	
Understand and document the current practice in the improvement area (4)	
Create an understanding of the initiative's necessity (3)	
Create positive expectations of the initiative (2)	
Base the initiative on facts and experiences (2)	
Exploit and adapt incentive schemes (3)	
Sell the idea (3)	

A.2 IMPROVEMENT IDEA

Table A.3 Risk Items Associated with the Improvement Idea

Risk Items	0–2
Is the improvement activity clearly focused?	
Does the PAT agree on the improvement idea's professional foundation and practical design?	
Has the improvement idea been adapted to the professional and business needs in the improvement area?	
Is the improvement idea culturally acceptable, and can it be adapted into the current practice?	
Are the improvement idea's consequences well understood?	
Does the PAT have sufficient knowledge about and experience with the improvement idea?	

Table A.3 *Risk Items Associated with the Improvement Idea*

Risk Items	0–2
Do the actors in the improvement area have sufficient knowledge about and experience with the improvement idea?	
Has the potential for innovation been exploited?	
Is the improvement idea coordinated with other ongoing improvement activities?	
Can the improvement idea's effect be measured?	
Total risk for improvement idea	/20

Table A.4 *Risk Resolution Actions Associated with the Improvement Idea*

Risk Resolution Actions	X
Formulate measurable goals (5)	
Create clear and shared visions (2)	
Initiate discussion about possible means of change (3)	
Identify and solve specific problems (2)	
Use an incremental improvement strategy (2)	
Evaluate the consequences of the improvement idea (4)	
Study the state of the art (4)	
Consider alternative improvement ideas (2)	
Reuse others' successes (2)	
Take advantage of experiences from other organizations (4)	
Adapt well-known standard solutions (2)	
Buy a tool or a method (2)	
Experiment (4)	
Consider identified improvement needs (1)	
Educate actors in the improvement area (2)	
Take advantage of the relationships to other improvement initiatives (2)	

A.3 IMPROVEMENT PROCESS

Table A.5 *Risk Items Associated with the Improvement Process*

Risk Items	0–2
Has an agreement or contract been made regarding how the improvement initiative is organized and conducted?	
Does the PAT have a well-defined criterion for success?	
Is the improvement process planned?	
Do resource organization and allocation for the improvement process correspond to the extent and complexity of the task?	
Are the relevant levels of management sufficiently committed to the improvement initiative?	
Is the improvement initiative sufficiently integrated with the rest of the organization?	
Has the rest of the organization been sufficiently informed?	
Have visible results at appropriate intervals been planned throughout the course of the initiative?	
Are improvements and progress documented?	
Are the PAT's results and progress monitored?	
Is there a realistic plan for implementing the improvement idea?	
Total risk for improvement process	/22

Table A.6 *Risk Resolution Actions Associated with the Improvement Process*

Risk Resolution Actions	X
Get sponsors (3)	
Organize the improvement initiative as a project (5)	
Establish a contract with management regarding the improvement initiative (5)	
Arrange an event to create attention at project start-up (3)	
Plan the improvement initiative (5)	
Adapt the strategy to the task (2)	
Coordinate with other improvement initiatives (5)	

Table A.6 *Risk Resolution Actions Associated with the Improvement Process*

Plan implementation from the outset (5)	
Plan visible results every six to nine months (2)	
Design effect measures (2)	
Initiate discussions about the improvement process (3)	
Create and maintain management commitment and backing (3)	
Establish and maintain collaboration with the improvement area (3)	
Try out improvement ideas in pilot projects (4)	
Communicate plans, problems, progress, and results (5)	
Conduct reviews at regular intervals (5)	
Make the results visible (5)	

A.4 IMPROVEMENT ACTORS

Table A.7 *Risk Items Associated with the Improvement Actors*

Risk Items	**0–2**
Do the participants in the process action team have sufficient resources to carry out the improvement?	
Does the PAT have concrete knowledge about the current practice in the improvement area?	
Does the PAT have sufficient knowledge about the improvement idea and its professional foundation?	
Does the PAT have sufficient knowledge about and experience with improvement work?	
Are all PAT participants sufficiently committed to the improvement initiative?	
Do PAT members function as a team?	
Do PAT members have the necessary expertise and experience?	
Does the PAT cooperate with all the relevant parts of the organization?	
Total risk for improvement actors	/16

Table A.8 *Risk Resolution Actions Associated with the Improvement Actors*

Risk Resolution Actions	X
Obtain resources for the actors (3)	
Educate the PAT members in the improvement idea's professional foundation (4)	
Find good facilitators (5)	
Incorporate experienced change agents (5)	
Exclude participants who do not contribute (5)	
Adjust the level of ambition (1)	
Involve voluntary actors from the improvement area (5)	
Educate the PAT in improvement work (4)	
Build stronger teams (5)	
Enter into alliances (3)	
Keep people informed about the group's work (5)	
Use consultants (4)	

Research Team

Improving Software Organizations: From Principles to Practice is based on a collaborative research effort between engineers and researchers. A detailed account of the research approach and setting can be found in *Collaborative Practice Research* by L. Mathiassen (in R. Baskerville, J. Stage, and J.I. DeGross, eds., *Organizational and Social Perspectives on Information Technology*, Kluwer Academic Publishers, 2000). Following is a list of the contributors to this book, along with their affiliations during the project and their current e-mail addresses.

Ivan Aaen	Aalborg University	ivan@cs.auc.dk
Carsten Andersen	Danske Bank A/S	cve@danskebank.dk
Jesper Arendt	Aalborg University	jar@tdk.dk
Stig Bang	Ericsson Denmark	stig.bang@lmd.ericsson.se
Gro Bjerknes	Aalborg University	gb@avenir.no
Mads Christiansen	Delta Software Engineering	mc@delta.dk
Anne Mette Jonassen Hass	Delta Software Engineering	amj@delta.dk
Jan Pries-Heje	Delta Software Engineering	jph.inf@cbs.dk
Jakob Iversen	Aalborg University	iversen@vaxa.cis.uwosh.edu
Jørn Johansen	Delta Software Engineering	joj@delta.dk
Karlheinz Kautz	Copenhagen Business School	karl.kautz@cbs.dk

Flemming Krath	Danske Bank A/S	fek@dendanskebank.dk
Carsten Kristensen	Systematic Software Engineering	chk@systematic.dk
Lise Kruchow	Danske Bank A/S	lk@dendanskebank.dk
Lars Mathiassen	Aalborg University	larsm@cs.auc.dk
Ojelanki Ngwenyama	Aalborg University	ojelanki@erols.com
Ann-Dorte Nielsen	Danske Bank A/S	anndn@dendanskebank.dk
Lars Birger Nielsen	Brüel & Kjær A/S	lbnielsen@bk.dk
Peter Axel Nielsen	Aalborg University	pan@cs.auc.dk
Jacob Nørbjerg	Technical University Denmark	jacob@cbs.dk
Morten Hvid Pedersen	Systematic Software Engineering	mhp@systematic.dk
Susanne Tryde	Danske Bank A/S	sus@dendanskebank.dk
Otto Vinter	Brüel & Kjær A/S	otv@delta.dk

Index

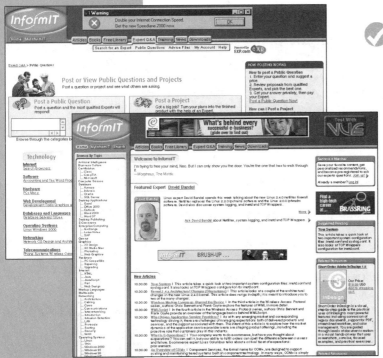